French
Warships
of
World War I

French
Warships
of
World War I

LONDON

IAN ALLAN LTD

First published 1974
ISBN 0 7110 0445 5

Published by Ian Allan Ltd., Shepperton, Surrey
and printed in Great Britain by the
Garden City Press Limited, Letchworth, Hertfordshire SG6 1JS

Contents

Title page: The battleships REPUBLIQUE (*top*),
CONDORCET (*centre*) and the submarine AIGRETTE (*foot*)

Preface

This book describes all the warships of the French Navy in World War I, including ships which were laid down before and during the war but not completed for war service; also requisitioned and purchased craft including river gunboats for French rivers, auxiliary vessels, auxiliary cruisers and hospital ships. It includes also a description of weapons and equipment fitted on these ships and notes on naval aircraft in service during this period.

The story of these ships and their equipment being inseparable from that of the Navy, it was decided to include in the foreword a brief account of the activities of the French Navy during the war. The reader will see that French naval activity, little known or totally ignored in British accounts, was very important and that the French Navy took a great and significant part in the Adriatic, Dardanelles and Near East operations as in anti-submarine warfare and the protection of troop transports and merchant ships on all oceans. Thus, the French Navy made a very efficient contribution to the Allied sea victory which enabled the land forces to win the war.

The author wishes to express his grateful thanks to those who assisted him with the task of writing this book, especially to:

Mr Froger, the well-known shiplover who had the kindness to authorise the author to publish several photographs from his splendid collection, the finest in France;

Mr Henri le Masson of Académie de Marine, the well-known French maritime writer and author of *Les Flottes de Combat*, the French Jane's, who gave him valuable documentation;

Mr Jean Meirat who is one of the most serious French naval historians, though his usual modesty does not accept this judgment. Thanks to his courtesy, this book includes a lot of information of great interest.

The author also thanks his friends and comrades of the French Naval Staff who had the kindness to help him with the work of translation.

In spite of extensive research some ships and details may have been omitted. The author will be grateful to the readers for any corrections, which may be addressed to him through the editor.

Paris, February 1974   *Jean Labayle-Couhat*

The French Navy of World War I

In 1914, France with her extensive coastline and vast colonial empire needed a strong Navy. Hence the importance of the New Era starting in 1909 after thirty-eight years of constant decline during which the French Navy, the world's second in 1871, came down to fifth rank among sea powers. Between 1898 and 1909 several politicians of the Pelletan type – (surnamed the 'naufrageur de la Marine') – had for their chief aim on arriving in office, the destruction of the work of their predecessors. The fact remains that during nearly forty years with 48 successive Ministers of Marine, there was never a well defined or stable French Naval policy. Too many armoured cruisers were launched instead of real battleships. Too often also, coastal flotillas of small torpedo boats were preferred to sea-going squadrons.

From 1909, Admiral Boué de Lapeyrere, M. Delcasse and M. Baudin the two latter both members of Parliament well acquainted with naval matters, took the necessary steps to bring about a prompt restoration of the naval prestige of their country. A naval programme was approved in 1912; it involved an establishment by 1920 of 28 battleships, 10 scouts, 52 destroyers and 94 submarines all of them to be under-age vessels. In 1914, the naval staff had foreseen an addition to this programme which would have included eight 'grands éclaireurs d'escadre' which would have been 25-knot battleships inspired by the British QUEEN ELIZABETH type.

From 333 million francs in 1909, the naval estimates rose to 415 million in 1911, 457 in 1912, 567 in 1913; the naval expenditure would have been considerably more than 600 million francs in 1914. While only six battleships (the DANTONS of 1906) had been approved from 1900 to 1909, sixteen dreadnoughts were authorised between 1910 and 1914 including seven of 23,500 tons, five of 25,300 tons, four of 29,000 tons, twelve of these with a main armament of 13·4in (340mm) guns.

Whilst content with a defensive position in Northern waters, the French government wished to master the Mediterranean and dominate the Austro-Italian combination so that from 1912, the French Navy was mainly concentrated in the Mediterranean. The so called 'armée navale' under command of Admiral de Lapeyrere, a competent leader, consisted on January 1st, 1914 of 18 battleships, 6 armoured cruisers, 40 destroyers and 25 submarines, all fully commissioned. The creation of this 'striking force' two years earlier had procured invaluable advantages from a training standpoint; in 1914 the French Fleet had acquired in manoeuvring, tactics, gunnery and torpedo exercises a proficiency it had never previously attained; it also had a remarkable morale.

On August 2nd, 1914, 19 battleships, 2 armoured coast-defence ships, 18 armoured cruisers, 14 protected cruisers, 86 destroyers, 13 seagoing torpedo boats, 115 coastal torpedo boats, 34 submarines, 8 gunboats, 4 minelayers, 7 minesweepers were operational. A new battleship, the PARIS, after completing trials, joined the fleet on August 22nd. To the above mentioned vessels there were added 3 large auxiliary cruisers, 14 others for patrol duty, several hospital ships and transports mobilised from the merchant service.

As soon as England had declared war on Germany (August 4th), 6 cruisers together with the submarines and torpedo boats of the Channel flotillas, were assigned for patrol duty in the Western Channel. In the Mediterranean, the battle squadrons first escorted the troop transports bringing to France several North African army divisions which later took part in the decisive Marne battle. From August 12th, a striking force numbering 12, and by the end of the month 14, battleships, 6 armoured cruisers, 30 destroyers and several submarines, based on Malta, patrolled the Adriatic to prevent an attack by the Austrian fleet. It shelled Cattaro and Lissa, destroyed the cruiser ZENTA, the Ragusa and Gravosa light-houses, protected the arrival of transports carrying stores and munitions to Montenegro.

In December 1914 the new battleship JEAN-BART was torpedoed in the upper Adriatic but succeeded in returning to Malta and the submarine CURIE was sunk while trying to enter the well defended Pola roadstead. As soon as Italy joined the Allies, an important part of the French Fleet,

A photograph showing some members of the Naval Parliamentary Commission inspecting astern main turrets of the dreadnought JEAN BART.

based on Corfu and Brindisi, continued to watch the Austrians in the Adriatic; its destroyers and submarines operating with Italian and British vessels, had many clashes with the enemy.

French ships took a prominent part in the Dardanelles and Suez operations. As early as September 25th, 1914 the two battleships VERITE and SUFFREN joined the British squadron watching the Dardanelles entrance and in January 1915 Rear-Admiral Guepratte's squadron (4 old battleships, 6 destroyers, 3 submarines, several sweepers and the seaplane carrier FOUDRE) became part of Vice-Admiral Carden's (later Admiral de Robeck's) fleet for the Dardanelles offensive. It took an important part in the actions of February 19th and March 18th, 1915. On this latter day, several allied battleships were sunk by mines or disabled by enemy coastal batteries, including the French BOUVET (sunk), the GAULOIS and SUFFREN (badly damaged); they were immediately replaced by the HENRI IV, JEANNE D'ARC and LATOUCHE TREVILLE. French ships supported the Allied forces which included two French divisions when they landed on April 25th. Four submarines (SAPHIR, JOULE, MARIOTTE and TURQUOISE) were lost while forcing the Dardanelles.

At Suez, French ships took part in the defence of the Canal. On February 3rd, 1915 the excellent gunnery of the coast defence ship REQUIN broke the main Turkish assault and together with the JAUREGUIBERRY renewed this success during the attack of August 7th/9th, 1916.

For four years, a number of French ships blockaded the Syrian coast and in 1917 greatly contributed to the progress of the British troops towards El Arish, Gaza and Jaffa. The cruiser AMIRAL CHARNER was lost with only one survivor, while on patrol off Syria.

After the failure of the Dardanelles campaign several British and French divisions were landed at Salonika. The Allied Armies in this new operational area were soon reinforced by the Serbian army which, in December 1915 had been forced to retreat in dramatic conditions to the coast of Albania. The French Navy took charge and successfully evacuated it, first to Corfu then to Bizerta where it was reformed; it was then transported to Salonika. Altogether 270,000 men and 86,000 horses were carried by sea without loss under French supervision, by means of 37 auxiliary cruisers and other transports (five of the latter British). The maintenance of the Salonika army required a huge transportation effort by the French Navy which, among other vessels, lost in so doing three large troop transports, the PROVENCE II (19,000 GRT) and GALLIA and BURDIGALA (12,000 GRT), also the 8000-ton cruiser CHATEAURENAULT which was acting as a fast transport between Taranto and Itea. All of them were torpedoed by German U-boats.

In December 1916, French ships operated off Athens for a pacific demonstration and landed a company to support the Allied policy in the conflict which had opposed for several months the Entente of the pro-German Hellenic government. French sailors fell into a murderous ambush causing numerous casualties and shots were fired by French ships to stop the Greek fire. Later a number of Greek warships were seized and commissioned under the tricolour to reinforce the Allied anti-submarine forces.

The French navy took an important part in the anti-submarine war, patrolling or escorting convoys. Excluding destroyers it comprised on November 1st, 1918, 9 patrol and escort commands totalling 111 torpedo boats, 35 submarines, 63 sloops and ASW gunboats, 153 submarine chasers, 734 armed trawlers, a large number of which had been newly built or purchased abroad. The Naval Air Service rose from an original force of eight seaplanes in August 1914 to a total in November 1918, of 37 airships and 1,264 aircraft mainly seaplanes or floatplanes with a naval personnel of more than 11,000 men. 1138 merchant ships were also provided with anti-submarine armament. This presented an enormous effort if one considers that, during the four years of war French naval dockyards were compelled to work mainly for the army, supplying it with 8500 guns and millions of shells. Thus they could not devote their important means of production exclusively to naval needs; they were obliged to abandon the construction of the 5 NORMANDIE class battleships already 60 per cent complete. They, succeeded however in completing the 3 BRETAGNE class battleships, 2 destroyers, 21 submarines and in building 80,000 tons of flotilla vessels including 45 sloops and ASW gunboats, 132 patrol vessels and minesweepers. It may be noted here that the submarine war cost the French merchant marine more than 500 vessels totalling 891,000 GRT.*

Within the limits of this chapter, it is impossible to give the full story of all the navy's war activities. In operations against raiders, it lost in the Indian Ocean the destroyer MOUSQUET and the gunboat ZELEE; two of its cruiser divisions took part, in 1917-18, in the protection of the ocean sea lanes and the armoured cruiser DUPETIT-THOUARS was lost in the North Atlantic. Off Dunkirk, French flotillas took part in many actions against German surface forces based on Zeebrugge and several light French ships were present at the assaults on Zeebrugge and Ostend. Altogether and excluding ships lost by other causes, the French Navy lost in action 4 battleships, 6 cruisers, 23 destroyers and torpedo boats, 14 submarines, 7 auxiliary cruisers, 49 sloops and other patrol vessels in addition to 26 requisitioned transports and other auxiliaries directly attached to the fleet.

Last but not least, French sailors took part in many fights on land. The French Navy does not have 'marines' but the so called 'Fusiliers marins' who are regular sailors trained for infantry duty. During the battle of Flanders (10.14) Admiral Ronarch's brigade – 6500 strong – which had been asked to resist for four days, held the vital position of Dixmude for 25 days against furious German attacks and lost 50 per cent of its force. Until the armistice, a battalion of 'fusiliers marins' fought on the Western Front while strong detachments of gunners (canonniers marins) commissioned twelve specially built river gunboats, several armed barges and manned long range batteries totalling 111 heavy naval guns, a valuable reinforcement considering the lack of such artillery in the French army of 1914 and 1915. Between 10.14 and 1.15 other gunners took part in the defence of Belgrade while 138·6mm guns were installed at the top of mount Lovcen (5100 feet) to shell Cattaro base. Others saw service at the Dardanelles manning a number of 138·6mm guns landed from auxiliary cruisers.

* To this tonnage must be added 5000 GRT of interned ships, 81,000 GRT at sea and 53,000 GRT sold to other nations.

The Admiral Guepratte's squadron in the Dardanelles. From left to right, the SAINT-LOUIS, the CHARLEMAGNE and the SUFFREN.

Old Battleships

Jaureguiberry – one ship

Displacement: 11,900 tons (full load).
Dimensions: 111m(wl) × 22m × 8·45m.
Machinery: 24 d'Allest boilers; 2 sets TE, 2 screws; IHP 15,000; speed 18·7 knots on trials. Coal 910 tons (max).
Radius (nm): 4000/10 knots
Protection: Main belt (steel): 250 – 430mm amidships, 100 – 150mm ends; Main deck: 70mm; Main turrets: 370mm; Small turrets: 100mm; Conning tower: 230mm.
Armament: 2 – 305mm[1], 2 – 274mm broadside[1], 8 – 138·6mm (2 × 4)[2], 4 – 65mm, 14 – 47mm[3], 2 – 350mm submerged tubes. 8 – 0·60m searchlights.
Complement: 31 officers, 566 crew.

[1]1887 model, [2]1891 model, [3]1885 model.

NAME	BUILDER	LAID DOWN	LAUNCHED	COMPLETED
JAURE-GUIBERRY	F. Ch. de la Méditerranée, La Seyne	1891	27.10.93	1.96

NOTES
1914: Special Squadron, escorting French North African and Indian troops to France; overhauled at Bizerta.
1915: Became flagship of Syrian Division based Port Said. In August 1915 replaced BOUVET and SUFFREN at the Dardanelles and became Admiral Guepratte's flagship; supported Gallipoli landings August 25th, 1915. On July 7th returned to Port Said and again flagship of Syrian Division until November 15th, 1915. On August 31st, 1915 destroyed railway station at Kaiffa with two 305mm shells; in September 1915 with JEANNE d'ARC took possession of Ruad Island, Syria.
1916: Sailed to Ismailia for defence of the Canal, later refitted at Malta.
1917: Part of armament removed for defence of the Canal.
1918: In reserve at Port Said; later sailed to Toulon and disarmed as accommodation ship for Mechanics' School.
Stricken June 20th, 1920; condemned in 1932.

Bouvet – one ship

Displacement: 12,200 tons (full load).
Dimensions: 118m(wl) × 21·40m × 8·40m.
Machinery: 32 Belleville boilers; 3 sets TE, 3 screws; IHP 14,000; speed 18 knots. Coal 630 tons (normal), 800 (max).

The old battleship JAUREGUIBERRY.

The old battleship BOUVET as she was in 1914.

Radius (nm):	4000/10 knots (nominal).
Protection:	Main belt (special hardened steel) 400mm amidships, 200mm ends; Upper belt 100mm; Main turrets 370mm; Small turrets 100mm; Conning tower 320mm.
Armament:	2 – 305mm[1], 2 – 274mm[1], 8 – 136·8mm[2], 8 – 100mm[3], 14 – 47mm[4], 10 – 37mm, 2 – 450mm tubes (above water). 6 – 0·6om searchlights.
Complement:	32 officers, 666 crew.

[1]1893 model. [2]1891–93 model. [3]1891 model. [4]1885 model.

NAME	BUILDER	LAID DOWN	LAUNCHED	COMPLETED
BOUVET	Lorient DY	16.2.93	27.4.96	1898

NOTES

1914: From August 3rd until December 16th assigned to the Special Squadron; escorted French North African and Indian transports.

1915: From December 16th to March 18th, 1915 took part in Dardanelles operations. Sunk March 18th on a mine with the loss of her commanding officer, Captain Rageot de la Touche and most of her crew. Posthumously awarded the 'Croix de Guerre' pennant to bear her name in the future.

Charlemagne class – three ships

Displacement:	11,300 tons (full load).
Dimensions:	118m(wl) × 20·50m × 8·40m.
Machinery:	20 Belleville boilers; 3 sets 4 cylinder TE, 2 screws; IHP 14,500; speed 18 knots. Coal 680/1100 tons.
Radius (nm):	3200/10 knots.
Protection:	Main belt (Harvey steel) 150 – 400mm amidships, 250mm ends; Main deck 40 – 90mm (flat below belt); Turrets 230 – 270mm.
Armament:	4 – 305mm (2 × 2)[1], 10 – 138·6mm[2], 8 – 100mm[3], 20 – 47mm[4], 2 – 450mm submerged tubes. 6 – 0·06m searchlights.
Complement:	25 officers, 702 crew.

[1]1893 model. [2]1891–93 model. [3]1893 model. [4]1885 model.

NAME	BUILDER	LAID DOWN	LAUNCHED	COMPLETED
CHARLEMAGNE	Brest DY	7.94	10.95	1899
SAINT-LOUIS	Lorient DY	28.3.95	8.9.96	1.9.00
GAULOIS	Brest DY	1.96	10.96	1899

NOTES

These three ships in August 1914 with SUFFREN, JAUREGUIBERRY and BOUVET formed a division which assumed the protection of Algerian, Tunisian and Indian troops for transport to France. GAULOIS and CHARLEMAGNE were later incorporated in Admiral Guepratte's division in the Dardanelles and took part in shore bombardments.

The old battleship CHARLEMAGNE as she was at the beginning of the war.

The old battleship CHARLEMAGNE with her lightened superstructures as she was during the Dardanelles operations.

Top: The old battleship SAINT-LOUIS with her lightened superstructures and blisters.

Above: The old battleship SAINT-LOUIS as she was in 1914.

GAULOIS on March 18th, 1915 was badly damaged by a mine and forced to beach near Drapano. She was later refloated but had the mishap to encounter the German submarine UB.47 which sank her on October 27th, 1915.

March 18th was a tragic day for the allied naval forces. BOUVET as she withdrew from action – being relieved by British battleships – struck a minefield and sank immediately with nearly all her crew. The British battleships OCEAN and IRRESISTIBLE were also sunk and a large breach was made in the hull of HMS INFLEXIBLE. After these disasters, the forcing of the Straits was abandoned and it was decided to attempt landings at Gallipoli and Koum Kale.

GAULOIS was awarded the 'Croix de Guerre' pennant.

CHARLEMAGNE

1914–15: Dardanelles from November 29th to April 1st, 1915. Refitted at Bizerta. Dardanelles May 14th to October 10th.

1915–16: Salonika October 10th to May 20th, 1916.

1916–17: Salonika August 5th to July 14th, 1918 after overhaul at Bizerta.

In September 1919 disarmed at Toulon; stricken June 21st, 1920.

ST LOUIS

1914: August, flagship of the 'Division de Complement'.

1915: Overhaul at Bizerta. From February 2nd to May 5th was flagship of the Syrian Division; in April shelled enemy installations at Gaza and El Arish. On May 9th rejoined the Dardanelles where for some time became Admiral Guepratte's flagship.

1915–16: Major refit at Lorient from November 1915 to May 1916, being fitted with bulges and her superstructure lightened.

1916–17: Assigned to 'Division Navale d'Orient' as flagship from October 26th to February 24th, 1917. April 1917 in reserve at Bizerta.

1919: Sailed to Toulon and became accommodation ship for the Mechanics' School. Stricken February 20th, 1920 and sold for scrap April 25th, 1933.

Suffren – one ship

Displacement:	12,750 tons (full load).
Dimensions:	126m(wl) × 21·40m × 8·40m.
Machinery:	24 Niclausse boilers; 2 sets TE, 3 screws; IHP 16,200; speed 18 knots. Coal 820/1150 tons.
Radius (nm):	5100/10 knots.
Protection:	Main belt 230 – 300mm; Cofferdams 70 – 130mm; Main turrets 300mm, Barbettes 250mm, Secondary turrets and casemates 120mm; Main deck 70mm; Conning tower 224 – 274mm.
Armament:	4 – 305mm (2 × 2)[1], 10 – 164·7mm (6 in turrets, 4 in casemates)[2], 8 – 100mm[3], 22 – 47mm[4], 4 – 450mm tubes (2 submerged, 2 above water).

[1]1893–96 model. [2]1893–96 model. [3]1893 model. [4]1902 model.

NAME	BUILDER	LAID DOWN	LAUNCHED	COMPLETED
SUFFREN	Brest DY	1.99	7.99	1.03

NOTES

Flagship of Vice-Admiral Guepratte's division (SUFFREN, BOUVET, GAULOIS, CHARLEMAGNE) during the Dardanalles Operations. She took part in the numerous bombardments with great accuracy, not hesitating to go very close inshore to reduce the Turkish fortresses.

SUFFREN was later torpedoed and sunk with her entire crew November 26th, 1916 off Lisbon by the German U.52 while sailing without escort to Brest for repairs. Posthumously awarded the 'Croix de Guerre' pennant.

Old Battleships, not commissioned

Four old battleships appeared on the Fleet List for 1914, out of commission and with armament probably disembarked for transfer either to the army or to equip auxiliary ships:

BRENNUS
Built:	1892.
Displacement	11,400 tons.
Armament:	3 – 370mm (2 × 1, 1 × 1), 10 – 164·7 mm, 4 – 65mm, 14 – 47mm.
Stricken:	1919.

CARNOT
Built:	1895.
Displacement:	12,150 tons.
Armament:	2 – 305mm, 2 – 274mm, 8 – 138·6mm, 4 – 65mm, 16 – 47mm
Stricken:	1919.

CHARLES MARTEL
Built:	1894.
Displacement:	11,900 tons.
Armament:	as CARNOT.
Stricken:	1919.

MASSENA
Built:	1898.
Displacement:	11,900 tons.
Armament:	2 – 305mm, 2 – 274mm, 8 – 138·6mm, 8 – 100m, 14 – 47mm.

After being reduced to a hulk, she was towed to the Dardanelles and scuttled November 9th, 1915 at Seddul-Bahr to serve as a breakwater.

Below: **The old battleship SUFFREN as she was rigged at the beginning of the war.**

Foot: **The old battleship SUFFREN as she was during the Dardanelles operations.**

Pre-Dreadnought Battleships

Republique class – two ships

Displacement:	14,865 tons (full load).
Dimensions:	134·8m(wl) × 24·46m × 8·50m.
Machinery:	24 Niclausse boilers; 2 sets TE, four cylinder, 3 screws; IHP 17,500; speed 18 knots (19+ on trials). Coal 905/1825 tons.
Radius (nm):	8100/10 knots (nominal).
Protection:	Main belt 260 – 280mm amidships, 180mm ends; Upper belt 240mm amidships, 180 and 76 mm ends; Main deck 60mm; Main turrets 320mm, Barbettes 280mm, Secondary turrets and casemates 180mm; Conning tower 280mm.
Armament:	4 – 305mm (2 × 2)[1], 18 – 164·7mm (turrets 2 × 6, casemates 6 × 1)[2], 13 – 65mm[3], 10 – 47mm[4], 5 – 450mm tubes (2 submerged, 3 above water).
Complement:	794.

[1]1902 model, [2]1893–96 model, [3]1902 model. [4]1902 model.

NAME	BUILDER	LAID DOWN	LAUNCHED	COMPLETED
REPUBLIQUE	Brest DY	12.01	9.02	1906
PATRIE	F. Ch. de la Méditerranée, La Seyne	1902	17.12.03	1906

NOTES

1900 programme. These fine ships had very good sea-keeping qualities, as had their successors the VERITE class, and were a turning point in French naval construction, breaking as they did with the troublesome tradition of the 'flotte d'échantillons' (Fleet of Specimens). Their building however was very slow because of the poor policy of M. Camille Pelletan, one of the most useless ministers the French Navy ever had and they unfortunately were obsolescent by the time they were completed. They were reputed to be economical steamers and their artillery was excellent.

From 1914 to 1917 they were incorporated in the 'Armée Navale' and in 1917 they formed with other ships the so called 'Division d'Orient'.

In 1915 PATRIE was fitted with a bow boom for the release of paravanes and in 1916 had taken part in the neutralization of the Greek navy at Salamis September 2nd, 1916. In 1918, four 164·7mm guns were removed at Salonika and given to the 'Armée d'Orient'. From 1920 to 1927 PATRIE was a training ship for electrical and torpedo apprentices at Toulon; she was condemned in 1927.

REPUBLIQUE was based at Toulon in 1918 for service with the Gunnery School, her 305mm turrets being removed and replaced by instruction facilities.

The battleship REPUBLIQUE.

The battleship REPUBLIQUE as she was in 1920 after her conversion into a school-ship.

The battleship PATRIE.

Verite class – three ships

Displacement:	14,900 tons (full load).
Dimensions:	134·8m(wl) × 24m × 8·40m.
Machinery:	22 or 24 Niclausse or Belleville boilers; 3 sets TE, 4 cylinder, 3 screws; IHP 17,500; speed 18 knots. Coal 905/1825 tons.
Radius (nm):	8400/10 knots (nominal).
Protection:	Main belt 260 – 280mm amidships, 180mm ends; Upper belt 240mm amidships, 180mm ends; Main deck 60mm; Main turrets 320mm, Barbettes 280mm, Secondary turrets and casemates 140mm; Conning tower 280mm.
Armament:	4 – 305mm (2 × 2)[1], 10 – 194mm (6 turrets, 4 casemates)[2], 13 – 65mm[3], 10 – 47mm[4], 4 – 450mm tubes (2 submerged, 2 above water broadside).
Complement:	32 officers, 710 crew (+ 12 and 55 as flagship).

[1]1902 model, [2]1902 model, [3]1902 model. [4]1902 model.

NAME	BUILDER	LAID DOWN	LAUNCHED	COMPLETED
DEMOCRATIE	Brest DY	1903	4.04	7.07
JUSTICE	F. Ch. de la Méditerranée, La Seyne	1903	27.9.04	1907
VERITE	Ch. de la Gironde, Bordeaux	1903	5.07	3.08

NOTES

A fourth ship, LIBERTE was blown up on September 25th, 1911.

These ships were similar to their predecessors of the REPUBLIQUE class but with a more powerful secondary armament. They steamed well and all exceeded 19 knots on trials; an average of 17·4 knots for three days had been sustained.

They had an excellent armament, chiefly the 194mm gun which had a very good reputation for accuracy. Light AA guns were installed during the war, DEMOCRATIE receiving 2 machine guns above the forward main turret, one above the port and starboard bow and midship 194mm turrets, two 47mm above the 194mm stern turrets and two more above the main stern turret. Her mainmast was cut down in 1918 for the towing of a kite balloon.

From August 1914 to May 1918 they were generally incorporated in the 'Armée Navale'; on September 25th, 1914 however, VERITE temporarily joined SUFFREN and British naval forces to reinforce the blockade of the Straits and to prevent a sweep by the battlecruiser GOEBEN into the Aegean. In 1916 the three ships took part in the events which brought about the pacific neutralization of the Royal Hellenic Navy at Salamis (September 2nd, 1916).

In May 1918 they joined the Aegean Squadron and in November of that

Top: **The battleship JUSTICE.**

Above: **The battleship VERITE.**

year JUSTICE and DEMOCRATIE moved to the Bosphorus to celebrate
the Allied victory. The former then sailed with FRANCE, JEAN BART,
VERGNIAUD, MIRABEAU and lighter vessels to the Crimea in order to
assist the Russian White army which was pressed by Bolshevik forces. The
French squadron and troops were soon forced to evacuate the district. Some
acts of indiscipline took place in a few ships because of Communist propa-
ganda and because of the slow demobilization of the crews. In April,
JUSTICE towed the damaged VERGNIAUD to Toulon.

These three battleships were condemned in 1921 (JUSTICE on November
29th, 1921, sold for scrap in 1922).

Danton class – six ships

Displacement:	18,318 tons (19,763 full load).
Dimensions:	146·60m(oa), 144·90m(pp) × 25·80m × 9·20m (full load).
Machinery:	26 Niclausse boilers; Parsons 4 shaft turbines; SHP 22,500; speed 19 knots (slightly exceeded on trials). Coal 2027 tons.
Radius (nm):	3370/10 knots, 1750/18 knots.
Protection:	Main belt 204 – 223mm ends, 255mm amidships; Main deck 65 – 75mm, Lower deck 75mm amidships; Main turrets 320mm, Barbettes 280mm, Secondary turrets 223mm; Conning tower 300mm.
Armament:	4 – 305mm (2 × 2)[1], 12 – 240mm (2 × 6)[2], 16 – 75mm[3]. 10 – 47mm[4], 2 – 450mm submerged tubes. 8 – 0.75m Breguet searchlights, 10 Barr and Stroud rangefinders.
Complement:	23 officers, 898 crew.

[1]1906 model, [2]1902 model, [3]1906 Schneider model. [4]1902
model.

NAME	BUILDER	LAID DOWN	LAUNCHED	COMPLETED
DANTON	Brest DY	2.06	1909	3.11
MIRABEAU	Lorient DY	5.08	1909	7.11
DIDEROT	Saint-Nazaire	1907	4.09	6.11
CONDORCET	Saint Nazaire	1907	4.09	6.11
VERGNIAUD	Ch. de la Gironde, Bordeaux	7.08	12.4.10	10.5.11
VOLTAIRE	F. Ch. de la Méditerranée, La Seyne	7.08	1.09	6.11

NOTES
1905 programme. Designed by M. L'Homme, the DANTONs were the
first big turbine-engined ships of the French fleet. They were not a great
success and their coal consumption was said to be heavy at cruising speed.
Nevertheless because of their number and their excellent artillery and

The battleship MIRABEAU as she was in 1914.

The battleship CONDORCET.

The battleship VERGNIAUD with her main mast cut down for the towing of a kite-balloon.

The battleship VOLTAIRE during her first trials.

weight of broadside, they were the 'force de frappe' of the 'Armée Navale.'

One triple mounting of 3·66m rangefinders (Triplex) was installed during the war above the conning tower and four supplementary searchlights fitted abaft and above the conning tower. The mainmast was in 1918 cut down in CONDORCET, VERGNIAUD and VOLTAIRE to the funnel height for the towing of kite balloons. The maximum range of the 240mm guns was increased from 13,700 to 18,000m and a fire-direction system identical to DREADNOUGHT's was fitted.

These 240mm guns, reinstalled at Dakar after the war as shore batteries, proved their accuracy and effectiveness when they caused great damage to cruisers HMS DELHI and CUMBERLAND during an unsuccessful attempt by the British and General de Gaulle to take the base (1940).

The six ships took part in the operations of the 'Armée Navale' in the Adriatic (the ZENTA affair).

In December 1916, VOLTAIRE, MIRABEAU, VERGNIAUD and CONDORCET moored off Athens with other ships for a pacific demonstration and landed a company to support the Allied policy in the conflict with the pro-German King Constantine and his government. The sailors fell into a murderous ambush causing 56 casualties and Vice-Admiral Dartige du Fournet commanding the combined forces had to open fire to stop the fight. Only some four rounds of intimidation from heavy guns were fired by MIRABEAU, one of them falling near the Royal Palace; the Greek government immediately agreed to Allied requests.

On March 19th, 1917, DANTON was torpedoed and sunk by the German U.64 south-west of San Prieto.

In 1918 German troops took possession of Sevastopol and captured some Russian warships. For fear they would achieve a sweep into the Mediterranean through the Straits, a powerful allied fleet was formed to counter this threat. DIDEROT, MIRABEAU and VERGNIAUD (plus VOLTAIRE later) left the 'Armée Navale' in Corfu and sailed to Mudros where they formed with the older battleships JUSTICE, VERITE, and DEMOCRATIE and some lighter vessels, the Aegean Sea Squadron. VOLTAIRE having been twice torpedoed without serious damage by the German submarine UB.48 (October 10/11th, 1918), the other ships moored on November 13th in front of Constantinople with allied warships to show their victorious supremacy to the enemy.

In 1919, two ships of the class, VERGNIAUD and MIRABEAU took part in unsuccessful fights off Sevastopol against the Bolsheviks. MIRABEAU stranded in a snowstorm on the Crimean coast near that port on February 8th. She was refloated in April after removal of the forward 305mm turret and side armour and towed to Toulon by JUSTICE. She was condemned October 27th, 1921 because of her damaged condition and used for experimental purposes before scrapping in 1928.

During 1920–22 the three surviving ships formed the Channel Division. Refitted between 1922 and 1925, they sailed in January 1927 to Toulon to form the training squadron. VOLTAIRE and DIDEROT were condemned in 1935 and 1936. CONDORCET was scuttled August 1944 by the Germans; refloated in September she was scrapped December 14th, 1945.

Battleships—Dreadnought Type

As was previously said, the 1912 programme should have provided a force of 28 battleships in 1920 including the ships of PATRIE-VERITE and DANTON classes and the four dreadnoughts of the COURBET type being built. The 13 warships to be built to complete the programme were to be laid down according to the following calendar:

3 in 1912 (the BRETAGNE class)
2 in 1913
2 in 1914
4 in 1915
2 in 1917

But owing to the rapid rearming of other navies, especially those of potential opponents to the French Fleet in the Mediterranean, it became necessary to remedy this dangerous situation. Consequently a financial law authorized the Navy to build, in 1913, four battleships of the NORMANDIE Class instead of two; likewise the financial law of 1914, tabled in November 1913, decided that the only battleship to be started in 1914 should be laid down January 1st instead of October 1st as had been planned and that she should be similar to NORMANDIE. There was another reason for advancing the laying down of this fifth ship: at the beginning of 1913, the Chief of Naval Staff had decided that each battle squadron should in the future be formed with eight ships in place of six as had been the case. He wished to oppose formations of the same composition and power as the foreign squadrons. This fifth NORMANDIE, named BEARN, was necessary to complete the division of the three BRETAGNE class ordered in 1912.

During the building of these battleships and of the NORMANDIE class, the Naval Staff studied and then fixed the characteristics of the four vessels which were to be laid down in 1915. They would have been the LYON Class which was never started because of the war which also forced the stopping of work on the five NORMANDIE Class. Finally the three BRETAGNEs only were commissioned and with the units of the COURBET class, the French Navy completed only seven dreadnoughts during the war.

Courbet class – four ships

Displacement:	23,189 tons (25,850 full load).
Dimensions:	165m(oa) × 27m × 9m.
Machinery:	24 (16 large, 8 small) Belleville boilers; Parsons 4-shaft turbines; SHP 28,000; speed 21 knots. Coal 906/2700 tons, fuel oil 310 tons.
Radius (nm):	4200/10 knots, 1140/20 knots.
Protection:	Main belt 270mm amidships, 180mm ends; Upper belt 180mm; Funnel uptakes 180mm; Forecastle deck 30mm,

The dreadnought JEAN BART.

	Upper deck 50mm, Main deck 70mm; Turrets 320mm, Barbettes 270mm, Casemates 180mm; Conning tower 300mm.
Armament:	12 – 305mm (2 × 6)[1], 22 – 138·6mm[2], 4 – 47mm (2 × 4)[3], 4 – 450mm submerged tubes.
Complement:	1108.

[1]1910 model, [2]1910 model. [3]1902 model.

NAME	BUILDER	LAID DOWN	LAUNCHED	COMPLETED
JEAN BART	Brest DY	15.11.10	26.9.11	5.6.13
COURBET	Lorient DY	9.10	23.9.11	9.13
PARIS	F. Ch. de la Méditerranée, La Seyne	11.11	28.9.11	8.14
FRANCE	Penhoet, Saint-Nazaire	11.11	11.12	7.14

NOTES

1910 programme. Designed by M. Lyasse, they were the first dreadnought type battleships in the French Navy; they were well constructed but had a very wet foredeck in a rough sea. This was due to the weight of the superimposed fore turrets and to the fact that the dimensions of the repair dock of the time had not allowed their hulls to be lengthened.

In August 1914 these four ships were the 'trump-card' of the 'Armée Navale'; they were fitted with modern fire-direction equipment (Lecomte-Aubry electric transmitters without intermediate transcription, Le Prieur graphic computators). Unfortunately the plastic breech-obturators of the 305mm guns were not adjusted, this meant that the guns would have to cease fire after a few salvoes. Happily enough for the 'Armée Navale', the artillery of DANTON was properly adjusted.

Astern view of the dreadnought COURBET bearing the flag of Vice Admiral Boué de Lapeyre C-in-C the 'Armée Navale'.

The dreadnought PARIS during her trials off Toulon.

The dreadnought FRANCE as she was at the end of the war.

COURBET was flagship of Vice-Admiral Boué de Lapeyrere when he commanded the 'Armée Navale'.

JEAN BART was torpedoed by the Austrian submarine U.12 in the Adriatic December 21st, 1914; the torpedo struck abreast of the wine-store just before the forward magazine. The crew were in despair by the loss of the wine but the magazine did not explode, thanks to the care given to its protection.

One triple mount of 3·66m rangefinders (Triplex) was installed during the war above the conning tower in all ships and searchlights added on a cradle abaft the second funnel in COURBET. This ship also had her mainmast removed to facilitate the towing of a kite balloon.

FRANCE, which took part with JEAN BART in the Sevastopol operations of 1919, foundered in Quiberon Bay (August 1922). The three others were largely refitted between 1926 and 1929 when the two forward funnels (except in PARIS) were trunked into a single heightened uptake, one tripod foremast replaced the pole mast and was stepped forward of the fore funnel; a modern fire director was installed and the range of the main guns increased from 14,500 to 23,000m. The AA armament was also increased.

JEAN BART was paid off in 1936 and renamed OCEAN and relegated to training duties. Before World War II, COURBET was used as a gunnery training ship and PARIS was attached to a signal training school.

In World War II, COURBET took part in the defence of Cherbourg, but was in Portsmouth at the time of the defeat of France; she was seized there by the British on July 3rd, 1940 (Operation Catapult). She was later turned over to the Free French Naval Forces and was used as a breakwater during the allied invasion of Normandy. PARIS was in Plymouth and was taken over on the same occasion by the British; she was eventually used as a barracks for Polish naval personnel. She had previously taken part in the defence of Le Havre where she was damaged by a bomb on June 11th, 1940. Turned over to the French, she was towed to Brest on August 21st, 1945; she was later paid off and scrapped in 1956, at that time the veteran of the French Navy.

OCEAN was used as a target ship by the Germans after November 1942.

Bretagne class – three ships

Displacement:	23,320 tons (circa 25,000 full load).
Dimensions:	166m(oa) × 27m × 8·90m.
Machinery:	Boilers, BRETAGNE: 24 Niclausse; LORRAINE: 24 Belleville; PROVENCE: 18 Guyot-du Temple; Parsons 4 shaft turbines; SHP 29,000; speed 20 knots. Coal 900/2680 tons, fuel oil 300 tons.
Radius (nm):	4700/10 knots, 2800/18¾ knots.
Protection:	Main belt 270mm amidships, 180mm ends; Upper belt 180mm; Focsle deck 30mm; Upper deck 50mm; Main deck 70mm; Turrets 340mm except superimposed turret 250mm and midship turret 400mm, Barbettes 270mm, Casemates 180mm; Conning tower 314mm.

Top: The dreadnought BRETAGNE moored at Brest in 1915.

Above: The dreadnought BRETAGNE as she was at the end of the war with a tripod mast.

Top: **The dreadnought PROVENCE during her trials off Toulon.**

Above: **The dreadnought PROVENCE as she was at the end of the war. Note that her forward 138·4mm guns are being disembarked.**

Armament:	10 – 340mm (2 × 5)[1], 22 – 138·6mm[2], 4 – 47mm, 2 – 1pdr, 4 – 450mm submerged tubes. 16 – 0·90m searchlights.			
Complement:	24 officers, 1109 crew.			

[1] 1912 model, [2] 1910 model.

NAME	BUILDER	LAID DOWN	LAUNCHED	COMPLETED
BRETAGNE	Brest DY	7.12	21.4.13	9.15
PROVENCE	Lorient DY	6.12	20.4.13	6.15
LORRAINE	Penhoet, St Nazaire	11.12	30.9.13	7.16

NOTES

1912 programme. The only French ships originally fitted with Bullivant net defence, removed in 1917. They were completed with triple mount 3·66m rangefinders (Triplex) with fire direction identical to that of the COURBET class. Also like the previous class, they were very wet forward in rough weather though otherwise splendid gun platforms, the 340mm having a good reputation but their maximum range (14,500m) was at the time less than that of other contemporary warships, especially the Austrian dreadnoughts.

However, the angle of laying of the stern turret of LORRAINE was in 1917 changed from 12 to 18 degrees and consequently the range increased to 18,000m. This modification should have been carried out in the other four turrets and also to her sister ships, but pressure of work in the dockyards made this impossible before the armistice.

On August 31st, 1918 it was decided to fit BRETAGNE, during her refit at Brest, with a tripod mast and fire directors; at the same time the range of

The dreadnought LORRAINE as she was in 1918.

her main guns was increased to 18,000m. Her fore funnel was raised, the bridge and the position of searchlights modified and a spotting plane added above the second forward turret. These were only completed in 1920.

It was later decided to carry out the same modifications to her sisters but with a gun-laying angle of elevation increased to 23 degrees, raising the range to 23,000m. This last alteration was later made in BRETAGNE at the same time as her mainmast which had been removed in 1920.

These ships were incorporated in 1916 in the 'Armée Navale', PROVENCE being flagship from 1916 to 1919.

PROVENCE took part in the Salamis and Athens operations in 1916. LORRAINE was detached to Cattaro in January 1919 in order to hasten repatriation of Austrian crews and in March to assist in the delivery of Austrian warships to Italy and France.

During 1932–35 BRETAGNE and PROVENCE were again refitted when they were provided with new 340mm guns originally intended for the NORMANDIE class battleships, were reboilered and converted to oil-firing; their SHP increased from 29,000 to 43,000. Eight 138·6mm guns and submerged torpedo tubes were also removed and AA guns augmented. LORRAINE was thoroughly reconstructed between 1932 and 1935 when the midship 340mm turret was replaced by an aircraft hangar and catapult.

BRETAGNE blew up and capsized during action at Mers-el-Kebir on July 3rd, 1940. PROVENCE during this same deplorable, stupid and finally vain action ordered by Churchill,* was so badly damaged that she had to be beached in the harbour. She was towed to Toulon in November 1940 and scuttled there on November 27th, 1942; later refloated, she was scrapped July 11th, 1943.

LORRAINE was disarmed in Alexandria in July 1940. On May 30th, 1943 she returned to action with other ships interned in the port. In 1944 she took part in the liberation of Toulon and in 1945, fired against German positions in the Atlantic pockets. She was scrapped on February 2nd, 1953.

Normandie class – five ships

Displacement:	25,230 tons (full load).
Dimensions:	176·40mm(oa), 175m(pp) × 27m × 8·65m.
Machinery:	Boilers, NORMANDIE and GASCOGNE: 21 small tube Guyot-du Temple; LANGUEDOC and FLANDRE: 28 small tube Belleville; BEARN: 21 small tube Niclausse. All except BEARN, 2 sets TE, 4 cylinder on lateral shafts, 2 Parsons or Rateau-Bretagne (GASCOGNE) or Zoelly (LANGUEDOC) direct action turbines on central shafts with no reversing gear; BEARN: 4 Parsons turbines only; HP 32,000; speed 21 knots. Coal 900/2700 tons, oil 300 tons.
Radius (nm):	1800/21 knots, 3375/16 knots and 6500/12 knots on TE only.

* The reader is asked to refer on this matter to the excellent book by Anthony Heckstall-Smith—*The Fleet That Faced Both Ways.*

Protection: Main belt 300mm amidships, 180 – 130mm ends; Upper
belt 240mm amidships, 160mm ends; Turrets 340 –
250mm, Barbettes 284mm, Casemates 180 – 160mm;
Conning tower 300mm; Double armoured deck and
efficient protection against torpedoes; Bullivant net defence.

Armament: 12 – 340mm (4 × 3)[1], 24 – 138·6mm[2], 6 – 450mm
submerged tubes. 5 – 3·66m rangefinders.

[1]1912 model, max range 16,500m. [2] 1910 model.

NAME	BUILDER	LAID DOWN	LAUNCHED	TRIALS (PROJECTED)
NORMANDIE	Ateliers et Ch. de la Loire, St Nazaire	18.4.13	19.10.14	3.16
LANGUEDOC	Forges et Ch. de la Gironde, Bordeaux	18.4.13	1.5.15	3.16
FLANDRE	Brest DY	1.10.13	20.10.14	6.17
GASCOGNE	Lorient DY	1.10.13	20.9.14	6.17
BEARN	F. et Ch. de la Méditerranée La Seyne	1.14	4.20	1917 when ordered

NOTES

1912 programme. In these vessels, designed by M. Doyere chief naval
constructor since 1911, the 340mm quadruple turret was finally adopted after
a variety of other gun dispositions had been considered in the limit of displacement tied down by the dimensions of French dry docks of the time.
This choice had allowed a total weight smaller than that of the five twin
turrets of the BRETAGNEs to obtain two additional guns with better
protection to each turret. The quadruple turret was adopted before World
War II in the French DUNKERQUE and RICHELIEU battleships and
also in the British KING GEORGE V class.

NORMANDIE's machinery was much criticized; it was a return to that
of former dreadnoughts, but chosen because the fuel consumption of turbines at the time was too great at cruising speeds. However, the turbine
drive was retained for the fifth of the class (BEARN) so as to constitute a
homogeneous division with the three BRETAGNEs.

At the outbreak of war in 1914, work was stopped on NORMANDIE and
the four most advanced were later launched to clear their building-berths.
There was no question of industrial mobilization in 1914 and only a short
war was expected; dockyard and private builders' workers put on their
uniforms and went to the war. All work consequently was disorganized or
stopped, but as soon as they were ready, the powerful 340mm and 138·6mm
guns that had been ordered for these ships were sent to the Front while
their water-tube boilers of a new, small and light design were used as spares
for destroyers or for new patrol vessels.

After the armistice, the Naval Staff studied the possibility of resuming the
construction of the four ships which had been put afloat, in order to keep

The dreadnought GASCOGNE after her launching. She was not completed.

an actual superiority over the Italian Navy which became the prime rival of the French Fleet. They hesitated between three options:

(a) to complete the ships without any change to the original design;
(b) to complete the NORMANDIE with the following ameliorations: strengthening of the horizontal protection and artillery, installation of anti-torpedo cofferdams, modernization of artillery especially in increasing the maximum range (26,000m as against 16,500m) and in fitting a modern fire control system, the installation of a tripod mast and more powerful searchlights;
(c) to lengthen the hull and build along the vital parts 2·70m-wide bulges and also to replace the machinery by turbines totalling 80,000 HP to obtain a speed of 26 knots and to modernize the guns as above mentioned.

But because of the lack of money and also of the opinion of a number of highly qualified naval experts who were of the feeling that the submarine was going to master the battleship, the Naval Staff gave up the idea of completing the NORMANDIE class and remained satisfied with the modernization of the seven dreadnoughts already in service. This was without doubt a political error, which was sanctioned by the Washington Treaty which put the French Navy, for this category of ships, on the same level as the Italian Fleet.

The BEARN, which was not well advanced, was launched in April 1920 to clear her building berth and converted between August 1923 and May 1927 into an aircraft carrier. She was equipped with the same propulsion system as NORMANDIE, and not with 4 Parsons Turbines as projected.

Lyon class – four ships

Displacement: 29,000 tons (full load).
Dimensions: 194·5m(oa), 190m(pp) × 29m × 8·65m.
Machinery: see notes.

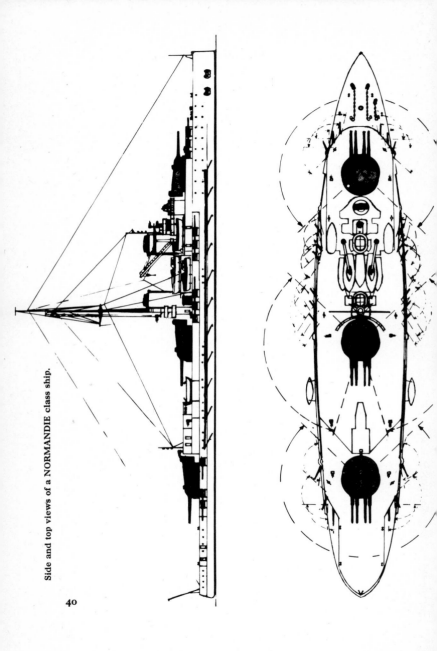

Side and top views of a NORMANDIE class ship.

40

Side and top views of a LYON class ship.

Protection:	see notes.	
Armament:	16 − 340mm (4 × 4)[1], 24 − 138·6mm[2], several AA guns.	

[1]1912M model. [2]1910 model *or* of a new semi-automatic type to be studied.

NAME	BUILDER	TO LAY DOWN
LYON	Penhoet, St Nazaire	1.1.15
LILLE	F. Ch. de la Méditerranée, La Seyne	1.1.15
DUQUESNE	Brest DY	1.4.15
TOURVILLE	Lorient DY	1.4.15

NOTES

1912 programme. Designed also by M. Doyere, these four vessels, whose displacement was not limited by dry dock dimensions,* were an extrapolation of the NORMANDIE class. They certainly would have been the most formidable among warships of their time.

Several projects, all turning around the 340mm gun as main artillery, had been presented to the Naval Staff. The choice of a 380mm gun had been also considered but it was finally rejected because of the long time the design of a new gun would have taken.

One of these projects provided for a ship of 27,500 tons with 14 - 340mm guns in three quadruple turrets (one forward, two superimposed astern) and a double turret amidships.

Two models of the 340mm gun were also considered:

a 45 calibre weapon identical to the one in BRETAGNE and NORMAN-DIE classes but with a longer, heavier and more efficient projectile with a greater range and a submerged trajectory. This type of shell was indeed at this time considered to be one of the most dangerous of threats owing to its double effect of torpedoing and perforation;

a 50 calibre weapon firing a heavier projectile (640 as against 590 kilos).

At last, the Naval Staff selected the first model above mentioned and decided that the LYON class would have four quadruple turrets with hydro-electric mountings and all-round loading position.

The propulsion considered was either of combined machinery as in the NORMANDIE class or by direct drive turbines as in BEARN and former dreadnoughts, but M. Doyere had not rejected geared turbines. This type of machinery had already made good progress by this time and good results were expected from the experiments which were to be undertaken aboard the destroyer ENSEIGNE GABOLDE. The power of the machinery was expected to reach 43,000 HP and the speed 23 knots.

The protection would have been generally similar to that in NORMAN-DIE with a strengthening of submerged parts to the slight detriment of the upper belt and casemate thicknesses.

* During their construction, dry docks would have been enlarged.

Coastal Defence Ships

Requin – one ship

Displacement: 7740 tons (full load).
Dimensions: 85·30m(oa) × 18m × 7·50m.
Machinery: 8 Niclausse boilers; 2 sets TE, 2 screws; IHP 11,200; speed 15 knots (12 knots by 1914). Coal 400 tons.
Radius (nm): 1500/10 knots.
Protection: Main belt (compound) 500mm amidships, 320mm ends; Main deck 80 – 100mm; Turrets (Harvey-nickel) 240mm, Barbettes 210mm; Conning tower 300mm.
Armament: 2 – 274mm[1], 6 – 100mm[2], 10 – 47mm[3].
Complement: 332.

[1]1893–96 model, [2]1893 model, [3]1885 model.

NAME	BUILDER	LAID DOWN	LAUNCHED	COMPLETED
REQUIN	F. Ch. de la Gironde, Bordeaux	1879	13.6.85	12.88

NOTES

This old battleship of the 1877 programme, was reconstructed between 1898 and 1901. Her initial armament (2 – 340mm, 4 – 100mm and 8 – 37mm revolving) was removed and she was rearmed as stated. New boilers were also fitted.

In 1913 she was in reserve at Bizerta. In October 1914 she was recommissioned and rated as formerly 'garde-côtes cuirassé' and sailed for Egypt. In December she shelled, near Alexandretta, the railway which supplied the Turkish forces preparing an attack on the Suez Canal. In January 1915 she cast anchor in the Timsah Lake along with the cruiser D'ENTRECAST-EAUX and the RIM ship HARDINGE and with accurate fire, forced the enemy to withdraw and the Canal was safeguarded.

From 1916 to 1918 she took part in the operations along the coast of Syria supporting the left of the Allied Offensive before Suza in spite of an enemy submarine which torpedoed her without success (UC.74 on April 19th, 1917). She was paid off in 1919, striken February 2nd, 1920 and scrapped in 1922. She was awarded the 'Croix de Guerre' pennant.

Henri IV – one ship

Displacement: 9000 tons (full load).
Dimensions: 108m(wl) × 22m × 7·50m.
Machinery: Niclausse boilers; 3 sets TE, 3 screws; IHP 11,500; speed 17·5 knots. Coal 820 tons.

The coastal defence ship REQUIN moored in the Timsah Lake.

The coastal defence ship HENRI IV.

Radius (nm):	5000/10 knots.
Protection:	Main belt (Harvey-nickel) 280mm amidships, 200mm ends; Upper belt 115mm; Main deck 75 – 115mm; Cofferdam and double bottom; Casemates 115mm, Main turrets 250mm, Secondary turrets 115mm.
Armament:	2 – 274mm[1], 7 – 138·6mm (4 casemates, 2 behind shields, 1 in stern turret)[2], 12 – 47mm[3], 2 – 450mm submerged tubes.
Complement:	460.

[1]1893–96 model, [2]1891–93 model, [3]1902 model.

NAME	BUILDER	LAID DOWN	LAUNCHED	COMPLETED
HENRI IV	Cherbourg DY	1897	8.99	1902

NOTES

This ship was rated as a 'garde-côtes cuirassé' and was a school ship before the war.

She joined the Dardanelles after the loss of GAULOIS.

Part of her secondary armament was disembarked in 1917 and sent to France for army use. She was condemned in 1921.

The two following coastal defence ships appeared in the Fleet List for 1914 but were not commissioned:

BOUVINES
AMIRAL TREHOUART

Built:	1893 (both)
Displacement:	6600 tons.
Armament:	2 – 305mm, 8 – 100mm, 8 – 47mm.

BOUVINES was based at Cherbourg and used as depot ship for the requisitioned interrogation boats.

Armoured Cruisers

In spite of their imposing silhouette and their numerous funnels, French armoured cruisers were slow and badly armed; slow speed and large size made them poor scouting vessels and poor protection and armament did not permit their challenging enemy battlecruisers. They resulted from the aberrant policy of the 'young school' which still prevailed at the turn of the century and was based on coast defence and commerce destroying.

Though French maritime history had in the past shown a use for this policy, it still unfortunately found support and a champion in the person of Camille Pelletan who has been referred to before. For the same reason the navy had no scouts of the small fast cruiser type which proved so useful during the war. However, with the advent of more competent ministers, especially of Vice-Admiral Boué de Lapeyrere in the 'seat of Colbert', sane concepts prevailed at last but too late.

It was thus proposed to build large fast warships of a type named 'cuirassé-croiseur' and ten light protected cruisers 'convoyeurs d'escadrilles'.

Inspired by the British QUEEN ELIZABETH battleships, the 'cuirassé-croiseur' would have had a speed of 25 knots with more guns and armour than contemporary battlecruisers; she would in fact have predated the new battleships of World War II. The project did not get further than the design stage and one such design, from the naval constructor Gille, had the following characteristics:

Displacement:	28,347 tons.
Dimensions:	205m(pp) × 27m × 9·03m (mean).
Machinery:	52 Belleville boilers; geared turbines, 4 screws; SHP 80,000; speed 28 knots.
Armament:	12 – 340mm (4 × 3), 24 – 138·6mm.
Complement:	41 officers, 1258 crew.

Another, designed by the future Admiral Durand-Viel, one of the most famous chiefs of the navy, foresaw 27,500 ton, 27 knot ships armed with eight 340 or 370mm guns in two quadruple turrets. A very similar armament was later adopted when Admiral Durant-Viel was chief of staff, in the fast battleships of the DUNKERQUE and RICHELIEU classes of World War II.

Amiral Charner class – three ships

Displacement:	4700 tons.
Dimensions:	110m × 14m × 6m.
Machinery:	Belleville boilers (without economisers); 2 sets horizontal TE, 2 screws; IHP 8300; speed 18·5 knots. Coal 600 tons maximum.
Protection:	Belt (steel) 90mm; Armoured deck 65 – 55mm, Splinter deck over vital parts; Turrets 100mm.

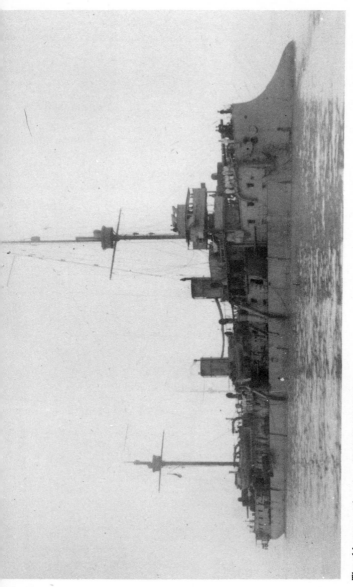

The old armoured cruiser AMIRAL CHARNER.

The old armoured cruiser LATOUCHE-TREVILLE.

Armament:	2 – 194mm[1], 6 – 138·6mm[1], 4 – 65mm[2], 8 – 47mm[3].	
	6 – 0·60m seachlights.	
Complement:	16 officers, 370 crew.	

[1] 1887 model. [2] 1891 model. [3] 1885 model.

NAME	BUILDER	LAID DOWN	LAUNCHED	COMPLETED
AMIRAL CHARNER	Rochefort DY	6.89	18.3.93	1895
LATOUCHE	Le Havre	1889	5,11.92	1895
BRUIX	Rochefort DY	1890	1894	1896

NOTES

These three ships were in reserve in 1914 or in use as school ships. A fourth of the class, CHANZY, was lost in 1907.

AMIRAL CHARNER: from August to November 1914 escorted troop transports from Morocco to France. In September 1915 was on a rescue operation in Antioch Bay evacuating 3000 Armenians escaping from the Turks. December 28, 1915 with JEANNE D'ARC took possession of Castellorizo Island.

On December 8th, 1916 was torpedoed and sunk west of Beirut with only one survivor; posthumously awarded the 'Croix de Guerre' pennant.

BRUIX: August to November 1914 with AMIRAL CHARNER. 1915 patrols in the Red Sea. December 1916 to June 1917 operations at Salamis and Athens; blockade of Greece. 1918 in reserve at Salonika.

LATOUCHE-TREVILLE: 1914 Morocco, Dakar, Bizerta and western Mediterranean. 1915: sailed for Syria February 12th, 1915 and captured the steamer INDIANA. Supported landings at Gallipoli and was damaged by Turkish gunfire; repaired at Toulon and rejoined ships off Salonika where she remained until January 16th, 1917, blockade of Greece January to June and later based at Corfu as gunlayers' schoolship. 1918 paid off at Toulon and condemned June 21st, 1920. Her hull was used as a caisson to raise the wrecked battleship LIBERTE.

Pothuau – one ship

Displacement:	5365 tons.
Dimensions:	113m × 15m × 6.50m.
Machinery:	16 old type Belleville boilers; 2 sets horizontal TE, 2 screws; IHP 10,400; speed 19 knots. Coal 538 tons.
Radius (nm):	4500/10 knots, 1400/full speed.
Protection:	Belt 60mm amidships, 35m ends; Deck 85 – 35mm; Main turrets 180mm, Casemates 55mm; Conning tower 240mm; Cellular cofferdam and cellular compartments to the waterline.
Armament:	2 – 194mm[1], 10 – 138·4mm in casemates or sponsons[2], 12 – 47mm[3], 8 – 37mm QF. 6 – 0·60m searchlights.
Complement:	21 officers, 434 crew.

[1]1893 model, [2]1891–93 model, [3]1885 model.

NAME	BUILDER	LAID DOWN	LAUNCHED	COMPLETED
POTHUAU	Le Havre	1893	1895	1896

NOTES

She was a good sea boat. In 1914 she was used as a gunnery school.

1914–15: after cruising in the Mediterranean, sailed for the Cameroun where her landing party took possession of Krivi. Replaced by FRIANT, she left for refit at Lorient at the end of 1915.

1916–17: At Port Said and took part in the defence of the Canal and Red Sea, then refitting at Saigon.

1917–18: Returned to Toulon where her mainmast was cut down and she was fitted for kite balloon towing; later became a gunnery school ship.

Post-war: Turrets replaced 1919 by AA gun prototypes and remained as gunnery school ship until 1929. Stricken November 3rd, 1927 and scrapped in 1929.

The armoured cruiser POTHUAU.

Jeanne d'Arc – one ship

Displacement:	11,270 tons.
Dimensions:	145m × 19·4m × 8·1m.
Machinery:	48 Normand-Sigaudy boilers; 3 sets vertical TE, 3 screws; SHP 28,000; speed 23 knots. Coal 1400 tons (normal).
Radius (nm):	13,500/10 knots.
Protection:	Belt 150mm amidships, 75mm end forward; Splinter deck 50mm; Turrets 200mm, Barbettes 167mm; Conning tower 150mm.
Armament:	2 – 194mm[1], 14 – 138·6mm[2], 16 – 47mm[3], 2 – 450mm submerged tubes.
Complement:	626.

[1]1893 model, [2]1891–93 model, [3]1902 model.

NAME	BUILDER	LAID DOWN	LAUNCHED	COMPLETED
JEANNE D'ARC	Toulon DY	10.96	8.6.99	1903

NOTES
Although designed by the naval constructor Emile Bertin, this cruiser was not a success; she never reached her contract speed and was a great coal consumer.

1912–14: In service as training ship.

August 1914; 2nd Light Squadron in the Channel, then joined Admiral Wemyss's squadron for patrols in the Western Channel.

1915: Eastern Mediterranean; took possession of Ruad Island with JAUREGUIBERRY and of Castellorizo with AMIRAL CHARNER. On May 31st, 1915 she destroyed the German consulate at Kaiffa and in September rescued the Armenians in Antioch Bay.

1916–17: Syrian division.

1918: Escorted troop convoys between the USA and France.

1919 to 1928: On training duties. 1929–33 in reserve.

February 2nd, 1933 unlisted; 1934 scrapped at Toulon.

Kleber class – three ships

Displacement:	7700 tons.
Dimensions:	130m × 17·75m × 7·4m.
Machinery:	20 Belleville boilers (except KLEBER 20 Niclausse); 3 sets vert TE, 3 screws; SHP 17,000; speed 21 knots. Coal: 880 tons (normal), 1200 (max including oil).
Radius (nm):	6400/10 knots.
Protection:	Belt 102mm waterline, 38mm below waterline; Deck 65 – 40mm; Turrets 100mm – 50mm; Conning tower 150mm.
Armament:	8 – 164·4mm (2 × 4)[1], 4 – 100mm[2], 10 – 47mm[3], 4 – 37mm. 6 – 0·60m searchlights.

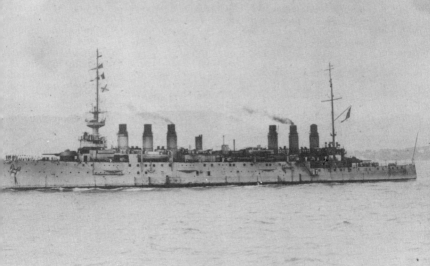

Top: The armoured cruiser JEANNE D'ARC seen in Port Said harbour.

Above: The armoured cruiser JEANNE D'ARC fitted as schoolship at the end of the war.

Complement: 19 officers, 551 crew (+5 and 33 as flagship).

^{1}1893–96 model, ^{2}1893 model, ^{3}1885 model.

NAME	BUILDER	LAID DOWN	LAUNCHED	COMPLETED
DUPLEIX	Rochefort DY	1899	4.00	1903
DESAIX	Penhoet, Saint-Nazaire	1.99	21.3.01	1904
KLEBER	Ch. de la Gironde, Bordeaux	1898	20.9.02	1903

NOTES

KLEBER was launched entirely complete but damaged her bottom in the process and remained in shipyard hands until November 1902, then suffered teething troubles up to the end of 1903.

In 1914 she was assigned to the 2nd Light Squadron in the Channel and Bay of Biscay. She went to the Mediterranean in May 1915 and later to the Dardanelles where she stranded and refloated under enemy gunfire May 29th/31st, 1915. Repaired at Toulon, she sailed to the Aegean where she shelled enemy shore installations. July 7th, 1915 she was seriously damaged in collision with a British cargo boat off Mudros; repaired at Mudros until October. In 1916 she was in the Eastern Mediterranean, later refitted at Bordeaux then flagship of the 6th Squadron based at Dakar. 1917: While returning to Brest, was mined in the Iroise (mine laid by UC.61) and sunk with the loss of 7 officers and 35 men (June 27th, 1917).

DESAIX in 1914 was on patrol in the Channel until December 1914 when she left for the Mediterranean. In 1915 took part with REQUIN and MONTCALM in the defence of the Suez Canal then joined the 3rd Squad-

The armoured cruiser DUPLEIX.

ron for the Syrian coast patrol. In September 1915 she was rescuing Armenians in Antioch Bay. In 1916 joined the 6th Squadron at Dakar. Her 100mm guns were removed in 1917 for the defence of merchant ships and two 47mm were fitted as AA guns. In 1918 she relieved GLOIRE in the West Indies for Atlantic patrol and in 1919 was in the Far East. Stricken June 30th, 1921, she was sold for scrap in 1927.

DUPLEIX was in the Far East from 1910 and attached to Admiral Jerram's squadron at Hong Kong in August 1914. On August 21st, 1914 captured the German collier SENEGAMBIA and cargo boat FERDINAND LAEISZ, both intended for supplying Admiral Graf Spee's squadron. She escorted several troop transports between India and Suez and took part in the search for the EMDEN. In May 1915 she was in the Mediterranean and shelled Boudrum. Suez Canal operations in 1917. She was unlisted in 1919 and scrapped 1922.

Gueydon class – three ships

Displacement:	9500 tons.
Dimensions:	138m(pp) × 19·4m × 7·45m.
Machinery:	Boilers: GUEYDON, Niclausse; MONTCALM, Normand; D. THOUARS, Belleville; 3 sets TE, 3 screws; IHP 20,000; speed 21 knots. Coal 1000/1600 tons.
Radius (nm):	10,000/10 knots nominal.
Protection:	Belt 150mm waterline, 60mm ends; Deck 50mm on slopes; Turrets 200mm, Casemates 100mm; Conning tower 160mm.
Armament:	2 – 194mm[1], 8 – 164·7mm in casemates[2], 4 – 100mm[3], 16 – 47mm[4], 2 – 450mm submerged tubes. 10 mines, Breguet type. 6 – 0.60m searchlights.
Complement:	26 officers, 565 crew (+9 and 64 as flagship).

[1]1893 model, [2]1893-96 model, [3]1895 model, [4]1885 model.

NAME	BUILDER	LAID DOWN	LAUNCHED	COMPLETED
GUEYDON	Lorient DY	8.97	20.9.99	1902
MONTCALM	F. et Ch. de la Méditerranée, La Seyne	1.98	27.3.00	7.01
DUPETIT-THOUARS	Toulon DY	4.99	7.01	1903

NOTES

GUEYDON. In 1914 in the Channel, 1915 Atlantic coast patrols between Brest and Gibraltar. In the S Atlantic and off S America in 1916 and in the W Indies 1917. In 1918 she was in N Russia, Murmansk and Archangel, supporting the White Russians and in the Baltic in 1919. In 1923 she had a major refit and became a gunnery training tender 1928–29. She was hulked July 24th, 1935 and used as accommodation ship at Brest. In 1942 she was destroyed during the German occupation.

Top: **The armoured cruiser GUEYDON as she was after her major refit of 1923.**

Above: **The armoured cruiser DUPETIT-THOUARS.**

MONTCALM. In 1914 she was on the S Pacific Station and joined the Australian Squadron for the capture of Samoa. 1915, Suez Canal operations. 1916, major refit January to September then joined the 4th Cruiser Squadron in the West Indies. From July to November 1918 she was escorting troop convoys between the USA and France, then to the Baltic and Murmansk. On October 28th, 1926 she was stricken but maintained as a barrack ship and from 1931 as a school tender. Renamed TREMINTIN October 1st, 1937. Dismantled during World War II.

DUPETIT-THOUARS. 1914, 2nd Light Squadron on Channel patrol until April 1915. 1916–17 was in the cruiser reserve division at Brest. From February 1918 she transported troops to Dakar then relieved CONDE in the West Indies and was on escort duty between the USA and France; she was refitted at Brooklyn. She left New York on July 24th, 1918, escorting 28 merchant ships and on August 7th, 1918 was torpedoed by U.62, 400 miles from Brest; most of her crew being rescued by American destroyers.

Amiral Aube class – four ships

Displacement:	10,400 tons.
Dimensions:	140m(pp) × 20·20m × 7·70m.
Machinery:	Boilers: Belleville (MARSEILLAISE and AMIRAL AUBE) or Niclausse (in the others); 3 sets TE, 3 screws; IHP 20,500; speed 21·4 knots. Coal 970/1590 tons.
Radius (nm):	12,000/10 knots nominal.
Protection:	Belt 170 – 140mm amidships, 106mm ends; Main deck 45 – 20mm; Splinter deck; Main turrets 200mm, other turrets 120mm, Barbettes 100mm.
Armament:	2 – 194mm[1], 8 – 164·7mm (4 in turrets, 4 casemates)[2], 6 – 100mm[3], 18 – 47mm, 5 – 450mm tubes (2 submerged).
Complement:	612.

[1]1893–96 model, [2]1893–96 model, [3]1893 model.

NAME	BUILDER	LAID DOWN	LAUNCHED	COMPLETED
GLOIRE	Lorient DY	9.99	12.6.00	1904
MARSEILLAISE	Brest DY	1.00	14.7.00	1903
CONDE	Lorient DY	3.01	3.02	1904
AMIRAL AUBE	Penhoët, St Nazaire	8.00	5.02	1904

NOTES

The following differences characterized the ships:

MARSEILLAISE	Large ventilation between funnels.
GLOIRE	Friatic wireless cable high up and steam pipes abaft first two funnels.
CONDE	Friatic wireless just above tops and steam pipes abaft first two funnels.
AMIRAL AUBE	Main top mast before instead of abaft.

The armoured cruiser MARSEILLAISE.

A fifth ship (SULLY) grounded February 1905 in Along Bay and later became a total loss.

GLOIRE. August 1914 to April 1915, 2nd Light Squadron on Channel patrols. 1916–18 in the S Atlantic, being relieved in February 1918 by DESAIX. In May 1918 she was damaged in collision with the US liner CITY OF ATHENS and repaired in New York; she then escorted troopships between the USA and France until November. On September 1st, 1919 with five destroyers, she escorted the liner LEVIATHAN from Brittany carrying General Pershing back home. She was with CONDE and MARSEILLAISE in the Atlantic Squadron in 1920 and was condemned in 1922.

MARSEILLAISE in 1914 was flagship of the 2nd Light Squadron on patrol in the western Channel. 1916–17 West Indies; 1918 US convoys in the North Atlantic. June 29th, 1920 with three destroyers, escorted the US liner GEORGE WASHINGTON carrying President Wilson back home. In 1920, with CONDE and GLOIRE in the Atlantic Squadron. 1925–29 Gunnery School, her 194mm turrets replaced by 164·7mm. Condemned in 1929.

CONDE in 1914 was in the West Indies and captured the Norwegian cargo boat HEINA on charter to the Hamburg-Amerika Line on August 10th, 1914. In 1918 she was with US convoys in the N Atlantic. In 1920 with GLOIRE and MARSEILLAISE in the Atlantic Squadron. She was unlisted in 1933, hulked and used as an accommodation ship at Lorient for Fusilier apprentices school. In 1940 she was taken by the Germans at

The armoured cruiser CONDE seen at Arkangelsk, 1919.

The armoured cruiser AMIRAL AUBE.

Lorient and used as a submarine depot ship and destroyed as an aircraft target at the end of the war.

AMIRAL AUBE was in the 2nd Light Squadron on patrol in the Western Channel in 1914 and in the E Mediterranean Squadron 1915–16; in November 1915 with two destroyers, patrolled the Sollum area (Libya) to intercept German U-boats which were landing troops and materials. Not traced after 1916, probably disarmed. She was condemned in 1922.

Leon Gambetta class – three ships

Displacement:	12,550 tons.
Dimensions:	148m(pp) × 21·4m × 8.20m.
Machinery:	Boilers: Niclausse (L. GAMBETTA), Guyot (J. FERRY), Belleville (V. HUGO); 3 sets, 4 cylinder TE, 3 screws; IHP 27,500; speed 22 knots. Coal 1320/2100 tons.
Radius (nm):	12,000/10 knots. 1500/22 knots.
Protection:	Belt 170 – 90mm; Upper deck 34 – 20mm, Lower deck 65 – 45mm, these two decks making a cofferdam with the belt; Main turrets 200mm, others 140mm; Conning tower 200mm.
Armament:	4 – 194mm (2 × 2)[1], 16 – 164·7mm (2 × 6 in turrets, 1 × 4 in casemates[2], 2 – 65mm, 22 – 47mm[3], 4 – 450mm tubes (2 submerged)[4].
Complement:	26 officers, 708 crew (+4 and 41 as flagship).

[1]1893–96 model, [2]1893–96 model, [3]1902 model. [4]1904 model torpedoes.

NAME	BUILDER	LAID DOWN	LAUNCHED	COMPLETED
LEON GAMBETTA	Brest DY	1.01	10.02	1903
JULES FERRY	Cherbourg DY	10.01	8.03	1906
VICTOR HUGO	Lorient DY	4.03	30.3.04	1906

NOTES

These ships were all good steamers.

LEON GAMBETTA, JULES FERRY and VICTOR HUGO took part with the 'Armée Navale' in the various operations in the Adriatic.

JULES FERRY was condemned in 1927.

LEON GAMBETTA was patrolling without escort in the Gulf of Otranto with Rear-Admiral Senes aboard commanding the 2nd Light Division, when on the night of April 24th, 1915 she was torpedoed and sunk by the Austrian submarine U.5; most of the crew and the admiral were lost.

VICTOR HUGO escorted the JEAN BART to Malta when the latter was torpedoed in 1916. She also took part with JULES MICHELET in the transportation of the Serbian army from Corfu to Bizerta. She was in the Far East in 1922. Stricken January 20th, 1928, she was sold for scrap November 26th, 1930.

Top: The armoured cruiser LEON GAMBETTA.

Above: The armoured cruiser JULES FERRY.

Jules Michelet – one ship

Displacement:	12,600 tons.
Dimensions:	148m(pp) × 21·4m × 8·20m.
Machinery:	20 du Temple-Guyot boilers; 3 sets TE, 3 screws; IHP 29,000; speed 23 knots. Coal 1400/2300 tons.
Radius (nm):	12,000/10 knots.
Protection:	Belt 170 – 90mm; Upper deck 34 – 20mm, Lower Deck 65 – 45mm, these two decks forming a cofferdam with the belt; Main turrets 20mm, others 140mm; Conning tower 200mm.
Armament:	4 – 194mm (2 × 2)[1], 12 – 164·7mm (8 turrets, 4 casemates)[2], 22 – 47mm[3], 4 – 450mm tubes (2 submerged)[4].

[1]1893–96 model, [2]1893–96 model, [3]1902 model. [4]1904 model torpedoes.

NAME	BUILDER	LAID DOWN	LAUNCHED	COMPLETED
JULES MICHELET	Lorient DY	6.04	8.05	1908

NOTES

This ship was similar to the GAMBETTA except that four 194mm guns were suppressed in the vain hope of gaining more speed. Her completion was consequently delayed for two years.

Her war service was very similar to that of the WALDECK ROUSSEAU class (qv).

In reserve in 1929, she was condemned in 1931 and used as an aircraft target and finally torpedoed and sunk by the submarine THETIS.

The armoured cruiser JULES MICHELET.

Ernest Renan – one ship

Displacement:	13,644 tons.
Dimensions:	157m(pp) × 21·36m × 8·20m.
Machinery:	40 Niclausse boilers; 3 sets TE, 3 screws; IHP 37,000; speed 23 knots (25·5 on trials). Coal 1350/2300 tons.
Radius (nm):	10,000/10 knots.
Protection:	Belt 170mm amidships, 90mm ends; Bulkhead 150mm (aft); Upper deck 34 – 20mm, Lower deck 65 – 45mm, these two forming a cofferdam with the belt; Main turrets 130mm, Single turrets 115mm; Conning tower 200mm.
Armament:	4 – 194mm (2 × 2)[1], 12 – 164·7mm (8 in turrets, 4 in casemates)[2], 16 – 65mm[3], 8 – 47mm[4], 2 – 450mm submerged tubes[5].
Complement:	750.

[1]1902 model, [2]1893–96 M. model, [3]1902 model. [4]1902 model. [5]1904 model torpedoes.

NAME	BUILDER	LAID DOWN	LAUNCHED	COMPLETED
ERNEST RENAN	Penhoët, St Nazaire	10.03	3.06	1908

NOTES

Her war service was similar to that of the WALDECK ROUSSEAU class (qv). At the end of the war her mainmast was removed for the towing of a kite balloon and AA guns were installed on the top of the after 164·7mm turrets. 1927–28 Gunnery School (mainmast reinstalled). Stricken 1931 and sunk as a target by aircraft and gunfire.

The armoured cruiser ERNEST RENAN as she was in 1914.

Waldeck Rousseau class – two ships

Displacement:	14,000 tons (full load).
Dimensions:	159m(oa), 157m(pp) × 21·36m × 8·40m.
Machinery:	40 Niclausse boilers; 3 sets TE, 3 screws; IHP 37,000; speed 23 knots. Coal 1242/2300 tons.
Radius (nm):	10,000/10 knots.
Protection:	Belt 170mm amidships, 90mm ends; Bulkhead 130mm (aft); Upper deck 34 – 20mm, Lower deck 65 – 45mm, these two forming a cofferdam with the belt; Turrets 150mm, Casemates 120mm; Conning tower 200mm.
Armament:	14 – 194mm (2 × 2 and 1 × 6 in turrets, 4 in casemates)[1], 18 – 65mm[1], 2 – 450mm submerged tubes[2]. (Later 2 – 75mm AA[3], 4 – 47mm and 8 – MG added).
Complement:	23 officers, 818 crew (34 and 890 as flagship).

[1]1902 model, [2]1904 model. [3]for flare fire.

NAME	BUILDER	LAID DOWN	LAUNCHED	COMPLETED
EDGAR QUINET	Brest DY	8.04	21.9.07	1910
WALDECK ROUSSEAU	Lorient DY	6.06	3.08	1910

NOTES

The last armoured cruisers built in France, these very handy ships were to have been similar to ERNEST RENAN, but during construction it was decided to equip them with a mono-calibre main armament. During the

The armoured cruiser EDGAR QUINET as she was in 1909.

The armoured cruiser WALDECK ROUSSEAU just sailing for the Far East where he served as flag ship for the admiral commanding the Far East French Naval Forces.

war one triple mount of 3·66m rangefinders (Triplex) was installed above the conning tower; the range of the main guns was increased from 14,000 to 18,000m.

EDGAR QUINET was with J. MICHELET and ERNEST RENAN in the 1st Light Division in 1914 and took part in the hunting of GOEBEN and BRESLAU and later on patrol in the Otranto Channel until 1915, based at Navarino. Also support of the sea-supplying of Montenegro and patrol off Tunisia. In 1916 present at the occupation of Corfu and the evacuation of the Serbian army and also at the Salamis and Athens operations. 1917 at Corfu; 1918 Corfu and Malta and patrol in the Eastern Mediterranean. From 1919 to 1922 she was in the Mediterranean and in this latter year with JEAN BART, gave hospitality to 1200 people during the burning of Smyrna. She was converted to a training ship 1925–27 to replace the JEANNE D'ARC, four 194mm guns being landed, two of her funnels removed and bridge modified for training purposes; two float-planes were also fitted. She was used as a schoolship until January 4th, 1930 when she stranded on an uncharted rock off Cape Blanc, Algeria and sank five days later.

WALDECK ROUSSEAU on August 9th, 1914 was on trials off Toulon after repair and from September operated in the Mediterranean with the 1st Light Division. On October 18th, 1914 she was attacked without success by a Austrian submarine off Cattaro and in the next month shelled enemy fortifications and made a demonstration off Lissa and again attacked by an Austrian submarine without success. For the rest of the war she cruised the Aegean and Ionian Sea and also took part in the Salamis–Athens operations. She was in the Black Sea in 1919–20 and took part in the withdrawal of General Wrangel's army. For some years she was flagship of the French Far East naval forces. She was stricken on June 14th, 1936.

Protected Cruisers

Friant class – three ships

Displacement:	3800 tons (FRIANT), 4000 tons (others).
Dimensions:	100m(pp) except FRIANT (95m) × 13m × 6·40m.
Machinery:	Lagrafel d'Allest boilers (FRIANT: Niclausse); 2 sets TE, 2 screws; IHP 10,000; speed 19 knots. Coal 684 tons maximum (FRIANT: 587 tons).
Radius (nm):	6000/10 knots.
Protection:	Deck 80mm; Gun shields 30mm; Conning tower 100mm; Cellular bulkhead.
Armament:	6 – 164·7mm[1], 4 – 100mm[2], 10 – 47mm[3], 2 – 450mm tubes (above water).
Complement:	393·

[1]1891 model, [2]1891 model, [3]1885 model.

NAME	BUILDER	LAID DOWN	LAUNCHED	COMPLETED
FRIANT	Brest DY	1891	1893	1895
DU CHAYLA	Cherbourg DY	1893	1895	1897
CASSARD	Cherbourg DY	1893	1896	1898

NOTES

Another ship of this type, CHASSELOUP-LAUBAT, was disarmed in 1913 and during the war used as a distilling vessel at Corfu.

FRIANT in 1914 was on the Newfoundland Station and joined the Special Division for escort duty and patrols in the Western Mediterranean. From 1915–16 she was on the Morocco Station. In 1918 she was based on Mudros as mother-ship for the 3rd Submarine Flotilla (at this time had only one funnel). She was condemned in 1920.

DU CHAYLA, with GALILEE, took part in the landing at Casablanca in August 1907. From 1914 she was in the Western Atlantic and from 1916–18 in the Red Sea Division on patrol between Suez and Sokotra Island; during 1917, with CASSARD, took part in search for German raiders. Her armament in 1918 comprised 2 – 164·7mm (with increased range), 4 – 75mm and 4 – 47mm, the rest of her original guns having been handed over for army use. On November 10th, 1918 took part in the last operations against the Turks in Lebanon; in 1919 she was in the Black Sea. She was condemned in 1933.

CASSARD: 1914, Special Division, Western Mediterranean; 1915 Morocco Station; 1916 Red Sea; 1917 with DU CHAYLA in the Indian Ocean; 1918 in the Red Sea; 1921–22 Syria Station; 1922–23 detached to the Gunnery School with turrets removed. She was condemned in 1924.

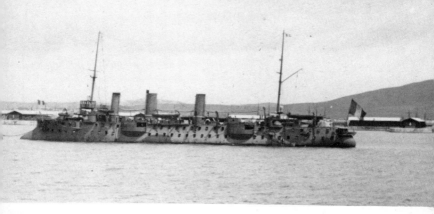

The protected cruiser DU CHAYLA moored in a Greek port during the war.

The protected cruiser CASSARD.

Top: The protected cruiser D'ENTRECASTEAUX as she was before the war.

Above: The protected cruiser BALTYK ex- D'ENTRECASTEAUX seen in Gdynia harbour where she served as schoolship for the Polish Navy.

D'Entrecasteaux – one ship

Displacement:	8114 tons.
Dimensions:	130m(pp) × 17·9m × 7·50m.
Machinery:	5 double-ended cylindrical boilers; 2 sets TE, 2 screws; IHP 13,500; speed 19·5 knots. Coal 650/1000 tons.
Radius (nm):	5000/10 knots, 2700/19 knots.
Protection:	Armoured deck 85 – 30mm, Splinter deck over vitals; Longitudinal bulkhead; Turrets (Harvey) 230mm, Gun shields 72mm, Casemates 52mm; Conning Tower 250mm.
Armament:	2 – 240mm[1], 12 – 138·6mm[2], 12 – 47mm[3], 6 – 37mm. 6 – 0·60m searchlights.
Complement:	521.

[1]1893 model. [2]1893 model. [3]1885 model.

NAME	BUILDER	LAID DOWN	LAUNCHED	COMPLETED
D'ENTRE-CASTEAUX	F. et Ch. de la Méditerranée, La Seyne	6.94	12.6.96	1898

NOTES

The hull of this ship was doubled with copper-covered teak for colonial service. She never attained her designed speed and by 1914 her maximum did not reach 17 knots.

In 1914 in reserve at Toulon; after commissioning, she joined the 'Armée Navale' and took part in surveillance of the Otranto Strait. On December 24th, 1914 she sailed for Syria and with REQUIN in 1915 and was engaged in the defence of the Suez Canal from the Timsah Lake. She shelled enemy installations at Gaza. Patrols off Syria and the Canal continued into 1916 after a brief stay off the Moroccan coast. In 1917–18 she escorted several convoys towards Madagascar and later, as a troopship, made numerous trips between Taranto and Itea. She continued in service as a trooper into 1919, bringing back to France demobilised soldiers of the Armée d'Orient. From October 1919 to 1921 she served as a schoolship for signalmen, shipwrights and reserve officers at Brest. In 1923 she was lent to Belgium as a schoolship and in 1927 to Poland for the same purpose, being renamed BALTYK and later KARL WLADISLAW IV. She ended her career in Poland, being scrapped at Gdynia in 1938.

Châteaurenault – one ship

Displacement:	8200 tons.
Dimensions:	140m(pp) × 18m × 7·50m.
Machinery:	28 Normand-Sigaudy boilers; 3 sets 4-cylinder TE, 3 screws; IHP 24,000; speed 23 knots. Coal 1460/2100 tons.
Radius (nm):	7500/12 knots.
Protection:	Armoured deck 100 – 60mm; Casemates 60 – 40mm, Gun shields 54mm; Cellular bulkhead, empty cofferdam.

A beautiful photo of the protected cruiser CHATEAURENAULT.

Armament:	2 – 164mm[1], 6 – 138·6mm (casemates)[2], 12 – 47mm[3], 3 – 37mm. 6 – 0·60m searchlights.
Complement:	18 officers, 569 crew.

[1]1893 model. [2]1893 model. [3]1885 model.

NAME	BUILDER	LAID DOWN	LAUNCHED	COMPLETED
CHATEAU-RENAULT	F. et Ch. de la Méditerranée La Seyne	1895	12.5.98	1900

NOTES

Commissioning was delayed because of considerable vibration which developed between speeds of 18 and 21 knots; various trials and return to dockyard from October 1899 to September 1902.

1914 was in the 2nd Light Squadron on patrol in the western Channel. She joined the 'Armée Navale' in 1915 and was used by the C in C for his own movements until detached on February 2nd, 1916 for the purpose of hunting for the German raider MOEWE in the South Atlantic. After refit at Bizerta she was assigned as troop transport for the Eastern Army. She picked up survivors from the AMC GALLIA south of Sardinia, sunk on October 5th, 1916 by a German submarine. On December 14th, 1917 she was hit by two torpedoes from the Austrian submarine UC.38 off Cephalonia and sunk. Troops and crew left the ship in perfect order while the submarine was pursued by escorts and sunk by destroyers MAMELUK and LANS-QUENET.

Jurien de la Graviere – one ship

Displacement:	5700 tons.
Dimensions:	137m(pp) × 15m × 6·40m.
Machinery:	Guyot boilers; 3 sets TE, 3 screws; IHP 17,000 (as designed); speed 23 knots (as designed but not made). Coal 600/900 tons.
Radius (nm):	6150/10 knots.
Protection:	Armoured deck 65mm (max); Gun shields 54mm; Casemates 46mm; Conning tower 160mm; Cellular bulkhead and cofferdam charged with zinc boxes.
Armament:	8 – 164mm[1], 10 – 47mm[2], 2 – 450mm tubes (above water).
Complement:	511.

[1]1887–93 model. [2]1885 model.

NAME	BUILDER	LAID DOWN	LAUNCHED	COMPLETED
JURIEN DE LA GRAVIERE	Lorient DY	11.97	7.99	1901

NOTES

Trials of this cruiser were long and difficult and her designed maximum speed was not reached. She differed in appearance from GUEYDON and AMIRAL AUBE by her foremast and generally smaller profile; she was also lower in the water.

From August 1st–3rd, 1914 she escorted the 2nd S/M Flotilla between

The protected cruiser JURIEN DE LA GRAVIERE during the war.

Below: **The protected cruiser GUICHEN during her trials.**

Foot: **The protected GUICHEN fitted as a troop transport. Note the life-rafts alongside the ship.**

Toulon and Bizerta. On August 16th, 1914 with destroyers, chased the Austrian destroyer UHLAN while the fleet was sinking the ZENTA. From September to November 1914 was on patrol in the Otranto Strait. On October 10th, 1916, with the C in C aboard, took part in bombarding operations by an Anglo-French force under French command, of Makry, Phineka, Marmarika, Myra and Mersina harbours on the Turkish coast. From December 1916 to June 1917 she took part in the Salamis and Athens operations, then in the blockade of Greece; during this period was also used as repeating ship and liaison for the C in C 'Armée Navale'. She was on the Syria Station in 1920 and was condemned in 1922.

Guichen – one ship

Displacement:	8300 tons.
Dimensions:	133m(pp) × 16·70m × 7·44m.
Machinery:	36 Lagrafel d'Allest boilers; 3 sets 4-cylinder TE, 3 screws; IHP 24,000; speed 23 knots. Coal 1460/2000 tons.
Radius (nm):	7500/12 knots.
Protection:	Armoured deck 100 – 6omm; Casemates 60 – 4omm, Gun shields 54mm; Conning tower 16omm; Cellular bulkhead, empty cofferdam.
Armament:	2 – 164mm[1], 6 – 138·4mm (in casemates)[2], 12 – 47mm[3], 2 – 450mm tubes (above water).
Complement:	625.

[1]1887–93 model. [2]1891–93 model. [3]1902 model.

NAME	BUILDER	LAID DOWN	LAUNCHED	COMPLETED
GUICHEN	Penhoët, St Nazaire	1895	5.98	1902

NOTES

1914, 2nd Light Squadron in the Channel, then patrols with SURCOUF in the Bay of Biscay; later operated off Morocco. In 1915 was detached to the 3rd Squadron, Levant and in September took part in rescuing Armenians in Antioch Bay. In 1917 with reduced crew, she was used as a fast transport between Taranto and Itea and in 1919 was operating in the Black Sea. She was stricken in 1921 and condemned in 1922.

Descartes – one ship

Displacement:	4000 tons.
Dimensions:	99m(pp) × 13m × 6·50m.
Machinery:	16 Belleville boilers without economisers; 2 sets TE, 2 screws; IHP 8500; speed 19 knots. Coal 680 tons max.
Radius (nm):	6000/10 knots.
Protection:	Armoured deck 50 – 2omm; Gun shields 54mm; Double bottom and cofferdam.

The protected cruiser DESCARTES as she was to her completing.

Armament: 4 – 164·7mm (in sponsons)[1], 10 – 100mm[2], 8 – 47mm[3],
                 2 – 356mm tubes (above water). 4 – 0·60m searchlights.

Complement: 19 officers, 402 crew.

              [1]1891 model. [2]1885 model. [3]1885 model.

NAME	BUILDER	LAID DOWN	LAUNCHED	COMPLETED
DESCARTES	Ch. de la Loire, Nantes	1892	27.9.94	1.96

NOTES

The single survivor of a class of four ships, the others being PROTET, PASCAL and CATINAT. She was designed by Louis de Bussy, one of the greatest of French naval constructors who was the 'father' of the REDOUTABLE, the world's first steel battleship and of DUPUY de LOME the first armoured cruiser, a type copied by all foreign navies.

1914, assigned to the Antilles Station, she suffered a collision with the Spanish cargo ship TELESFORA on September 23rd, 1914 off St Lucia. After repair at Fort de France, she was again in collision off St Lucia, with the British merchant STRATHMORE and again repaired at Fort de France. In 1915 she was at Port au Prince protecting French nationals. She remained in the West Indies until 1917 when she went into reserve at Lorient, her secondary armament being removed into anti-submarine vessels and her 164·7s being given to the army. She was stricken on May 10th, 1920 and sold for scrap on May 10th, 1921.

Third Class Cruisers

Surcouf class – three ships

Displacement:	1850 tons.
Dimensions:	95m × 9m × 5·20m.
Machinery:	2 sets TE, 2 screws; IHP 6000; speed 19 knots.
Radius (nm):	1800/17·5 knots.
Protection:	Armoured deck 40mm; Splinter deck over vital parts.
Armament:	4 – 138·6mm (in sponsons), 9 – 47mm, 5 tubes (above water).

NAME	BUILDER	LAID DOWN	LAUNCHED	COMPLETED
SURCOUF	Cherbourg DY	1886	1889	1891
COSMAO	Bordeaux	1887	1889	1891
FORBIN	Rochefort DY	3.86	14.1.88	1890

NOTES

Sometimes rated as 'avisos', they were also designed by de Bussy and belonged to a class which included the COETLOGON, LALANDE and TROUDE.

SURCOUF in 1914 joined the 2nd Light Squadron in the Channel and in September 1914 with GUICHEN on patrol in the Bay of Biscay. She was in the Ocean Patrol Force 1915–17 based on Brest and in 1918 was probably disarmed, her guns being used elsewhere. Condemned in 1921.

COSMAO joined the Special Division from Morocco in 1914 and was on escort and patrol in the Western Mediterranean. She was back on the Morocco Station 1915–18 and was condemned in 1922.

FORBIN was on the Morocco Station in 1914, with D'ENTRE-CASTEAUX in 1916 and at Gibraltar 1917–18 as depot ship for the Morocco Submarine Flotilla. Unlisted in 1919, she was condemned and sold for scrap in 1921.

D'Estrées – one ship

Displacement:	2450 tons.
Dimensions:	95m × 12m × 5·40m.
Machinery:	Lagrafel d'Allest boilers; 2 sets TE, 2 screws; IHP 8500; speed 21 knots. Coal 345 tons (480 max).
Radius (nm):	5700/10 knots.
Protection:	Deck 40 – 10mm (hard steel); Cellular bulkhead.
Armament:	2 – 138·6mm[1], 4 – 100mm[2], 8 – 47mm.
Complement:	250.

[1]1891–93 model. [2]1893 model.

NAME	BUILDER	LAID DOWN	LAUNCHED	COMPLETED
D'ESTREES	Rochefort DY	1886	10.97	1899

The third class cruiser SURCOUF.

The third class cruiser COSMAO.

The third class cruiser d'ESTREES.

NOTES
Sometimes rated as 'aviso'.

1914, 2nd Light Squadron in the Channel. 1915, 3rd Squadron in the Levant; patrols off Syrian and Turkish coasts and in September 1915 took part in the rescue of Armenians in Antioch Bay. From December 12th/15th, 1915 she was in the Sollum area to intercept German submarines which were landing men and material. In the summer of 1916, she was at Djibouti to protect the place against attack by Ethiopian forces. From 1917–18 on patrol in the Red Sea followed by a major refit at La Ciotat. She was in the Far East Squadron 1920–21; stricken in October 1922, she was condemned in 1924.

Lavoisier – one ship

Displacement:	2300 tons.
Dimensions:	100m × 11m × 5·45m.
Machinery:	16 Belleville boilers; 2 sets TE, 2 screws; IHP about 7000; speed 20 knots. Coal 380 tons max.
Radius (nm):	3000/10 knots, 600/20 knots.
Protection:	Armoured deck 40mm; Gun shields 54mm; Conning tower 100mm; Cofferdam and double bottom.
Armament:	4 – 138·6mm (in sponsons)[1], 2 – 100mm[2], 10 – 47mm, 2 – 450mm tubes (above water).
Complement:	248.

[1]1891–93 model, [2]1893 model.

The third class cruiser LAVOISIER.

NAME	BUILDER	LAID DOWN	LAUNCHED	COMPLETED
LAVOISIER	Rochefort DY	1893	17.4.97	12.97

NOTES

She was sometimes rated as 'aviso'.

She was on the Iceland fishery survey service in April 1914 and in August 1914 joined the 2nd Light Squadron in the Western Channel and was on the same patrol in December 1915. By December 30th, 1915 she was at Port Said detached to the Armée Navale and in February 1916 was in the Western Mediterranean Patrol Force. She was appointed to the Atlantic Patrol in April 1916 but had a major refit at Brest and went to the Morocco Station in September 1916 with FORBIN. Refitted June 1917 at Bordeaux then back to Morocco by January 1918. She was in the Levant Squadron by July 1918 and on the Syria Station in 1919. Disarmed in August 1919 at Rochefort, she was condemned in 1920.

Scouts

Lamotte Picquet class – ten projected ships

These ships rated as 'convoyeurs d'escadrilles' and would have been similar to the scouts in service in the Austrian and Italian navies. The construction of ten ships was planned and it was decided in 1914 to order two of them from private builders and the prototype, LAMOTTE PICQUET from the Toulon naval dockyard, but because of events, none was laid down. They were to have had the following characteristics:

Displacement:	4500 tons (6000 tons full load).
Dimensions:	138m × 13·80m × 4·80m.
Machinery:	12 Du Temple Guyot boilers; 4 turbines; 4 screws; SHP 40,000, max speed 29 knots. Coal 300 tons, oil 500 tons.
Radius (nm):	3300/16 knots, 1280/26 knots, 775/29 knots.
Protection:	Belt 28mm over vital parts.
Armament:	8 – 138·6mm, 2 – 47mm, 4 – 450mm tubes.
Complement:	17 officers, 340 crew.

NOTES

The project was re-examined in 1915 and modified for increased speed, increased gun range and the fitting of AA guns. The whole project was finally cancelled.

Aircraft Carriers

Foudre – one ship

Displacement:	5971 tons (6089 full load).
Dimensions:	118·70m(oa) × 17·20m(oa), 15·60m(wl) × 5·40m/7·20m.
Machinery:	2 sets TE, 2 screws; IHP 11,800; speed 19·6 knots. Coal 798 tons.
Radius (nm):	7500/10 knots, 1395/19 knots.
Protection:	Deck 105·40mm; Conning tower 100mm; Gunshields 54mm; Cofferdam.
Armament:	8 – 100mm[1], 4 – 65mm[2], 4 – 47mm[3].
Complement:	22 officers, 409 crew.

[1]1891 model; [2]1891 model; [3]1885 model.

NAME	BUILDER	LAID DOWN	LAUNCHED	COMPLETED
FOUDRE (ex-La Seine)	Ch. de la Gironde, Bordeaux	9.6.92	20.10.95	1896

NOTES
The building of this ship was inspired by the fallacious theories of the 'Jeune Ecole'; originally a special depot ship for ten small torpedo boats (14 tons, 17 knots, 1 – 380mm tube) which she carried on cradles. The TBS reheated their boilers with the steam of the mother-ship and were put afloat from a rolling deck, though only in a calm sea.

In 1907 she was converted into a repair ship and in 1910 to a minelayer (80 mines). In 1911 she was once more altered – into an aircraft depot ship; a hanger being fitted between the rear funnel and the mainmast and a crane added. In 1913 she underwent a third conversion into a seaplane carrier for from 4 to 8 flying-boats.

During the war she helped in the construction of seaplane bases at Port Said and at Mudros and was also used as a submarine tender. From January 10th, 1916 to March 21st, 1916 she served as command ship for the Eastern Mediterranean Patrols; some of her 100mm guns were disembarked in 1918 and replaced by modified army 90mm guns.

Campinas – one ship

Displacement:	3319 tons.
Dimensions:	102·40m × 12·85m × 7·08m.
Machinery:	2 boilers; 1 set TE; IHP 1460; speed 11·5 knots. Coal 988 tons.

NAME	LAID DOWN	LAUNCHED	COMPLETED
CAMPINAS	1894	1896	1897

Top: **The aircraft carrier FOUDRE.**

Above: **The aircraft carrier CAMPINAS.**

Ex-liner taken over during the war and converted in 1915 into a seaplane
carrier fitted with two hangars for from 6 to 10 flying-boats or float-planes.
In January 1916 appointed to the Suez Canal Seaplane Flotilla; numerous
operations off the Syrian coast; September 1916 to March 1917, Salamis and
Athens operations; 1917–18 in the Levant.

Auxiliary Seaplane Carriers
(Requisitioned Channel packets)

Tonnage: 1541 GRT.
Dimensions: 102·97m × 10·65m × 3·30m.
Machinery: Reciprocating, paddle; IHP 7800; speed 21 knots.

NAME	LAID DOWN	LAUNCHED	COMPLETED
NORD	1897	1898	1899
PAS-DE-CALAIS	1897	1898	1899

NOTES
NORD: 1914 requisitioned as light auxiliary cruiser, 2nd Light Squadron,
Channel; October 1914 lent to British Red Cross; 1916–17 used as seaplane
carrier based on Dunkirk; 1919 returned to owners.

PAS-DE-CALAIS: 1914 requisitioned as light auxiliary cruiser, 2nd
Light Squadron, Channel; 1915, based at Cherbourg, patrols in the eastern
Channel; 1916 used as seaplane carrier with NORD; 1919 returned to
owners.

Tonnage: 1656 GRT.
Dimensions: 92m × 10·57m × 2·95m.
Machinery: 3 turbines, 3 screws; SHP 8000; speed 24 knots.

NAME	LAID DOWN	LAUNCHED	COMPLETED
ROUEN	1911	1912	1912

NOTES
1914 requisitioned as light auxiliary cruiser (2 – 47mm guns), 2nd Light
Squadron, Channel; October 1914 Captain, Eastern Channel Flotillas; 1915
R. Admiral, commanding Channel Flotillas; December 29th, 1916 disabled
by a mine off Brittany, repaired and converted to seaplane carrier; 1917
Mediterranean, convoys between Italy and Greece; 1919 returned to owners.

1940 requisitioned as ammo storeship for Flanders operations, then as
trooper for the Dunkirk withdrawal; derequisitioned in June 1940. On
August 30th, 1940 seized at Bordeaux by the Germans and converted into
minelayer WULLENWEVER; found badly damaged at Kiel in 1945 and
scrapped in 1946.

Destroyers

(Rated as Torpilleurs d'Escadre)

The French destroyer force was not adapted to the task which faced it in 1914; most of the ships were too small for escort work, especially in rough weather. The modern craft were fragile and were not homogeneous and their fire-control system was often inferior to that of enemy destroyers.

The Naval Staff was conscious of all these deficiencies and intended to launch a new construction programme which would provide the French navy by about 1920, with thirty-two 1200 to 1500-ton geared turbine vessels fitted with two or three 138·6mm QF guns and at least four 450 or 500mm torpedo tubes. The declaration of war stopped this project and only the building of near-completed ships was resumed while four ex-Argentine destroyers were requisitioned. In 1917 twelve ships were ordered in Japan to replace losses.

The 300-ton type

Designed by the famous naval constructor A. Normand, 55 destroyers of the so-called '300 tonners' were built between 1900 and 1908. All were equipped with a 'caillebotis' deck, the main feature of the class. In spite of their small size they were excellent sea boats and, except for two ships, all exceeded their contract speed. In 1908 mainmasts were removed to improve stability and replaced in 1911 by a small aerial mast.

In August 1914 they represented two-thirds of the destroyer force and were very active during the war, assigned as follows:

29 in the North, 21 in the Mediterranean and three in the Far East.

Because of their age and an average of 50 tons overload, the best could reach only 25 knots and normal speed was only 22 – 23 knots, especially when in formation. However they were very good patrol and escort vessels, at their best in the Adriatic, Dardanelles and Channel coastal waters. In these latter areas, German aircraft were very active, consequently it became necessary to give them an AA armament and in 1915 the two rear 47mm guns were so modified and in 1917 an 8mm Hotchkiss or Saint-Etienne machine gun was fitted over the stern torpedo tube. When this tube was removed, the machine gun was relocated above the rear bridge. By the end of the war many destroyers of this type had two AA guns.

Armament was also modified as a consequence of the submarine threat; on several units the 65mm gun being replaced by a 75mm of army type. One Thornycroft DC thrower and racks for from six to twelve 75 kilo depthcharges were also fitted on the quarterdeck. Meanwhile the stern tube was coupled with the midship one until 1918 when it was reinstalled in its initial position and the DC thrower removed.

Most of the 300 tonners after arduous war service could barely reach 20 knots and were stricken between 1919 and 1921. Two however (CAR-QUOIS and TRIDENT) were used as auxiliary school ships and were stricken in December 1930 and November 1932, respectively.

All of this class were initially fitted with 65mm on a platform before and after the bridge and six 47mm, three on each beam; the 65mm was an 1891 model and the 47mm an 1885 model in the early boats and 1902 models from CLAYMORE on. Two single 381mm revolving tubes were in the first 32 units (1887 model torpedoes) and two 450mm of 1906 model in later boats; two reserve torpedoes were also carried.

MACHINERY NOTES
All of this type steamed well with a relatively low coal consumption. Their machinery was strongly built and included two return-flame boilers generally of the Normand type (water tube) and two sets of triple expansion engines developing 6800 to 7200 HP. These were set up amidships between the two boiler rooms.

Durandal class – three ships

Displacement:	300 tons (343/344 tons full load).
Dimensions:	57·64m(oa), 56m(wl) × 5·95/6·30m × 3·20m.
Machinery:	See above notes. *Designed speed:* 26 knots.
Radius (nm):	2300/10 knots, 217/26 knots.
Complement:	4 officers, 48 crew.

NAME	BUILDER	LAUNCHED	TRIALS	SPEED
DURANDAL	Normand	11.2.99	4.7.99	27·42
HALLEBARDE	Normand	8.6.99	7.8.99	27·20
FAUCONNEAU	Normand	2.4.00	5.7.00	27·14

The destroyer FAUCONNEAU.

ESPINGOLE of this type was sunk in 1903.

DURANDAL on October 12th, 1914 with ESCOPETTE and PAS-DE-CALAIS, shelled and chased the German U.20 off Cape Gris-Nez. From 1915 to 1916 she was based on Dunkirk. Sold for scrap February 22nd, 1921.

HALLEBARDE with ARBALETE was attached to 1st Submarine Flotilla in the Armée Navale in 1914 and in 1916–17 was in the 7th Destroyer Flotilla based on Brindisi on escort and patrol in the Adriatic. She was in the 8th Flotilla in 1918 based in Southern France. Unlisted March 4th, 1920, she was sold for scrap April 20th, 1921.

FAUCONNEAU was Command ship of the 1st S/M Flotilla (Cherbourg) in November–December 1914 and left for the Mediterranean in 1915, serving off the Syrian coast and later, until March 1919, with the 10th Flotilla based at Salonika. She was stricken January 15th, 1921 and sold for scrap April 20th, 1921.

Pique class – three ships

Displacement:	319 tons (348 tons full load).
Dimensions:	58·20m(oa), 56·22m(wl) × 5·86/6·31m × 3·03m.
Machinery:	See note below. *Designed speed:* 26 knots.
Radius (nm):	2055/10 knots, 194/26 knots.
Complement:	4 officers, 44 crew.

NAME	BUILDER	LAUNCHED	TRIALS	SPEED
YATAGAN	Ch. de la Loire, Nantes.	20.7.00	5.10.00	27·07
PIQUE	F. et C. de la Méditerranée, Granville-Le Havre	31.3.00	7.5.01	25·88
EPEE	F. et C. de la Méditerranée, Granville-Le Havre	27.7.00	1.7.01	26·19

NOTES

These ships differed from the DURANDAL class in having four boilers instead of two and consequently had four funnels. Their two sets of TE engines developed only 4200/5200 HP and their designed speed was reached with difficulty after arduous trials. They were on the whole less successful than their predecessors and the type was not repeated in the French navy.

FRAMEE of this type was rammed and sunk on August 11th, 1900 by the battleship BRENNUS.

YATAGAN spent the war in the Channel as fishery protection vessel; she was rammed and sunk off Dieppe on November 3rd, 1916 by the British cargo vessel TEVIOT.

The destroyer PIQUE as she was to her completing.

The destroyer PIQUE after the modifications fitted during the war.

The destroyer FLAMBERGE.

PIQUE 1916–17 was at Brindisi in 7th Flotilla on escort and patrol in the Adriatic. In 1918 was in the 4th Flotilla, South France. She was sold for scrap on July 28th, 1921. The silhouette of PIQUE was modified during the war. In 1916 she was fitted with a large bridge around the mast and first funnel; her stern tube was transferred to between the two gun groups and a 65mm (or 75mm army?) gun fitted on a platform in place of the transferred torpedo tube.

EPEE in February 1917 while escorting a convoy in the western Mediterranean, attacked and chased the German U.64. She was in the 8th Flotilla in South France in 1918. Unlisted October 1st, 1920, she was sold for scrap January 8th, 1921.

Pertuisane class – four ships (also known as 'les Rochefortais'*)

Displacement:	300 tons (343/344 full load).
Dimensions:	57·64m(oa), 56m(wl) × 5·95/6·30m × 3·20m.
Machinery:	See notes above. *Designed speed:* 26 knots.
Radius (nm):	2300/10 knots, 217/26 knots.
Complement:	4 officers, 48 crew.

*Because their builder, the Rochefort Naval Yard, was for several years the leading yard for destroyers.

Name	Builder	Laid Down	Launched	Trials	Speed
PERTUISANE	Rochefort DY	6.99	5.12.00	9.02	26·96
ESCOPETTE	Rochefort DY	1.00	20.12.00	1.03	26·5
FLAMBERGE	Rochefort DY	15.6.99	28.10.01	7.03	26·8
RAPIERE	Rochefort DY	2.1.00	16.7.01	5.03	26·9

NOTES

PERTUISANE spent six hours during the night of February 22nd, 1917 in a thick fog and flat calm, trying to locate and attack the German UB.40 anchored on the surface in Le Havre Roads and whose w/т could be clearly heard; she got away. Unlisted March 16th, 1923 and used for fire-control tests; sold for scrap April 20th, 1928.

ESCOPETTE spent the war in the Channel. Stricken April 4th, 1921.

FLAMBERGE spent the war in the Mediterranean from 1915. In 1918 joined the 10th Flotilla (Salonika). Stricken October 1st, 1920 and sold for scrap January 8th, 1921.

RAPIERE was in the 3rd Flotilla (North) from January 1913, then sailed to the Mediterranean where she served in the Patrol Boat Division off Bizerta. Stricken October 27th, 1921 and sold for scrap.

Arquebuse class – twenty ships

Displacement:	302·7 tons (designed), 318/320 tons (normal).
Dimensions:	58·26m(oa), 56·30m(wl) × 5·95/6·38m × 3·20m.
Machinery:	2 Normand Du Temple boilers; 2 sets TE, 2 screws; IHP 6300; designed speed 28 knots. Coal 26·6/46·6 tons.
Radius (nm):	with 20 tons coal: 2300/10 knots, 220/26 knots.
Complement:	4 officers, 56 crew.

Name	Builder	Laid Down	Launched	Trials	Speed
CARABINE	Rochefort DY	5.01	21.7.02	5/9.03	30·16
SARBACANE	Rochefort DY	5.01	12.3.03	10/12.03	29·50
ARQUEBUSE	Normand	1901	15.11.02	1/5.03	30·76
ARBALETE	Normand	1901	28.4.03	5/8.03	31·37
MOUSQUET	Ch. Loire, Nantes	11.00	7.8.02	2/5.03	29·12
JAVELINE	Ch. Loire, Nantes	11.00	15.10.02	3/6.03	29·14
SAGAIE	F. et Ch. de la Méditerranée, Graville-Le Havre	1901	15.11.02	10.02/4.03	30·62
EPIEU	F. et Ch. de la Méditerranée, Graville-Le Havre	1901	17.1.03	3/6.03	31·21

HARPON	Ch. de la Gironde, Bordeaux	11.00	20.10.02	11.02/3.03	30·70
FRONDE	Ch. de la Gironde, Bordeaux	1.01	17.12.02	1/3.03	30·71
FRANCISQUE	Rochefort DY	1902	2.3.04	3/4.04	30·09
SABRE	Rochefort DY	1902	15.4.04	5/6.04	29·73
DARD	Penhoët, Rouen	1901	19.9.03	12.03/4.04	29·55
BALISTE	Penhoët, Rouen	1901	22.10.03	12.03/6.04	29·90
MOUSQUETON	Schneider	1901	4.11.02	9.03/8.04	28·78
ARC	Schneider	1901	24.12.02	7.03/7.04	28·89
PISTOLET	Ch. Loire, Nantes	9.01	29.5.03	6/8,03	28·94
BELIER	Ch. Loire, Nantes	9.01	29.5.03	1/3.04	29·93
CATAPULTE	F. et Ch. de la Méditerranée, Graville-Le Havre	1901	1.4.03	5/9.03	30·90
BOMBARDE	F. et Ch. de la Méditerranée, Graville-Le Havre	12.01	26.6.03	8/11.03	30·48

NOTE: First ten were 1900 programme, second ten, 1901 programme.

The destroyer ARBALETE.

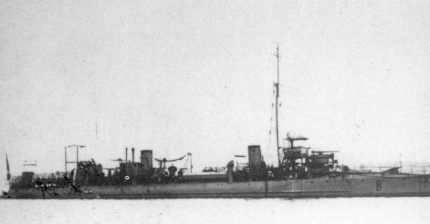

Top: **The destroyer HARPON.**

Above: **The destroyer BALISTE.**

88

Because of increased power, all of the ARQUEBUSE class exceeded their contract speed, especially the Normand boats; stability was improved by the removal of the mainmast, the boats having rather too much top-hamper. In 1903-04, ARBALETE and MOUSQUETON carried out the first wireless telegraphy trials in the French navy.

CARABINE from 1915 to 1918 served in the Mediterranean where on October 1st, 1918 she was in collision with the British merchant ship MENTOR; her foredeck and bridge were wrecked; towed to Palermo for temporary repair then to Bizerta where she was condemned January 8th, 1919.

SARBACANE was in the 2nd Flotilla at Brindisi in 1916 and operated in the Adriatic. In 1918 she was in the South France Patrol Force.

ARQUEBUSE was in the 2nd Light Squadron, Channel, in 1914 and in the Mediterranean 1916 where in April 1916 with other destroyers she made a vain search for U.34. On June 15th, 1916 sighted U.35 which was sinking the British cargo ship UGANDA, and attacked her and on October 2nd, 1916 she assisted the sinking sloop RIGEL. She was sold for scrap on March 2nd, 1921.

ARBALETE on April 16th, 1917 with REQUIN and others, operated in support of the British army and bombarded Gaza. On May 29th, 1917 while escorting a convoy off Crete with HM sloop LILY, attacked the German UC.74. She again attacked this same submarine on September 6th, 1917 while escorting a convoy off Cerigo Island. She was sold for scrap on May 10th, 1921.

MOUSQUET was sunk on October 28th, 1914 off Penang by the German cruiser EMDEN after a glorious but vain fight.

JAVELINE, SAGAIE, EPIEU and HARPON were all in the 2nd Light Squadron (Channel) in 1914. JAVELINE stricken January 12th, 1920, SAGAIE sold April 12th, 1921 and EPIEU sold May 20th, 1922. HARPON, based at Dunkirk 1915-16 rescued some British seaplanes found drifting off the enemy coast. She was sold for scrap July 10th, 1922.

FRONDE, in reserve at Saigon, was commissioned March 1915 and sent to the Mediterranean; on June 3rd, 1917 attacked the German UB.47 off Messina. Condemned October 30th, 1919, she was sold for scrap on May 6th, 1920.

FRANCISQUE was stricken April 4th, 1921 and sold July 10th, 1922; her war service was in the Channel.

SABRE was command ship of the 1st S/M Flotilla June 1913 to April 1915 then in the Eastern Mediterranean until 1918. In March 1916 she carried the King of Serbia from Valona to Corfu.

DARD, in the Mediterranean 1915-18, was escorting the GAULOIS when she was sunk by UB.47 on October 27th, 1916 and from 1917 was at Port Said in the 7th Flotilla. She was stricken April 3rd, 1919 and sold for scrap May 6th, 1920.

BALISTE served in the 9th Flotilla (Bizerta) then the 10th (Salonika). She was stricken October 30th, 1919.

MOUSQUETON was in the 4th Flotilla, Mediterranean 1915-17 then the 8th at Toulon in 1918. She was stricken May 10th, 1920.

ARC 1914 attached 2nd S/M Flotilla; 1916 7th Destroyer Flotilla in the Adriatic; 1918 8th Flotilla, South Provence. Unlisted October 1st, 1920 and sold for scrap January 9th, 1921.

PISTOLET attacked U.35 after the submarine had sunk the British cargo boat SILVERTON on July 13th, 1916 in the western Mediterranean. By 1918 she was in the 8th Flotilla. She was sold for scrap May 6th, 1920.

BELIER, CATAPULTE and BOMBARDE were all in the 2nd Light Squadron (Channel) in 1914. BELIER was 9th Flotilla in 1918 (Tunisia); unlisted January 25th, 1921 and sold May 20th, 1922. CATAPULTE was with ARQUEBUSE on October 2nd, 1916 assisting the RIGEL and with BELIER in 1918. May 18th, 1918 she was rammed and sunk off Bone by the British cargo boat WARRIMOO. BOMBARDE was sold April 20th, 1921.

Claymore class – thirteen ships

Displacement:	356 tons (323·45 on trials).
Dimensions:	58m(wl) × 6·20/6·53m × 2·95m.
Machinery:	2 Normand boilers (except COGNÉE, HACHE and MASSUE: 2 Du Temple boilers); 2 sets TE, 2 screws; IHP 6800; Designed speed 28 knots.
Radius (nm):	2300/10 knots, 1170/14 knots, with 30 tons coal.
Complement:	4 officers, 56 crew.

NAME	BUILDER	LAID DOWN	LAUNCHED	TRIALS	SPEED
STYLET	Rochefort DY	21.3.04	18.5.05	1/4.04	27·12
TROMBLON	Rochefort DY	8.7.04	17.6.05	12.06/4.07	28·48
PIERRIER	Rochefort DY	6.10.04	28.2.05	7/11.08	27·12
OBUSIER	Rochefort DY	10.5.04	9.3.05	6/9.07	28·30
MORTIER	Rochefort DY	12.9.04	23.3.06	10.07/1.08	29·50
CLAYMORE	Normand	1904	14.3.06	4/5.06	30·35
CARQUOIS	Rochefort DY	10.7.05	29.6.07	4/8.08	30·10
TRIDENT	Rochefort DY	1905	5.12.07	10.08/1.09	28·15
FLEURET	Rochefort DY	5.05	14.12.07	8.07/3.08	28·98
COUTELAS	Rochefort DY	3.2.06	12.1.07	9.07/3.08	29·57
COGNEE	Toulon DY	1905	26.11.07	8/12.08	27·04
HACHE	Toulon DY	1.8.06	15.2.08	12.08/6.09	28·48
MASSUE	Toulon DY	1.11.06	19.9.08	2/6.09	28·47

The destroyer PIERRIER

The destroyer MASSUE.

This class differed from the preceding group in being heavier with hull of different form, the tumble-home under the 'caillebotis'–deck being more abrupt. The galley was under the bridge which was consequently higher and the funnels were taller. The class was also the first to be fitted with the 450mm torpedo tube, but on the whole they were less successful.

The trials of PIERRIER were long and difficult because her machinery had experimental force-feed lubrication which was unsatisfactory.

TROMBLON, OBUSIER, CLAYMORE, CARQUOIS and FLEURET were all in the 2nd Light Squadron (Channel) in 1914.

TROMBLON on November 23rd, 1914 attacked U.21 off Le Havre and was on patrol off the Flanders coast in 1917.

PIERRIER was unlisted July 27th, 1921.

OBUSIER assisted the sinking BRANLEBAS September 29th, 1915 and was with the British force in the raid on Ostend April 23rd, 1918.

MORTIER was with the ERNEST RENAN in the attack on Pelagosa, Adriatic, September 17/18th, 1914 and was still in the Adriatic in 1916–17 where she was involved in collision with the passenger ship ASIE. From June 1919 to October 1923 she was a torpedo school tender and was stricken May 27th, 1927.

CLAYMORE was in the Baltic in 1920.

CARQUOIS, on May 24th, 1916 towed the disabled OBUSIER to port.

TRIDENT, 1914–15 Dardanelles; 1916–17 Adriatic. November 13th, 1931 unlisted and sold for scrap November 29th, 1932.

HACHE, COUTELAS and COGNEE were all in the Adriatic 1916 and the latter two were with REQUIN April 16th, 1917 in the bombardment of Gaza.

MASSUE in 1912 was temporarily fitted as a minesweeper. She was in the Dardanelles in 1915 and Adriatic 1916. On March 19th, 1917 she depthcharged the German U.64 and assisted the sinking DANTON. From 1919–26 she was in the Mediterranean Training Division and was unlisted March 30th, 1927.

Branlebas class – ten ships

Displacement:	344 tons (328·14 on trials).
Dimensions:	58m(pp) × 6·28/6·56m × 1·57m (forward), 2·37m (stern).
Machinery:	2 Normand or Guyot Du Temple boilers; 2 sets TE, 2 screws; IHP 6800; designed speed 27·5 knots. Coal 30/80 tons.
Radius (nm):	2100/10 knots, 1170/14 knots, with 30 tons coal.
Complement:	4 officers, 56 crew.

NAME	BUILDER	LAID DOWN	LAUNCHED	TRIALS	SPEED
GLAIVE	Rochefort DY	5.05	10.9.08	4/9.10	27·09
POIGNARD	Rochefort DY	5.05	3.7.09	4/11.10	28·65

Top: **The destroyer GABION.**

Above: **The destroyer BRANLEBAS.**

SABRETAGNE	De La Brosse et Fouché, Nantes	6.06	5.2.08	4/9.08	29·65
ORIFLAMME	De La Brosse et Fouché, Nantes	6.06	4.4.08	5/9.08	29·49
ETENDARD	Dyle et Bacalan, Bordeaux	12.05	20.3.08	5.08/2.09	28·53
FANION	Dyle et Bacalan, Bordeaux	12.05	4.5.08	7.08/2.09	29·06
SAPE	Penhoët, Rouen	11.05	23.9.07	3/11.08	29·82
GABION	Penhoët, Rouen	11.05	21.12.07	2/11.08	29·77
BRANLEBAS	Normand	11.05	8.10.07	11.07/7.08	28·76
FANFARE	Normand	11.05	19.12.07	1/9.08	28·91

NOTES

These ten were also designed by A. Normand and were similar but slightly heavier than the CLAYMORE class. Boilers and machinery were protected by a light 20mm belt. They (and the CLAYMOREs) had a bridge which was relatively large for the size of the ship; they were excellent sea boats.

GLAIVE: 1914, 2nd Light Squadron (Channel); August 12th, 1917 with GABION, was local escort for the first US troop convoy arriving at Brest, and attacked the German UC.69.

POIGNARD and SABRETAGNE both on Adriatic operations in 1916.

ORIFLAMME: August 22nd/23rd, 1915 with BRANLEBAS, sank the torpedo-boat A.15 and on March 2nd, 1916 with the FRANCIS GARNIER captured a German seaplane off Ostend. In 1917 part of her crew were Belgians. January 1919 in the Baltic, she captured the German cargo ship ELBE and the tug BERGER I and took them to Dunkirk through the Kiel Canal despite opposition from German sluice-keepers.

ETENDARD in 1914 was in the 2nd Light Squadron. April 25th, 1917 blown up by German destroyers; no survivors.

FANION on February 11th, 1917 depthcharged the German UC.21 off Brest.

SAPE was in the Mediterranean, 4th Flotilla 1912–15 and at the Dardanelles. 5th Flotilla, 'Division Navale d'Orient' Salonika 1916–18. Stricken May 3rd, 1926.

BRANLEBAS was in the North Sea Flotilla and took part in the destruction of the German torpedo boat A.15. She sank on a mine off Nieuport September 30th, 1915.

FANFARE in 1916 Adriatic operations and in 1918 in the Algerian Patrol Force.

The 450-ton type

Thirteen destroyers were ordered between 1906 and 1910; in spite of several common features, displacement, armament and engine power, they differed by the type of machinery used. Consequently naval reference books usually divide them into three sub-classes:

1. Seven coal-burning ships with reciprocating engines (SPAHI group);
2. Two ships with a combined propulsion of two turbines and a reciprocating engine (VOLTIGEUR group);
3. Four turbine-driven vessels (CHASSEUR group).

All thirteen had four boilers and were equipped with six 1902 model 65mm guns and three 450mm torpedo tubes (1906 model torpedoes) including a bow tube.

On the whole they were more or less experimental ships; the most robust as was proved during the war, were the SPAHIs with their reciprocating engines.

Spahi class – seven ships

Displacement: 530/550 tons (designed as 450).
Dimensions: LANSQUENET, ENSEIGNE HENRY and ASPIRANT HERBER: 64m(pp) × 6·60m.
SPAHI: 64·60m(pp) × 6·05m(wl).
HUSSARD and MAMELUK: 65·80m(pp) × 6·60m.
CARABINIER: 64·20m(pp) × 6·48m(wl).
Machinery: 4 Normand boilers (SPAHI, LANSQUENET); 4 Du Temple boilers (HUSSARD, MAMELUK); 4 Guyot boilers (in others); 2 sets TE, 2 screws; designed HP 7500 (SPAHI: 9000); designed speed 28 knots. Coal 95 tons (except LANSQUENET, 115 tons and greater radius).

The destroyer SPAHI

The destroyer HUSSARD

Radius (nm): LANSQUENET: 2880/10 knots, 960/20 knots. Others: 1000–1200/10 knots.

Complement: 77 to 79.

NAME	BUILDER	LAUNCHED	COMPLETED	SPEED
SPAHI	F. et Ch. de la Méditerranée, La Seyne	3.5.08	7.10	29·43
HUSSARD	Ch. de la Loire	12.9.08	9.11	29·80
CARABINIER	Penhoët, St Nazaire	10.10.08	10.09	27·05
LANSQUENET	Dyle et Bacalan, Bordeaux	20.11.09	10.10	28·84
MAMELUK	Ch. de la Loire	10.3.09	6.11	29·75
ENSEIGNE HENRY	Rochefort DY	12.5.11	4.12	28·46
ASPIRANT HERBER	Rochefort DY	30.4.12	8.12	28·25

NOTES

These were well-built vessels and their sea-keeping qualities, because o heavier displacement, were better than the 300-ton series though this dis placement was still insufficient to make them good long-distance escorts.

SPAHI in May 1915 chased an Austrian submarine which attempted t attack HM cruiser AMETHYST. December 14th, 1917 she assisted th sinking CHATEAURENAULT. She was condemned in December 1927.

HUSSARD was condemned in March 1922.

The destroyer LANSQUENET.

The destroyer LANSQUENET in a dock at Bizerta.

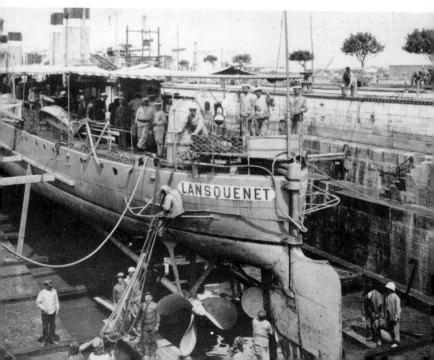

CARABINIER on May 11th, 1915 attacked the German U.21 while entering the Mediterranean. On November 13th, 1918 she stranded near Lataquie, Syria and was scuttled under Turkish fire two days later.

LANSQUENET was present at the raid on Lissa Island, Adriatic on November 1st, 1914.

MAMELUK in the night of June 5th, 1916 rammed and sank the FANTASSIN, and with LANSQUENET sank the UC.38 which had just torpedoed the escorted cruiser CHATEAURENAULT, which was being used as a troop transport. The two destroyers rescued 1,162 men, including 60 members of the crew of UC.38. Both ships were awarded the 'Croix de Guerre' pennant.

ENSEIGNE HENRY with the ASPIRANT HERBER attacked the Austrian U.3 on August 12th, 1915 and on February 17th, 1917 while escorting a convoy, attacked the German U.65. She was condemned in June 1928.

ASPIRANT HERBER was condemned in July 1930.

Voltigeur class – two ships

Displacement	450 tons (as designed), 590 (full load).
Dimensions:	VOLTIGEUR: 65·50m(pp) × 6·82m(wl).
	TIRAILLEUR: 63m(pp) × 6·40m(wl).
Machinery:	4 Normand boilers (V) or 4 du Temple (T); 1 set TE, 3 cylinder on central shaft, 2 Rateau (V) or Breguet (T) on the lateral shafts; 3 screws; designed HP 7500; speed 28 knots. Coal 118 tons.
Radius (nm):	1520/10 knots, 1010/16 knots, 560/20 knots.
Complement:	76/77.

The destroyer VOLTIGEUR.

The destroyer TIRAILLEUR

NAME	BUILDER	LAUNCHED	COMPLETED
VOLTIGEUR	A. Ch. de Bretagne, Nantes	25.3.09	4.10
TIRAILLEUR	Ch. de la Gironde, Bordeaux	27.11.08	7.10

NOTES

VOLTIGEUR 1917: operations near Castellorizo Island. Condemned in May 1920.

TIRAILLEUR 1916–17 Adriatic Sea operations. Condemned July 1921.

The combined propulsion system of these two destroyers was regarded as less flexible than that of ships fitted with the single type of machinery.

Chasseur class – four ships

Displacement:	450 tons (designed), 520 (full load).
Dimensions:	CHASSEUR: 64·20m(pp) × 6·54m(wl).
	JANISSAIRE: 64·50m(pp) × 6·60m(wl).
	FANTASSIN: 65·40m(pp) × 6·65m(wl).
	CAVALIER: 64·20m(pp) × 6·60m(wl).
Machinery:	4 Normand boilers except JANISSAIRE 3 Foster Wheeler; 3 Parsons turbines, 3 screws; designed SHP 7200 (8/9000 on trials); designed speed 28 knots. Fuel: 99 tons coal (CHASSEUR), 135 tons oil (others).

The destroyer JANISSAIRE.

Radius (nm):   1400/1500/10 knots, 420/560/20 knots.
Complement: 77/79.

NAME	BUILDER	LAUNCHED	COMPLETED	SPEED
CHASSEUR	Normand	20.2.09	11.09	30·39
JANISSAIRE	Penhoët, St Nazaire	12.4.10	6.11	28·57
FANTASSIN	F. de Ch. de la Méditerranée, La Seyne	17.6.09	6.11	30·04
CAVALIER	Normand	9.5.10	1.11	31·02

NOTES

As in the VOLTIGEUR type, the four boilers were placed before the engine room. All had oil-fired boilers, except CHASSEUR, the first of this type in the French Fleet. Their trials on the whole were a success but there was disappointment at the fragility of their turbines.

CHASSEUR: 1915–17 2nd Flotilla Brindisi. Stricken in October 1919.

JANISSAIRE: 1915–16 patrols near Castellorizo. Stricken in October 1920.

FANTASSIN: On June 5th, 1916 while hunting a submarine, was rammed by MAMELUK; her wreck was destroyed by gunfire from FAUCONNEAU.

CAVALIER: On August 17th, 1914 collided with FANTASSIN; repaired at Malta and bow tube removed. Used as schoolship for mechanics, stokers and divers.

The 800-ton type

After the 450-tonners came the so-called '800-ton series'. The increase in displacement was noteworthy and followed the trend seen in all navies especially the Royal Navy.

Like the former classes, the 'Service Technique des Constructions Navales' simply fixed one general programme and notified the private yards leaving them a great latitude in the design and the choice of machinery; this however was to include turbines and oil-fired boilers. The first twelve 800-tonners consequently presented marked differences between each other, especially in hull form and in accommodation details and machinery. Builders accordingly used various types of turbines and boilers, totalling 13 to 14,000 SHP.

Except BOUCLIER which was shorter (72·32m oa) the waterline length and beam of the first units varied between 74 and 78·28m and 7·57 and 8·05m respectively. The mean draught varied between 2·90 and 3·26m. All had two screws except BOUCLIER and CASQUE which had three shafts. These two destroyers had the best fuel consumption and were also the fastest. The vessels equipped with Breguet turbines were the fastest at raising steam.

In service the hull, especially in the first group, showed weakness and parts had to be reinforced; machinery also was fragile. The silhouette was thought to be too high, the bridge too light and guns and torpedoes insufficient; these faults had to be remedied during hostilities. One good point was that these vessels were homogeneous.

The armament initially included two 1893 model 100mm and four 1902 model 65mm guns with four 450mm torpedo tubes in twin staggered mounts. During the war, one 47mm AA gun or one 75mm and two St Etienne 8mm machine guns were added, also 8 to 10 depthcharges of the Guiraud type.

The fore funnel was raised or equipped with a cowl to protect the bridge. All this increased the ships' initial displacement to 900/950 tons and consequently the operational speed rarely exceeded 26 knots.

Bouclier class – twelve ships

Displacement: 800 tons (designed).
Dimensions: see notes above.
Machinery: 4 Normand, Normand-Sigaudy, du Temple or Dyle et Bacalan boilers; 2 – (a) Parsons, (b) Zoelly, (c) Breguet, or (d) Rateau turbines, 2 screws; designed SHP 13,000; designed speed 30 knots.
NOTE: BOUCLIER and CASQUE had 3 Parsons turbines and 3 shafts.
Oil: varied between 120 and 160 tons.
Radius (nm): 1200 to 1400/12 to 14 knots.
Complement: 5 to 6 officers, 75 to 77 crew.

Top: The destroyer BOUCLIER as she was in 1911.

Above: The destroyer BOUCLIER as she was at the end of the war with her modified bridge and the forefunnel heightened.

Top: The destroyer CASQUE as she was in 1914.

Above: The destroyer CASQUE at the end of the war with her enlarged bridge
and a depth charges rack astern.

NAME	BUILDER	LAID DOWN	LAUNCHED	COMPLETED	SPEED
BOUCLIER (a)	Normand	1090	29.6.11	1911	35·53
BOUTEFEU (b)	Dyle et Bacalan, Bordeaux	1909	2.5.11	1911	31·42
CASQUE (a)	F. Ch. de la Méditerranée, Le Havre	1909	25.8.10	1911	34·89
CIMETERRE (c)	F. Ch. de la Gironde	1909	13.4.11	1912	31·15
DAGUE (c)	F. Ch. de la Gironde	1909	13.4.11	1912	32·81
FAULX (d)	De la Brosse et Fouché, Nantes	1909	2.2.11	1912	32·01
FOURCHE (d)	De la Brosse et Fouché, Nantes	1909	21.10.10	1912	32·11
CAPITAINE MEHL (a)	A. Ch. de la Loire, St Nazaire	1910	20.4.12	1912	31·77
COMMANDANT BORY (d)	Dyle et Bacalan, Bordeaux	1910	14.9.12	1913	30·68
COMMANDANT RIVIERE (c)	F. Ch. de la Gironde	1910	2.10.12	1913	32·35
DEHORTER (a)	Penhoët, Rouen	1910	18.4.12	1913	29·31
FRANCIS GARNIER (a)	Normand	1910	1.10.12	1913	29·38

NOTES

All except CASQUE had four funnels, of variable height, vertical or slightly inclined, equidistant (BOUTEFEU and C^{dt} BORY) or arranged in two more or less near pairs. Because CASQUE's two boilers were back to back this ship had only three uptakes, the central being larger than the others. As has been said, BOUCLIER and CASQUE were the fastest; on the other hand, BORY's speed was the lowest and she reached 24 knots with difficulty. DAGUE had an experimental tripod mast for a time.

BOUCLIER: On September 6th, 1914 carried Prince Danilo of Montenegro to Antivari; on May 26/27th, 1915 escorted British battleships from Malta to Taranto; January 27th, 1916 while escorting a damaged Italian cruiser, gave chase to Austrian cruiser NOVARA. In December 1916 she was based on Dunkirk and on May 20th, 1917 was damaged in action with German destroyers. On October 17th, 1917 present at the bombardment of Ostend. Her poop was destroyed December 8th, 1917 by one of her depth-charges while attacking a U-boat. March 21st, 1918 with CAPITAINE MEHL, sank the German destroyer A.7. April 23rd, 1918 took part in the

The destroyer CIMETERRE as she was in 1914.

The destroyer CIMETERRE at the end of the war.

Top: **The destroyer FAULX.**

Above: **The destroyer FOURCHE.**

p: The destroyer CAPITAINE MEHL. Note the position of the 75mm army gun.

ove: The destroyer COMMANDANT RIVIERE. Note her heightened forefunnel
d the two Thornycroft throwers amidship.

attack on Zeebrugge and May 10th, 1918 the operation against Ostend. She was awarded the 'Croix de Guerre' in 1919 and condemned in February 1933.

BOUTEFEU: 1915–17 in the 1st Flotilla at Brindisi; operations in the Adriatic. December 22nd, 1916 in action with Austrian destroyers in the Otranto Strait. She was cut in two and sunk May 15th, 1917 off Brindisi by a mine laid by UC.25; posthumously awarded the 'Croix de Guerre'.

CASQUE: 1915–17 1st Flotilla. In chase of Austrian forces November 2nd, 1914 off Lissa and on December 29th, 1915 finished off the Austrian destroyer TRIGLAV by gunfire after she had been mined. December 22nd, 1916 was in action with Austrian forces in the Otranto Strait and on the following day the Italian destroyer ABBA rammed her at 31 knots causing serious damage. May 15th, 1917 she attacked the German UC.25 which had torpedoed HMS DARTMOUTH. August 29th, 1918 she again received serious damage by being rammed, this time by PLUTON off the Dardanelles. In 1919 she was awarded the 'Croix de Guerre' and was condemned in March 1926.

CIMETERRE: Was in action with Austrian forces on May 14th, 1917 and again on April 22nd, 1918. She was condemned in July 1926.

DAGUE was sunk February 24th, 1915 on a drifting mine in Antivari Roads.

FAULX: 1915–17, 1st Flotilla at Brindisi; on February 9th, 1916 attacked an Austrian submarine off Durazzo and in action with Austrian forces May 14th, 1917. On April 18th, 1918 she was rammed and sunk by the MAN-GINI in the Otranto Strait.

FOURCHE: 1915–16, 1st Flotilla at Brindisi; escort to supply ships for Montenegro in 1915. On June 23rd, 1916 was torpedoed by the Austrian U.15 and sunk. Posthumously awarded the 'Croix de Guerre' pennant.

CAPITAINE MEHL: 1914, 2nd Light Squadron (Channel); 1915–18 based on Dunkirk, Flanders operations; on November 8th, 1916 escorted the damaged HMS ZULU to Calais; in July 1916 attacked U.51 in the Channel. On October 27th, 1917 she was in action with German destroyers and on March 21st, 1918 with BOUCLIER, sank the German destroyer A.7. She was condemned in July 1926.

COMMANDANT BORY: On May 26/27th, 1915 escorted British battleships from Malta to Taranto; June 5th, 1915 bombardment of Ragusa; June 9th, 1915 attacked the Austrian U.4; on December 29th, 1915 and August 15th, 1916 in action with Austrian forces, in latter action was straddled by the cruiser ASPERN; again in action with Austrian forces on May 13th, 1917. In 1919 awarded the 'Croix de Guerre' and condemned in July 1926.

COMMANDANT RIVIERE: 1914–15 escorting supply ships to Monte-negro; June 5th, 1915 bombardment of Ragusa; July 11th, 1915 raid on Pelagosa; October/December 1915 operations near Salonika; December 22nd, 1916 and May 15th, 1917 in action with Austrian forces, in former hit the DINARA but had her boiler room out of action. She was based on Mudros in 1918, in 1919 awarded the 'Croix de Guerre' pennant; con-demned in June 1933.

DEHORTER: 1915–18, 1st Flotilla at Brindisi; December 1916 Athens and Salamis operations; December 22nd, 1916 in action with Austrian forces. Condemned in 1933.

The destroyer DEHORTER. Note her damaged bow.

The destroyer FRANCIS GARNIER at the end of the war. Note the astern 75mm army gun.

Top: The destroyer BISSON as she was in 1914.

Above: The destroyer BISSON at the end of the war with her enlarged bridge.
Note also the cowl to protect the bridge on the forefunnel.

FRANCIS GARNIER: 1915, 2nd Light Squadron (Channel); October/December 1914 shelled German positions in Flanders in support of the left wing of the British Army; had General Foch aboard on December 1st, 1914. On March 2nd, 1916 with ORIFLAMME, captured a German seaplane off Ostend; slight damage on October 27th, 1917 while in action with German destroyers. She was condemned in July 1926.

Bisson class – six ships

Displacement:	850 to 880 tons (as designed).
Dimensions:	78·10m(pp) × 8·63m × about 3·10m (for 4 built in the Naval Dockyards).
Machinery:	4 boilers; 2 Breguet (in (a)), Parsons (b), Zoelly or Rateau (d) turbines, 2 screws; SHP 15,000 (designed); speed 30 knots (designed). Oil 160 tons.
Radius (nm):	1350 – 1400/14 knots.
Complement:	5/6 officers, 75/77 crew.

NAME	BUILDER	LAID DOWN	LAUNCHED	COMPLETED	TRIALS SPEED
BISSON (a)	Toulon DY	1.11	12.9.12	1913	31·05
RENAUDIN (a)	Toulon DY	2.11	20.3.13	1913	30·55
COMMANDANT LUCAS (a)	Toulon DY	2.12	11.7.14	1914	30·02
PROTET (b)	Rochefort DY	7.12	15.10.13	1914	
MANGINI (c)	Schneider, Chalon-sur-Saone	1911	31.3.13	1914	30·93
MAGON (d)	A. Ch. de Bretagne, Nantes*	1911	19.4.13	1914	32·02

NOTES
On these destroyers the four funnels were distributed in two pairs, those of the four ships built in the naval dockyards being higher.
As designed, MAGON had a slightly incurved bow. MANGINI built by Schneider in its river plant, went down the Rhône on a specially built barge without her masts and funnels. CDT LUCAS was fitted with a tripod mast. These destroyers had the same disadvantages and qualities as their predecessors.
BISSON: 1915–17, 1st Flotilla at Brindisi; numerous escorts to Montenegro during 1915. August 7th, 1915 raid on Lagosta; August 13th, 1915 shelled and sank the Austrian U.3; August 15th, 1916 and May 13th, 1917 in action with Austrian forces. In 1918 she was based on Mudros and in 1919 in the Black Sea. She was awarded the 'Croix de Guerre' pennant. Unlisted in June 1933 she was broken up in 1939.

* Ex Ch. de la Brosse et Fouché.

Top: The destroyer RENAUDIN as she was in 1914.

Above: The destroyer COMMANDANT LUCAS entering Brindisi harbour after a war mission. In the background the very old Italian battleship ANDREA DORIA

Top: The destroyer PROTET.

Above: The destroyer MANGINI at the end of the war.

The destroyer MAGON in a dock.

RENAUDIN: 1915–16 based at Brindisi and escorting to Montenegro. On March 17th, 1916 was cut in two and sunk by the Austrian U.6 off Durazzo; awarded a posthumous 'Croix de Guerre' pennant.

COMMANDANT LUCAS: Based at Brindisi 1915–17 operating in the Adriatic and in action with Austrian forces May 13th, 1917. Based on Mudros 1918. Condemned in June 1933.

PROTET: May 26/27th, 1915 escorted British battleships from Malta to Taranto. 1915–17 based at Brindisi and in action December 22nd, 1916 with Austrian forces in Otranto Strait. 1918 based on Mudros and in 1919 in the Black Sea. From 1921 to 1932 she was a Signal School tender; unlisted February 1933 and sold June 1936.

MANGINI: 1915–16 Adriatic; 1917 blockade of Greece. In 1918 based on Mudros. On November 10th, 1918 with HM destroyer SHARK, was the first to anchor at Constantinople. She was in the Black Sea 1919 and in 1934 was condemned.

MAGON: 1915-16 based at Brindisi; in December 1916 she was in the Dunkirk Flotilla and in action with German destroyers on April 25th, 1917, May 20th, 1917, October 27th, 1917 and March 21st, 1918. On October 4th, 1918 with British monitors at the bombardment of German positions in Flanders. She was condemned in February 1926.

Enseigne Roux class – three ships

Displacement:	1075 tons (full load).
Dimensions:	82·60m × 8·60m.
Machinery:	4 boilers; 2 Parsons turbines (geared turbines in ENSEIGNE GABOLDE, see notes), 2 screws; SHP 17.000; designed speed 300 knots. Oil 175 tons.
Radius (nm):	about 1400/14 knots.
Complement:	5/6 officers, 71/75 crew.

NAME	BUILDER	LAID DOWN	LAUNCHED	COMPLETED	SPEED
ENSEIGNE ROUX	Rochefort DY	13.12.13	13.7.15	1916	30·41
MÉCANICIEN PRINCIPAL LESTIN	Rochefort DY	12.11.13	15.5.15	1916	31·21
ENSEIGNE GABOLDE	A. Normand	26.6.14	23.4.21	1923	33·43

NOTES

The first two of this group were an extrapolation of the preceding ships; the third unit was experimental and not completed until after the war.

It was arranged that her sisters could be fitted for minelaying or for minesweeping. Their armament, similar to the other 800-tonners was reinforced during the war by a 75mm AA gun, ten depthcharges (Guiraud type) and a Pinocchio towed torpedo; they had tripod masts.

It was intended that ENSEIGNE GABOLDE should be fitted with Parsons geared turbines but the war prevented this and her building was only resumed just prior to the war's end; meanwhile she was cannibalised, her four boilers being put into the ex-Argentine OPINIATRE and TEMERAIRE and the ex-Greek AETOS and PANTHER chartered after the Athens events of 1916. ENSEIGNE GABOLDE finally had the following characteristics:

Dimensions:	83·60m(oa), 82·07m(wl) × 8·21m × 3·12m.
Machinery:	4 vertical tube Normand boilers; 2 Parsons geared turbines, 2 screw; designed SHP 20,000; speed 31 knots. Oil 196 tons.
Radius (nm):	1300/14 knots as designed.
Armament:	3 – 100mm (2 forward superimposed, 1 astern), 1 – 75mm AA, 2 twin 550mm tubes.
Complement:	80

Her bridge was of an enlarged design and like the others of the class, she had four funnels, the forward pair being taller than the rear pair. On trials she made more than 33 knots with 26,000 SHP. She was condemned just prior to World War II.

ENSEIGNE ROUX: 1915–18 Dunkirk Flotilla and on May 20th, 1917 was in action with German destroyers. On April 22nd/23rd, 1918 took part in the blocking of Zeebrugge and Ostend and again Ostend on May 10th 1918. On October 14th, 1918 with British monitors shelling German positions in Flanders. Condemned 1936.

The destroyer ENSEIGNE ROUX.

MECANICIEN PRINCIPAL LESTIN: March 1916, Mediterranean Fleet, escort and patrol in the Aegean. November/December 1916 Athens and Salamis operations; January/June 1917 blockade of Greece. In April 1918 she was in the Dunkirk Flotilla and took part in the operations against Zeebrugge and Ostend. October 14th, 1918 bombardment of German positions in Flanders. In 1930 she was in the Baltic Division. Condemned in 1935.

Aventurier class – four ships (ex-Argentine)

Displacement:	990/1000 tons (on trials), 1250 (full load).
Dimensions:	88·53m(oa), 86·28m(wl) × 8·62/8·75m.
Machinery:	5 White Foster Wheeler boilers; 2 Rateau turbines, 2 screws; designed SHP 18,000; designed speed 32 knots. Coal 230 tons, oil 72 tons.
Radius (nm):	1850/10 knots, 1180/18 knots with about 300 tons fuel.
Armament:	see notes

NAME	BUILDER	LAUNCHED	COMPLETED
OPINIATRE (ex-Rioja)	Dyle et Bacalan, Bordeaux	1911	16.9.14
AVENTURIER (ex-Mendoza)	Dyle et Bacalan, Bordeaux	18.2.11	29.9.14
TEMERAIRE (ex-San Juan)	A. Ch. de Bretagne, Nantes	8.12.11	2.11.14
INTREPIDE (ex-Salta)	A. Ch. de Bretagne, Nantes	25.9.11	2.11.14

NOTES
These four destroyers were requisitioned on August 9th, 1914 while completing for the Argentine navy; they had been ordered at the same time as four ships in Germany which had been taken into the German navy.

The French-built vessels had a displacement of about 950/1000 tons and armed with 6 – 457 or 2 – 557mm tubes and 4 – 102mm guns supplied by the USA. Under the French flag this initial armament was replaced by four Canet 100mm guns and four 1902 model 450mm single tubes.

AVENTURIER and INTREPIDE joined the 2nd Light Squadron (Channel) in October 1914 and took part in the action before Nieuport and the shelling during the Yser battle of enemy positions around Lombaertzydt. On October 30th, 1914 Admiral Hood, commanding the Dover Patrol, hoisted his flag in INTREPIDE, the first time a French warship went to fight in this condition.

At the end of December 1914 the 100mm guns having worn out their tubes, were replaced in one ship by obselescent 100mm from the battleship DEVASTATION (1879) and in the other by new Canet guns.

Both ships remained in the North until 1917 then went to the Mediterranean to replace their sisters OPINIATRE and TEMERAIRE whose boilers were getting into a bad state and who went to Brest for repairs.

The destroyer AVENTURIER.

Each then received an oil-fired boiler intended for ENSEIGNE GABOLDE and three coal-fired du Temple from the incomplete battleships NORMANDIE and GASCOGNE and also a reserve boiler from a 300-ton destroyer. They then had four funnels, a silhouette different from the other two ships and could reach only 22 knots; they had become a fast type of gunboat!

In 1919-20 the four ships were assigned to the Baltic Division. Between 1924 and 1927 AVENTURIER and INTREPIDE were refitted with three Schulz-Thornycroft boilers from the ex-German V.100 and V.126 transferred to the French navy in 1920. This conversion was a success and they maintained 26 knots under full load. Like their sisters, they were converted in 1926 into fast minesweepers. OPINIATRE was discarded 1933, TEMERAIRE 1936, INTREPIDE 1937 and AVENTURIER 1938.

Arabe class – twelve ships

Displacement:	685 tons (690/750 on trials).
Dimensions:	82·96m(oa), 79·40m(wl) × 7·33m × 2·39m (mean).
Machinery:	4 Japanese Admiralty (Yarrow type) boilers; 3 sets TE, four cylinder and forced-feed lubrication, 2 screws; IHP 10,000; speed 29 knots. Coal 102 tons, oil 118 tons.
Radius (nm):	2000/12 knots, 1600/14-15 knots, 1100/19 knots.
Armament:	1 – 120mm, 4 – 76mm (one = AA), 4 – 450mm tubes (2 × 2).
Complement:	5 officers, 81 crew.

The destroyer TEMERAIRE as she was in 1916.

The destroyer TEMERAIRE after her reconstruction in 1917.

Top: **The destroyer ARABE entering Bordeaux harbour.**

Above: **The destroyer TOUAREG.**

Name	Builder	Laid Down	Launched
ALGERIEN	Yokosuka DY	1917	1917
ANNAMITE	Yokosuka DY	1917	1917
ARABE	Kure DY	1917	1917
BAMBARA	Kure DY	1917	1917
HOVA	Sassebo DY	1917	1917
KABYLE	Sassebo DY	1917	1917
MAROCAIN	Maizuru DY	1917	1917
SAKALAVE	Maizuru DY	1917	1917
SENEGALAIS	Kawasaki, Kobe	1917	1917
SOMALI	Kawasaki, Kobe	1917	1917
TONKINOIS	Mitsubishi, Nagasaki	1917	1917
TOUAREG	Mitsubishi, Nagasaki	1917	1917

All were completed between July and September 1917.

NOTES

As it was not possible to get urgently required modern destroyers from Great Britain or the USA, the French Government ordered twelve from Japan in 1917. Similar to the Japanese KABA class, they were built and delivered in record time. Unfortunately their armament was Japanese, but they were good sea boats and rendered good service during the last months of the war in the Mediterranean where seven were assigned to the 11th Flotilla (TOUREG, BAMBARA, KABYLE, SAKALAVE, SENEGALAIS, SOMALI and ANNAMITE) and escorted troop transports between Taranto and Itea. The five others joined the 3rd Destroyer Division based on Mudros in 1918.

After the war, most of this class were assigned to the North Squadron based at Brest. During the Riff campaign (1924–25) some of them were operating along the coast of Morocco.

ANNAMITE and BAMBARA stricken 1933; MAROCAIN, SOMALI and TOUAREG in 1935 and the others in 1936.

D'Iberville – one ship

Displacement:	925/960 tons.
Dimensions:	81·90m(oa), 79·80m(wl) × 8·80/8·23m × 3·10m (mean).
Machinery:	8 vertical small-tube Lagrafel d'Allest boilers; 2 sets quad. expansion, 2 screws; IHP 5000; speed 21 knots. Coal 188 tons.
Protection:	Slight belt over machinery; protective deck 15mm.
Armament:	1 – 100mm (forward), 3 – 65mm, 7 – 47mm, and initially 3 torpedo tubes which were soon removed.

Name	Builder	Laid Down	Launched	Completed
D'IBERVILLE	Ch. de la Loire, Nantes	26.8.91	11.9.93	1894

Two others of this type, CASSINI and CASABIANCA, were fitted as minelayers (qv).

Designed by M. de Bussy, these three initially rated as 'avisos-torpilleurs', were the first French warships fitted with quadruple expansion engines.

D'IBERVILLE at the outbreak of the war was at Penang where luckily she was not spotted by the German cruiser EMDEN which sank the French destroyer MOUSQUET and the old Russian cruiser JEMTCHOUG. She later sailed to the Mediterranean where she was assigned until 1917 to the Algerian Patrol Division. At the end of the war she was disarmed at Toulon. Condemned in July 1919 and sold for scrap in 1920.

Dunois class – two ships

Displacement:	890 tons.
Dimensions:	78m(oa), 77·60m(wl) × 8·22/8·43m × 3·10m (mean).
Machinery:	4 small-tube Normand-Sigaudy boilers; 2 sets TE, 2 screws; IHP 6400; speed 21·7 knots. Coal 137 tons.
Radius (nm):	less than 5000/10 knots.
Protection:	Belt 25mm machinery rooms; deck 14mm.
Armament:	6 – 65mm[1], 6 – 47mm[1].
Complement:	8 officers, 120 crew.

[1]1902 model.

NAME	BUILDER	LAID DOWN	LAUNCHED	COMPLETED
DUNOIS	Cherbourg DY	5.96	6.10.97	1898
LA HIRE	Cherbourg DY	5.96	3.11.98	1898

NOTES
Designed by M. Trogneux and were initially rated as 'avisos-torpilleurs'.

DUNOIS: 1914 commanding Channel Destroyer flotillas, 2nd Light Squadron. In November 1914 was based on Dunkirk and took part in bombardments of German positions in support of the British army in Flanders. February 1914 appointed to Western Channel Patrol Force.

LA HIRE was assigned before 1914 to the Gunnery School at Toulon for rapid fire training. In November 1914 was used for patrols for the control of neutral shipping between Bizerta and Sardinia; captured the Spanish cargo boat TRES AMIGOS carrying 30 mobilised Germans to Italy. In 1916 was on anti-submarine patrol between Crete and Rhodes and 1917–18 in the Tunisian Patrol Force. Later she was again attached to the Gunnery School for gun-laying training and received two 1917 model 100mm guns, six 47mm and depthcharges. Condemned October 31st, 1922.

Below: **The destroyer DUNOIS.**

Foot: **The destroyer LA HIRE.**

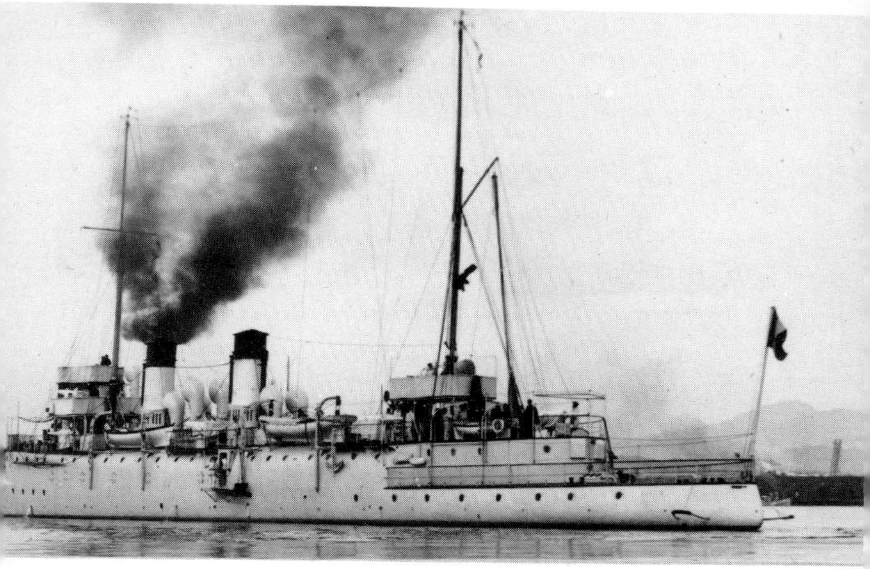

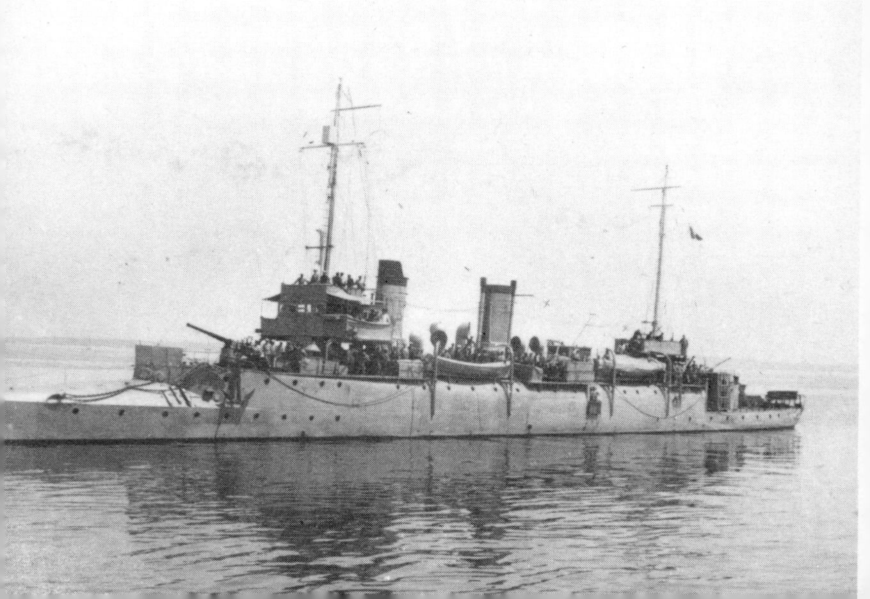

Torpedo Boats

Chevalier – one ship

Displacement: 120 tons (designed), 137 (full load).
Dimensions: 43·78m(pp) × 4·37m × 1·45m.
Machinery: 2 du Temple boilers; 2 sets TE, 2 screws; IHP 2000, speed
24·5 knots (as designed). Coal 16·8 tons.
Radius (nm): 2000/10 knots, 100/14 knots.
Armament: 2 – 37mm guns, 2 – 450mm tubes.

NAME	BUILDER	LAID DOWN	LAUNCHED	COMPLETED
CHEVALIER	Normand	7.91	15.6.93	1894

NOTES
From 1914 to 1918 Division des Patrouilles de Provence. Stricken on
October 1st, 1919.

Cyclone class – eleven ships

Displacement: 152 to 180 tons (full load).
Dimensions: (a) 46·35m(oa), 45m(wl) × 4·68m × 1·40/1·50m.
(b) 46·57m(oa), 45m(wl) × 4·78m × 1·50m.
(c) 46·50m(oa), 45m(wl) × 5·04m × 1·60m.
Machinery: 2 return-flame Normand boilers; 2 sets TE; IHP 3800 to
4200, speed 29 knots (as designed) (26 in MISTRAL
group). Coal 17 to 25 tons.
Radius (nm): generally 2000 to 2500/10 knots, 1000/14 knots, 200 at
full speed.
Protection: slight protection around machinery in MISTRAL group.
Armament: 2 – 47mm guns, 2 – 381mm tubes.*

NAME	BUILDER	LAID DOWN	LAUNCHED	COMPLETED	SPEED
CYCLONE (a)	Normand	11.96	21.5.98	1899	30·38
BOURRASQUE (b)	Normand	6.99	31.8.01	1902	31·94
RAFALE (b)	Normand	7.00	27.11.01	1902	31·41
BOREE (b)	A. Ch. de la Gironde, Bordeaux	1900	23.3.01	1901	29·01
TRAMONTANE (b)	A. Ch. de la Gironde, Bordeaux	1900	21.5.01	1902	29·72
MISTRAL (c)	Normand	8.98	4.5.01	1902	28·24
SIROCO (c)	Normand	8.98	20.2.01	1901	28·72

* Group 'c' originally had a third tube, soon removed.

The First Class torpedo boat BOURRASQUE.

SIMOUN (c)	F. Ch. de la Méditer-ranée Graville, Le Havre	11.99	23.3.01	1902	27·77
TYPHON (c)	F. Ch. de la Méditer-ranée Graville, Le Havre	12.99	15.6.01	1903	28·24
TROMBE (c)	A. Ch. la Loire, Nantes	1.8.98	30.7.00	1902	26·60
AUDACIEUX (c)	A. Ch. la Loire, Nantes	1.8.98	29.8.00	1901	26·19

NOTES
CYCLONE: local defence of Algiers. Stricken October 1st, 1920.
    BOURRASQUE: local defence, Bizerta; on patrol with the S/M ARIANE when the latter was sunk. Stricken in September 1921.

RAFALE: Dunkirk Flotilla; accidently sunk December 1st, 1917 at Boulogne by depthcharge explosion, raised and repaired. Stricken April 4th, 1921.

BOREE: at Brindisi 1915–16; local defence of Toulon 1918. Stricken in October 1920.

TRAMONTANE: Dunkirk Flotilla 1914–15 then Algiers local defence. Stricken in October 1920.

MISTRAL: local defence, Brest. Renamed BOREE in 1925, stricken May 17th, 1927.

SIROCO: local defence of Cherbourg, Algiers and Oran. Stricken May 5th, 1925.

SIMOUN: October 15th, 1915 entered Ostend under enemy fire and took to Dunkirk the first report of its occupation by the enemy.

TYPHON: March 12th, 1918 the first ship sent to investigate the area where HM submarine D.3 had been mistakenly sunk by a French balloon.

TROMBE: April 5th, 1916 depthcharged the German UB.26 then shelled her on the surface, which led to her capture off Le Havre.

AUDACIEUX: local defence of Brest. Stricken in February 1923.

Forban – one ship

Displacement:	123 tons (152 full load).
Dimensions:	44m(wl) × 4·64m × 1·30/1·40m.
Machinery:	2 direct-flame Normand boilers; 2 sets TE, 2 screws; IHP 3200; speed 29 knots (designed). Coal 18 tons.
Radius (nm):	1300/8 knots, 250/20 knots, 100/26 knots (in 1897).
Armament:	2 – 37mm guns, 2 – 381mm tubes.
Complement:	1 officer, 28 crew.

NAME	BUILDER	LAID DOWN	LAUNCHED	COMPLETED
FORBAN	Normand	4.93	25.7.95	1896

NOTES
In 1914 pre-war was on fishery protection service. War service on local defence of Algiers, Oran and Bizerta. Stricken in 1920.

Torpedo Boats—2nd class

Rated as 'Torpilleurs de 1° classe' and known as 'Torpilleurs de defense mobile' or 'Torpilleurs numerotes'.

Existing in 1914 were:

37 of the so called '37-metres' type, all built between 1895 and 1903 (Nos 206, 224, 231, 236, 238, 239, 251–3, 258, 260, 263–9, 273–6, 278–83, 288 and 289; also 6S (ex-242), 16S (ex-255), 17S (ex-284), 18S (ex-285), 19S (ex-286), 20S (ex-291), 21S (ex-242) which were assigned to the local defence of Saigon, Indochina.

Displacement:	80 to 90 tons.
Machinery:	2 Normand or du Temple boilers; 1 set TE, 1 screw; IHP 1500 to 2000; speed 24 knots (designed).
Armament:	as designed; 2 – 37mm guns, 3 – 381 or 450mm tubes.

95 of the so-called '39-metres' type, all built 1903-4 (Nos 295 to 369).

Displacement:	103 to 105 tons.
Machinery:	2 Normand or Guyot-du Temple boilers; 1 set TE, 1 screw; IHP 2000 (except 368, 369; 1800); speed 26 knots (designed), 23 knots in service).
Armament:	as designed; 2 – 37mm guns, 3 – 450mm tubes.

NOTES

At the beginning of the war about 100 torpedo boats were in commission or reserve and these were the survivors of the era when the fallacies of the 'Young School' prevailed; during the war most of them were assigned to local defence of naval ports and bases; some were sent to the Eastern Mediterranean where they were utilized as boom defence vessels, though their poor range necessitated their coaling seven times for the journey.

Of the boats remaining in France, only those of the Dunkirk Flotilla retained their initial armament since there was the possibility of their encountering German vessels based at Zeebrugge; four depthcharges and one 8mm machine gun were added. Other boats had their original armament replaced by one army 75mm gun (Guiraud type) and from four to eight depthcharges and so equipped were generally utilized for local escort or fishery protection.

A number were converted into inshore minesweepers (252, 266, 278, 297, 301, 304, 306, 308, 313, 315, 316, 320–2, 324, 327, 341 and 352). The following were war losses:

300 mined November 1st, 1916 off Le Havre
317 mined November 27th, 1916 off Calais
319 mined January 19th, 1915 off Nieuport
325 mined January 22nd, 1919 off Kerkenah Island
225 lost in collision with destroyer ORIFLAMME October 26th, 1914
331 lost in collision with a British cargo vessel off Barfleur

333 lost in collision March 12th, 1917 off Kelibia
347 lost in collision with No. 348 off Toulon October 10th, 1914
348 lost in collision with No. 347 off Toulon October 1st, 1914
289 stranded late 1918 near Bizerta.

Engines from some of the boats condemned before the war had been preserved, being in excellent condition, and were used in anti-submarine gunboats of the 1916 programme.

War service; patrol and escort duties,

In the Channel: Nos 302, 306, 308, 316, 326, 327, 334 and 340.

Atlantic Patrol Force (1915–18): Nos 275, 279, 301 and 307.

Dunkirk and Flanders: Nos 231, 258, 259, 279, 280, 305, 314, 318, 320, 321, 322, 323, 341–6, 350, 351 and 365.

Bay of Biscay 1916–18: Nos 303, 324, 334, 338 and 367.

Southern France 1916–18: No 310 and detached to Brindisi: 349, 360 and 369.

Tunisian Patrol Force 1916–18: Nos 263, 274, 289, 328–30, 333, 355, 356, 361, 362 and 366.

Brindisi 1915–18: Nos 281, 288, 349, 360, 368 and 369.

Dardanelles 1915: Nos 309–11, 353, 357 and 359.

The French Navy also used during the war the old TB ARVERNE (1895); she had the following characteristics:

Displacement: 133 tons (full load).
Machinery: 2 du Temple boilers; 2 TE engines; IHP 1750; speed 23·5 knots.
Armament: 2 – 47mm guns, 2 – 381mm tubes.

She was attached Toulon S/M Flotilla 1914 and Brindisi S/M Flotilla 1915–18. Condemned 1919 and sold for scrap in 1920.

Requisitioned Greek Destroyers and Torpedo Boats

After the events in Greece in 1916, the French Navy requisitioned and manned under French colours the following destroyers and torpedo boats:

Aetos class – three ships

AETOS (ex-Argentine San Luis)
HIERAS (ex-Argentine Santa Fe)
LEON (ex-Argentine Tucuman)

All were built in 1910 by Cammell Laird, launched 1911 and acquired by the Greek navy in 1911.

Displacement: 980 tons (1300 full load).
Dimensions: 90m × 8·40m × 2·50m.
Machinery: 5 White Forster boilers; Parsons and Curtis turbines, 2 screws; SHP 20,000; speed 30/32 knots.
Armament: 4 – 102mm guns, 6 – 533mm tubes.
Complement: 102.

The Second Class torpedo boats Nos. 206 and 268 (to the right) in the Caen harbour.

The Second Class Torpedo-boat No. 339. Note her 75mm army gun in place of the torpedo tubes.

The Second Class Torpedo-boat No. 357, with Gen Gouraud aboard, at the Dardanelles.

Seized in December 1916 and under the French flag from 1917–18. For some unknown reason the fourth of the class, PANTHER, does not seem to have been seized.

Niki class – four ships

ASPIS, DOXA, NIKI, VELOS.
Built 1905–6 by Vulkan at Stettin, launched 1906.

Displacement: 350 tons (full load).
Dimensions: 67m × 6·4m × 2·70m.
Machinery: Turbines; 2 screws; SHP 6400; speed about 28 knots.
Radius (nm): 1140 to 1280/15 knots.
Armament: 2 – 12pdr, 4 – 6pdr, 2 – 450mm tubes.
Complement: 70.

Thyella class – four ships

LONGHI, NAVKRATOUSSA, SPHENDONI, THYELLA.
Built 1906 by Yarrow, launched 1907.

Displacement: 390 tons.
Dimensions: 67m × 6·25m × 2·70m.
Machinery: Reciprocating, 2 screws; IHP 7000; speed 29/30 knots.
Radius (nm): 1100/15 knots.
Armament: 2 – 88mm German guns, 2 – 457mm tubes.
Complement: 70.

Doris class – six ships

AIGLI, ALKYONE, ARETHOUSA, DAPHNI, DORIS, THETIS.
Built 1913 by Vulkan at Stettin, launched 1913.

Displacement: 120 tons.
Dimensions: 75m × 5m × 1·20m.
Machinery: Reciprocating, 2 screws; IHP 2400; speed 28 knots.
Armament: 2 – 57mm American Bethlehem guns, 2 – 457mm tubes.

NOTES
Seized in December 1916 at Salamis; manned under French flag from 1917–18 (patrols in the Aegean). Returned late 1918. It is not certain that THETIS was commissioned.

Submarines

Built during a period of Franco-British tension, the French submarines had been designed for attacks on British merchant shipping. Though far from perfect, they were fairly well adapted for this role. But, after the 'Entente Cordiale' the new military problems to be solved were not properly defined and the concept came to the idea of using them in fleet combat, which was absurd. The result was that these ships were totally unfit for the tasks they were given during the war.

They however had some good qualities; they were good sea boats, their submerged speed and manoeuvrability were excellent; generally speaking, all the problems of underwater navigation had been solved in theory but their effective operation proved far from satisfactory:

Either because of insufficient testing (until the advent of the AMPHI-TRITE type the French boats had three pairs of hydroplanes when two pairs, if correctly placed, would have been enough. Their very simple accommodation made them so difficult to live in that their autonomy was limited in time).

Or for technical reasons (diesel engines, electric equipment and periscopes were of bad quality; furthermore the absence of standardization made maintenance difficult).

Or because of non-military design (the launching apparatus left the torpedoes exposed to the sea, which limited the diving depth to 30 metres and made the armament unreliable. Steam propulsion gave good results on the surface but proved unsafe).

Most of these defects were due to the building of many submarines before their equipment had been perfected. Furthermore, the building of these sophisticated vessels made an adaptation of the classical shipbuilding methods very necessary; this was not done, in spite of the recommendations of M. Laubeuf.

On the whole, with all the restrictions to their design, it was only by a narrow margin that the French submarines were not good ones. The example of the CURIE is typical: this ship belonged to a class which gave much trouble, but when refloated and refitted by the Austrian navy, she became one of their best submarines.

Circe – one ship

Displacement	351 tons (surface), 491 (submerged).
Dimensions:	47·10m × 4·90m × 3m.
Machinery:	2 – 315 BHP Man diesels, 2 – 230 SHP electric motors, 2 screws; speed 11·9 knots (surface), 7·7 knots (submerged).
Radius (nm):	2160/8 knots (surface), 98/3·5 knots or 44/5 knots (submerged).

The submarine CIRCE.

| *Armament:* | 1 – 47mm gun, 2 Drzewiecki launching systems, 4 external cradles, 6 – 450mm torpedoes. |
| *Complement:* | 22. |

NAME	BUILDER	LAID DOWN	LAUNCHED	COMPLETED
CIRCE	Toulon DY	1905	13.9.07	1909

NOTES

Designed by M. Laubeuf. Another of the class, CALYPSO, was sunk in collision July 7th, 1914 by CIRCE.

CIRCE sank the German minelaying submarine UC.24 on May 25th, 1917 in the Adriatic. She herself was torpedoed and sunk by U.47 off Cattaro on September 20th, 1918. Awarded the 'Croix de Guerre' pennant.

Sirène class – four ships

Displacement:	157 tons (surface), 213 (submerged).
Dimensions:	32·50m × 3·90m × 2·50m.
Machinery:	1 – 250 HP steam, 1 – 100 HP electric, 1 screw; speed 9·75 knots (surface), 5·80 knots (submerged).
Radius (nm):	430/7·75 knots (surface), 55/3·75 knots (submerged).

Armament:	4 Drzewiecki launching systems, 4 – 450mm torpedoes.			
Complement:	13.			

NAME	BUILDER	LAID DOWN	LAUNCHED	COMPLETED
SIRENE	Cherbourg	5.00	4.5.01	12.01
TRITON	Cherbourg	6.00	13.7.01	12.01
ESPADON	Cherbourg	1900	7.9.01	6.02
SILURE	Cherbourg	1900	29.10.01	6.02

NOTES

Designed by the famous naval constructor Laubeuf, they were the first double-hulled French submarines.

Based at Cherbourg during the war, they were stricken in November 1919.

Aigrette class – 2 ships

Displacement:	178 tons (surface), 253 (submerged).
Dimensions:	35·85m × 4·05m × 2·63m.
Machinery:	1 – 150 BHP diesel, 1 – 130 SHP electric, 1 screw; speed 9·25 knots (surface), 6·20 knots (submerged).
Radius (nm):	1300/8 knots (surface), 65/3·8 knots and 23/6·2 (submerged).
Armament:	2 Drzewiecki launching systems, 2 external cradles, 4 – 450mm torpedoes.
Complement:	14.

NAME	BUILDER	LAID DOWN	LAUNCHED	COMPLETED
AIGRETTE	Toulon DY	1903	23.1.04	1905–08
CIGOGNE	Toulon DY	1903	11.11.04	1905–08

NOTES

Designed by M. Laubeuf; experimental ships.

AIGRETTE was based at Cherbourg during the war for local defence and was fitted with special devices for cutting defence nets.

CIGOGNE went to Brindisi and was on local defence there 1916–18.

Argonaute – one ship

Displacement:	306 tons (surface), 409 (submerged).
Dimensions:	48.90m × 4.20m × 2.83m.
Machinery:	2 du Temple boilers, 1 – 350 IHP reciprocating, 1 – 230 SHP electric, 1 screw; speed 10·2 knots (surface), 6·02 knots (submerged).
Radius (nm):	1076/8 knots (surface), 45/5 knots (submerged).
Armament:	2 superimposed bow tubes, 2 Drzewiecki systems, 2 aft-trained external cradles, 6 – 450mm 1904 model torpedoes.
Complement:	22.

Top: **The submarine SIRENE.**

Above: **The submarine ESPADON.**

The submarine AIGRETTE.

The submarine CIGOGNE.

The submarine ARGONAUTE.

NAME	BUILDER	LAID DOWN	LAUNCHED	COMPLETED
ARGONAUTE	Toulon DY	1.03	28.11.05	1.11

NOTES

Designed by M. Emile Bertin and M. Petithomme, she was originally fitted with a special diesel engine for both surface and submerged propulsion using while submerged a mixture of air and exhaust gas compressed under 150 and 12 kilos respectively. This engine was not a success and she was later fitted with the half of the engine fitted in the PLUVOISE class. She was stricken in 1919.

Eméraude class – six ships

Displacement:	392 tons (surface), 425 (submerged).
Dimensions:	44·90m × 3·90m × 3·68m.
Machinery:	2 – 300 BHP Sautter Harlé diesels, 2 electric motors, 2 screws; speed 11·5 knots (surface), 9·2 knots (submerged).
Radius (nm):	2000/7·3 knots (surface), 100/5 knots (submerged).
Armament:	6 – 450mm tubes (4 forward, 2 aft), 6 1904 model torpedoes.
Complement:	23.

NAME	BUILDER	LAID DOWN	LAUNCHED
EMERAUDE	Cherbourg DY	10.03	6.8.06
RUBIS	Cherbourg DY	10.03	26.6.07
TOPAZE	Toulon DY	10.03	2.7.08
OPALE	Cherbourg DY	10.03	20.11.06
SAPHIR	Toulon DY	10.03	6.2.08
TURQUOISE	Toulon DY	10.03	3.8.08

All were 1903 programme and completed between October 1908 and December 1910.

NOTES

Designed by M. Maugas, these were of mono-hull type; they were true submarines but with poor surface buoyancy. Trials were long and difficult because of the weakness of their diesels.

SAPHIR was lost in a daring attempt to sail submerged through the Dardanelles in order to attack Turkish shipping; she hit a mine and sank with most of her crew and her commanding officer January 15th, 1915.

TURQUOISE, which had succeeded in getting into the Sea of Marmara, was hit by enemy gunfire and forced to beach on October 30th, 1915. Refloated by the Turks, she was renamed MUSTADIEH OMBASHI but not commissioned; she was retroceded to the French in 1919 but soon condemned.

RUBIS: 1916, 2nd Flotilla (Mudros); stricken 1919.

TOPAZE: 1915–16 2nd Flotilla; 1918 3rd Flotilla (Mudros); she then had a 47mm gun. Stricken in 1919.

OPALE: 1915–16 2nd Flotilla; 1918 3rd Flotilla; stricken in 1919.

The submarine TOPAZE. Note her lengthened conning tower and the position of the 37mm gun.

The submarine SAPHIR seen in a dock.

The submarine TURQUOISE.

Pluviôse class – seventeen ships

Displacement:	398 tons (surface), 550 (submerged).
Dimensions:	51·12m × 4·97m × 13·04m.
Machinery:	2 du Temple boilers, 2 – 350 IHP reciprocating, 2 – 225 SHP electric, 2 screws; speed 12 knots (surface), 8 knots (submerged).
Radius (nm):	1500/9 knots or 900/12 knots (surface), 50/5 knots (submerged).
Armament:	4 external cradle tubes (2 abeam conning tower trained forward 6° from axis; 2 trained aft 1° from axis), 2 Drzewiecki systems fixed inboard; 8 – 450mm torpedoes, 1904 model. VENTOSE, GERMINAL, FLOREAL, VENDEMAIRE and MONGE in 1914 also had an originally fitted bow tube, removed from others after an accident in FRESNEL.
Complement:	24.

NAME	BUILDER	LAUNCHED
PLUVIOSE	Cherbourg DY	27.5.07
GERMINAL	Cherbourg DY	7.12.07
PRAIRIAL	Cherbourg DY	26.9.07
THERMIDOR	Cherbourg DY	3.7.07
FRESNEL	Rochefort DY	16.6.08
VENTOSE	Cherbourg DY	15.9.07
FLOREAL	Cherbourg DY	18.4.08
MESSIDOR	Cherbourg DY	24.12.08
FRUCTIDOR	Cherbourg DY	13.11.09
PAPIN	Rochefort DY	4.1.08
BERTHELOT	Rochefort DY	19.5.09
MONGE	Toulon DY	31.12.08
GAY-LUSSAC	Toulon DY	17.3.10
CUGNOT	Rochefort DY	14.10.09
AMPERE	Toulon DY	30.10.09
WATT	Rochefort DY	18.6.09
GIFFARD	Rochefort DY	10.2.10

These were all of the 1905 programme, laid down in 1906 and completed between October 1908 and January 1911.

NOTES
These submarines, designed by M. Laubeuf, had excellent sea-keeping capabilities but because of their steam propulsion they submerged too slowly. However, they gave good service and were very active during the war, notably in the Adriatic.

FRESNEL, on watch off Cattaro was surprised by Austrian aircraft and attacked by the TB WARADISNER and forced to beach. Her commander gave the order to abandon ship before he blew her up (December 5th, 1915).

FLOREAL was sunk in collision with the British armed boarding steamer HAZEL on August 2nd, 1918 off Mudros.

Top: Details of the submarine GERMINAL.

Above: The submarine VENTOSE. Note her bow tube.

The submarine MESSIDOR and in the background the armoured cruiser LEON GAMBETTA.

The submarine PAPIN.

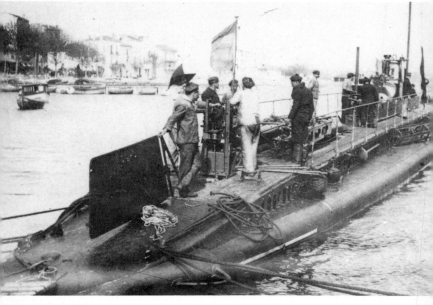

The submarine WATT. Note the position of her 47mm gun.

PRAIRIAL was also lost in collision, off Le Havre with a British cargo ship on April 29th, 1918.

MONGE penetrated Cattaro but missed a minelayer; on August 17th, 1915 she attacked the Austrian cruiser HELGOLAND but missed. During the night of December 28th, 1915 she was sunk by gunfire from this same cruiser and five destroyers while attempting to attack them off Cattaro; she was awarded the 'Croix de Guerre' pennant.

AMPERE, CUGNOT and FRESNEL all got into Cattaro harbour and fired torpedoes at destroyers without effect. CUGNOT later spent several hours exploring Cattaro base but saw no worthwhile target, avoiding attack from three destroyers. She was awarded the 'Croix de Guerre' pennant.

PAPIN on September 8th, 1915 made an unsuccessful attack on the Austrian destroyer LIKA but managed to blow off the bows of TB.51 with a torpedo.

AMPERE torpedoed the unmarked hospital ship ELEKTRA on March 8th, 1916, which ship was later salved.

VENDEMAIRE, the eighteenth ship of the class was lost before the war. All survivors were stricken in 1919.

Brumaire class – sixteen ships

Displacement:	397 tons (surface), 551 (submerged).
Dimensions:	52·15m × 5·42m × 3·13m.
Machinery:	2 – 420 BHP four-stroke six-cylinder diesels, 2 – 230 SHP electric, 2 screws; speed 13 knots (surface), 8·8 knots (submerged).

The submarine BERNOUILLI the day of her launching.

Radius (nm):	1700/10 knots (surface), 84/5 knots (submerged).	
Armament:	1 – bow tube, 4 Drzewiecki systems, 2 external cradles abeam conning tower, 8 – 450mm 1904 model torpedoes.	
Complement:	29.	

NAME	BUILDER	LAUNCHED
BRUMAIRE	Cherbourg DY	29.4.11
NIVOSE	Cherbourg DY	6.1.12
EULER	Cherbourg DY	12.10.12
FARADAY	Rochefort DY	27.6.11
NEWTON	Rochefort DY	20.5.12
BERNOUILLI	Toulon DY	1.6.11
COULOMB	Toulon DY	13.6.12
CURIE	Toulon DY	18.7.12
FRIMAIRE	Cherbourg DY	26.8.11
FOUCAULT	Cherbourg DY	16.6.12
FRANKLIN	Cherbourg DY	22.3.12
VOLTA	Rochefort DY	23.9.11
MONTGOLFIER	Rochefort DY	18.4.12
JOULE	Toulon DY	7.9.11
ARAGO	Toulon DY	29.6.12
LE VERRIER	Toulon DY	31.10.12

All of the 1906 programme, laid down 1906–7, completed March 1913 to July 1914.

NOTES

Several of these were fitted with a 47 or 75mm gun during the war.

BERNOUILLI was lost February 15th, 1918, probably mined.

FOUCAULT was sunk September 15th, 1916 by Austrian aircraft.

JOULE was mined May 1st, 1915 in the Dardanelles.

CURIE had an epic history. She was captured on December 20th, 1914 at Pola after penetrating that well-defended base, and refloated by the Austrians, given good motors, a new battery and an 88mm gun and renamed U.14; her radius was increased to 6500 miles on the surface. She was then one of the best boats in the Austrian Navy and under the command of Lt. Von Trapp, the submarine officer who sank the cruiser LEON GAMBETTA. She was recovered by the French after the war and awarded the 'Croix de Guerre' pennant.

FARADAY: 1915, Dardanelles; 1916–18 in the Adriatic.

BERNOUILLI got into Cattaro on April 4th, 1916 and blew up the stern of the Austrian destroyer CSEPEL but did not sink her; she also attacked the destroyer BALATON May 14th, 1917. Awarded the 'Croix de Guerre'.

LE VERRIER: 2nd Flotilla at Bizerta 1914; Dardanelles in 1915 then the Adriatic 1916–18. On July 28th, 1918 she was accidentally rammed by the German U.47 and exchanged torpedoes without result.

All the surviving boats were stricken between 1919 and 1923 except LE VERRIER (1925), NEWTON (1926), CURIE (1928) and BRUMAIRE (1930).

The submarine FRIMAIRE. Note her 75mm army gun before the conning tower.

The submarine FOUCAULT.

Details of the submarine FRANKLIN.

The submarine LE VERRIER before her modernisation.

Archimede – one ship

Displacement:	598 tons (surface), 810·5 tons (submerged).
Dimensions:	60·54m × 5·63m × 4·17m.
Machinery:	2 boilers; 2 – 850 IHP reciprocating, 2 – 615 SHP electric, 2 screws; speed 14·92 knots (surface), 10·95 knots (submerged).
Radius (nm):	1160/10 knots or 680/15 knots (surface), 100/4·5 knots (submerged).
Armament:	1 – bow tube, 4 Drzewiecki systems, 2 external cradles (abeam conning tower), 8 – 450mm 1904 model torpedoes.
Complement:	26.

NAME	BUILDER	LAID DOWN	LAUNCHED	COMPLETED
ARCHIMEDE	Cherbourg DY	2.1.08	4.8.09	9.11

NOTES

1906 programme, designed by M. Hutter and was an amelioration of the PLUVIOSE class with better machinery and equipment. She reached 15·2 knots on the surface.

She was lucky enough to sink four enemy transports, the DUBROVNIK on May 9th, 1916, the ALBANIEN on May 12th, 1916 and two others unidentified. She was stricken in November 1919.

Mariotte – one ship

Displacement:	530 tons (surface), 627 (submerged).
Dimensions:	64·75m × 4·30m × 3·83m.
Machinery:	2 – 700 BHP six-cylinder Sautter Harlé diesels, 2 – 700 SHP electric, 2 screws; speed 14·26 knots (surface), 11·66 knots (submerged).
Radius (nm):	1050/10 knots (surface), 100/5 knots (submerged).
Armament:	4 – 450mm inboard tubes, 2 Drzewiecki systems, 8 – 1904 model torpedoes.
Complement:	26.

NAME	BUILDER	LAID DOWN	LAUNCHED	COMPLETED
MARIOTTE	Cherbourg DY	30.3.08	2.2.11	1.13

NOTES

1906 programme, designed by M. Radiguer, MARIOTTE was an extrapolation of the EMERAUDE type, ie a true submarine. In order to improve her sea-keeping capabilities most of the buoyancy tanks were moved forward, only two being amidships.

MARIOTTE was sunk in a vain attempt to force the Dardanelles straits on July 27th, 1915, she was trapped in the net defences and destroyed by Turkish gunfire.

Top: **The submarine ARCHIMEDE.**
Above: **The submarine MARIOTTE.**

Amiral Bourgois – one ship

Displacement: 555 tons (surface), 735 (submerged).
Dimensions: 56·20m × 5·50m × 3·63m.
Machinery: 2 – 700 BHP Schneider diesels, 2 – 500 SHP electric,
2 screws; speed 13·85 knots (surface), 8·65 (submerged).
Radius (nm): 2500/10 knots (surface), 100/5 knots (submerged).
Armament: 4 – 450mm inboard tubes (2 forward, 2 aft).
Complement: 25.

NAME	BUILDER	LAID DOWN	LAUNCHED	COMPLETED
AMIRAL BOURGOIS	Rochefort DY	19.5.08	25.11.12	8.14

NOTES
1906 programme; 1914–18 served in the Channel. Stricken in November
1919.

Gustave Zédé class – two ships

Displacement: G. ZEDE: 849 tons (surface), 1098 (submerged);
NEREIDE: 820 tons (surface), 1047 (submerged).
Dimensions: 74m × 6m × 3·74m.
Machinery: G. ZEDE: 2 return-flame du Temple boilers; 2 – 1750
IHP reciprocating three-cylinder Delaunay-Belleville,
2 – 820 SHP electric, 2 screws; speed 17·5 knots (surface),
11·44 knots (submerged).

The submarine AMIRAL BOURGOIS.

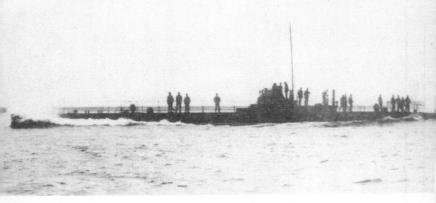

The submarine NEREIDE.

NEREIDE: 2 – 1200 BHP Schneider-Carels diesels,
2 – 820 SHP electric, 2 screws; speed 17·3 knots (surface),
10·5 knots (submerged).

Radius (nm): G. ZEDE: 1400/10 knots (surface), 135/5 knots
(submerged); NEREIDE: 1550/16 or 3120/10 knots
(surface), 90/4 knots (submerged).

Armament: 1 – 75mm, 1 – 47mm guns, 8 – tubes (2 bow, 4 inboard,
2 external cradles).

Complement: 47.

NAME	BUILDER	LAID DOWN	LAUNCHED	COMPLETED
GUSTAVE ZEDE	Cherbourg DY	2.11	20.5.13	10.14
NEREIDE	Cherbourg DY	7.11	9.5.14	1.16

NOTES

1909 programme; designed by M. Simonot, both were to have been diesel
engined but in 1912 it was decided to equip GUSTAVE ZEDE with steam
propulsion. The diesels of NEREIDE reached only half of their projected
power. Post-war she was given additional air vents, a new bridge and periscope and a twin revolving torpedo tube. GUSTAVE ZEDE after the war
was reconstructed; she was given diesels from ex-German submarines, a
new conning tower and bridge and had the two after ballast tanks turned
into fuel tanks. During the war GUSTAVE ZEDE operated in the Adriatic
and NEREIDE in the Atlantic; they were stricken 1937 and 1935 respectively.

Clorinde class – two ships

Displacement:	413 tons (surface), 567 (submerged).
Dimensions:	53·95m × 5·10m × 3·41m.
Machinery:	2 – 400 BHP two-stroke Man-Loire diesels, 2 – 350 SHP electric, 2 screws; speed 13 knots (surface), 9 knots (submerged).
Radius (nm):	1300/10 knots (surface), 100/5 knots (submerged).
Armament:	1 – 75mm gun, 8 – 450mm tubes (2 forward external cradle and 6 Drzewiecki).
Complement:	29.

NAME	BUILDER	LAID DOWN	LAUNCHED	COMPLETED
CLORINDE	Rochefort DY	11.10	2.10.13	10.16
CORNELIE	Rochefort DY	11.10	29.10.13	9.17

NOTES

1909 programme. Both boats operated in the Atlantic 1917–18.

CLORINDE was stricken in January 1926 and her sister in December 1926.

Amphitrite class – eight ships

Displacement:	414 tons (surface), 609 (submerged) (except ASTREE and AMARANTE see notes).
Dimensions:	53·95m × 5·41m × 3·31m.
Machinery:	2 – 400 BHP two-stroke Man-Loire diesels, 2 – 350 SHP electric, 2 screws; speed 12/13 knots (surface), 9·5 knots (submerged).
Radius (nm):	1300/10 knots (surface), 100/5 knots (submerged).
Armament:	8 – 450mm tubes (2 forward external cradles, 6 Drzewiecki).
Complement:	29.

NAME	BUILDER	LAUNCHED	COMPLETED
AMPHITRITE	Rochefort DY	9.6.14	1915
ARTEMIS	Toulon DY	14.10.14	1915
ATALANTE	Toulon DY	14.4.15	1915
ARIANE	Cherbourg DY	5.9.14	1915
ASTREE	Rochefort DY	6.12.15	6.18
ARETHUSE	Toulon DY	20.4.16	1916
AMARANTE	Toulon DY	11.11.15	9.18
ANDROMAQUE	Cherbourg DY	13.2.15	1916

NOTES

1909 programme and laid down in 1911 and 1912. After launch, ASTREE and AMARANTE were towed to Le Havre and completed in 1918 as mine-laying submarines.

AMPHITRITE was renamed AMPHITRITE II on April 20th, 1928, her name being given to a new boat; stricken in September 1935.

Top: **The submarine CLORINDE.**

Above: **The submarine ARTEMIS.**

ARTEMIS in 1916–18 was engaged in Adriatic Sea operations and on June 23rd, 1918 was attacked in error by British aircraft and on July 14th, 1918 for three hours by British destroyers; she was stricken in 1927.

ATALANTE 1916–18 Adriatic. Renamed ATALANTE II on April 20th, 1928, her name being given to a new boat; stricken in 1931.

ARIANE was torpedoed and sunk June 19th, 1917 by the German UC.22 north of Bizerta while on trials after repairs.

ARETHUSE: 1917–18, Adriatic operations; stricken in 1927.

AMARANTE in company with ENGAGEANTE made tests with the Walser hydrophone. She was stricken in 1925.

ASTREE was stricken in 1928 and ANDROMAQUE in 1931.

Gorgone class – three ships

Displacement:	523 tons (surface), 788 (submerged).
Dimensions:	60·60m × 5·40m × 3·52m.
Machinery:	2 – 820 BHP two-stroke Sabathé diesels (except GORGONE, Sulzer), 2 – 400 SHP electric, 2 screws; speed 14·7 knots (surface), 9·5 knots (submerged).
Radius (nm):	2300/10 knots (surface), 100/5 knots (submerged).
Armament:	1 – 75mm gun, 8 – 450mm tubes.
Complement:	4 officers, 34 crew.

NAME	BUILDER	LAID DOWN	LAUNCHED	COMPLETED
BELLONE	Rochefort DY	12.12	8.7.14	10.16
HERMIONE	Toulon DY	12.12	15.3.17	12.17
GORGONE	Toulon DY	12.12	23.12.15	7.16

The submarine GORGONE.

1912 programme. Modernized post-war; air vents being grouped in order to reduce diving time and a 7·50m periscope installed in the conning tower.

   BELLONE served in the Atlantic 1917–18 and the other two in the Adriatic; all were discarded in 1935.

Diane class – two ships

Displacement:	633 tons (surface), 891 (submerged).
Dimensions:	68m × 5·53m × 3·72m.
Machinery:	2 – 900 BHP 4-stroke Vickers (DIANE) or 2-stroke Sulzer (DAPHNE) diesels, 2 – 700 SHP electric, 2 screws; speed 17 knots (surface), 11·5 knots (submerged).
Radius (nm):	2500/10 knots (surface), 130/5 knots (submerged).
Armament:	1 – 75mm gun (DAPHNE only), 10 – 450mm tubes.
Complement:	4 officers, 39 crew.

NAME	BUILDER	LAID DOWN	LAUNCHED	COMPLETED
DIANE	Cherbourg DY	12.12	30.9.16	8.17
DAPHNE	Cherbourg DY	12.12	25.10.15	7.16

NOTES

1912 programme.

   DIANE was lost with all hands by unknown cause on the night of February 11th, 1918 off La Pallice while escorting the four-master QUEVILLY. After the war her sister ship was modernized on the lines of the ATALANTE and GORGONE classes. She was stricken in February 1935.

The submarine DAPHNE.

Top: The submarine DUPUY DE LOME fitted with a 75mm army gun before her conning tower and a 47mm gun astern.

Above: The submarine DUPUY DE LOME after her large reconstruction after the war. Note her new conning tower and that the position of her 75mm and 47mm guns had been inversed.

The submarine SANE as she was during the war.

Dupuy de Lôme class – two ships

Displacement:	833 tons (surface), 1287 (submerged).
Dimensions:	75m × 6·40m × 4·6m.
Machinery:	2 return-flame du Temple boilers; 2 – 1750 IHP 3-cylinder Delaunay-Belleville, 2 – 820 SHP electric, 2 screws; speed 17 knots (surface), 11 knots (submerged).
Radius (nm):	2350/10 knots (surface), 120/5 knots (submerged).
Armament:	1 – 47mm AA gun as designed, but 2 – 75mm later, 8 – 450mm tubes (10 torpedoes).
Complement:	4 officers, 39 crew.

NAME	BUILDER	LAID DOWN	LAUNCHED	COMPLETED
DUPUY DE LOME	Toulon DY	3.13	9.9.15	8.16
SANE	Toulon DY	11.13	27.1.16	8.16

NOTES

1913 programme. After the war these two boats were widely reconstructed. Their steam engine was replaced by a 1200 BHP diesel taken from ex-German submarines with greatly increased radius; they also had new equipment as fitted in the GUSTAVE ZEDE class. They were discarded in July 1935.

From 1917 to the close of the war they served in the Morocco Flotilla based on Gibraltar.

Joessel class – two ships

Displacement:	870 tons (surface), 1247 (submerged).
Dimensions:	74m × 6·40m × 3·62m.
Machinery:	2 – 450 BHP 8-cylinder Schneider-Carels diesels, 2 – 850 SHP electric, 2 screws; speed 16·5 knots (surface), 11 knots (submerged).
Radius (nm):	4300/10 knots (surface), 125/5 knots (submerged).
Armament:	2 – 75mm guns, 8 – 450 tubes (10 torpedoes)
Complement:	4 officers, 43 crew.

NAME	BUILDER	LAID DOWN	LAUNCHED	COMPLETED
JOESSEL	Cherbourg DY	11.13	21.7.19	2.20
FULTON	Cherbourg DY	11.13	1.4.19	7.20

NOTES

1914 programme. Designed by M. Simonot as steam submarines with two 2000 SHP geared turbines but altered while building to diesel propulsion; their turbines were used for anti-submarine avisos of the AILETTE class. After completion a new cylindrical conning tower was fitted with a bridge and new periscopes, one of 7·50m in the conning tower and one of 9·50m in the central operation room.

JOESSEL was stricken in April 1935 and FULTON in July 1935.

Lagrange class – four ships

Displacement:	920 tons (surface), 1318 (submerged).
Dimensions:	75·20m × 6·39m × 3·62m.
Machinery:	2 – 1300 BHP Sulzer diesels, 2 – 820 SHP electric, 2 screws; speed 16·5 knots (surface), 11 knots (submerged).

The submarine FULTON as she was after her modernization.

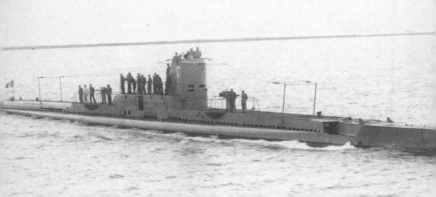

The submarine LAPLACE. She was completed after the war.

Radius (nm):	4300/10 knots (surface), 125/5 knots (submerged).			
Armament:	2 – 75mm guns, 8 – 450mm tubes (10 torpedoes).			
Complement:	4 officers, 43 crew.			

NAME	BUILDER	LAID DOWN	LAUNCHED	COMPLETED
LAPLACE	Rochefort DY	1913	12.8.19	1921
REGNAULT	Toulon DY	1913	25.6.24	1924
LAGRANGE	Toulon DY	1913	31.5.17	2.18
ROMAZOTTI	Toulon DY	1914	31.3.18	9.18

NOTES

1913 programme. Designed by M. Hutter and were to have been steam driven as the JOESSEL class, but completed with diesels; were widely constructed post-war. LAPLACE and LAGRANGE were stricken in July 1935 and the others in 1937.

Minelaying Submarines
Maurice Callot – one ship

Displacement:	931 tons (surface), 1298 (submerged).
Dimensions:	75·50m × 6·70m × 3·57m.
Machinery:	2 – 450 BHP 2-stroke Schneider diesels, 2 – 850 SHP electric, 2 screws; speed 16·5 knots (surface), 10·5 knots (submerged).

Radius (nm):	2800/11 knots (surface), 118/5 knots (submerged).			
Armament:	1 – 75mm gun, 6 – 450mm tubes (4 forward, 2 aft), 8 torpedoes, 27 mines.			
Complement:	3 officers, 45 crew.			

NAME	BUILDER	LAID DOWN	LAUNCHED	COMPLETED
MAURICE CALLOT	F. et Ch. de la Gironde, Bordeaux	5.17	26.3.21	1922

NOTES

The mines were stored in the superstructure and laid by the Laubeuf system, a method later recognized as inferior to the Fenaux system in which mines were stowed in wells in the outer ballast tanks with direct release mechanism. MAURICE CALLOT was discarded in 1936.

Pierre Chailley – one ship

Displacement:	884 tons (surface), 1191 (submerged).
Dimensions:	70m × 7·52m × 4·04m.
Machinery:	2 – 900 BHP 2-stroke Sulzer diesels, 2 – 700 SHP electric, 2 screws; speed 13·75 knots (surface), 8·5 knots (submerged).
Radius (nm):	2800/11 knots (surface), 80/5 knots (submerged).
Armament:	1 – 100mm gun, 4 – 450mm tubes, 40 mines (200 kilo type).
Complement:	4 officers, 40 crew.

NAME	BUILDER	LAID DOWN	LAUNCHED	COMPLETED
PIERRE CHAILLEY	Normand, Le Havre	5.17	19.12.22	1922

NOTES

This submarine of the Normand-Fenaux type was the prototype for the successful minelaying submarines of the SAPHIR class of World War II.

Requisitioned Submarines
Armide class – three ships

Displacement:	457 tons (surface), 670 (submerged).
Dimensions:	56·20m × 5·20m × 3·02m.
Machinery:	2 – 1100 BHP 2-stroke Schneider diesels, 2 – 450 SHP electric, 2 screws; speed 17·4 knots (surface), 11 knots (submerged).
Radius (nm):	2600/11 knots or 900/13 (surface), 160/5 knots (submerged).

Top: The minelaying submarine MAURICE CALLOT. She was completed after the war.

Above: The minelaying submarine PIERRE CHAILLEY which was also completed after the war.

Armament: 1 – 47mm gun (except AMAZONE: 1 – 75mm),
             4 – 450mm tubes.

Complement: 31.

NAME	BUILDER	LAID DOWN	LAUNCHED	COMPLETED
ARMIDE (ex-Japanese 14)	Schneider, Chalon-sur-Saône	1912	7.15	6.16
ANTIGONE (ex-Greek)	Schneider, Chalon-sur-Saône	1912	10.16	1.17
AMAZONE (ex-Greek)	Schneider, Chalon-sur-Saône	1913	8.16	6.17

NOTES

ARMIDE was assigned to the 3rd Flotilla based at Mudros; stricken in July 1932.

ANTIGONE: 1917, Bizerta Flotilla patrolling in company with Q ships; 1918, 3rd Flotilla, Mudros; stricken in August 1935.

AMAZONE: 1917, Adriatic operations; 1918, 3rd Flotilla, Mudros; stricken in July 1932.

O'Byrne class – three ships

Displacement: 342 tons (surface), 513 (submerged).
Dimensions: 52·40m × 4·70m × 2·72m.
Machinery: 2 – 510 BHP 4-stroke Schneider diesels, 2 – 200 SHP electric, 2 screws; speed 14 knots (surface), 8 knots (submerged).
Radius (nm):   1850/10 knots (surface), 55/5 knots (submerged).
Armament: 1 – 47mm gun, 4 – 450mm tubes.
Complement: 2 officers, 23 crew.

NAME	BUILDER	LAID DOWN	LAUNCHED	COMPLETED
O'BYRNE (ex-Rumanian)	Schneider, Chalon-sur-Saône	4.17	22.5.19	1921
HENRI FOURNIER (ex-Rumanian)	Schneider, Chalon-sur-sur-Saône	4.17	30.9.19	1921
LOUIS-DUPETIT-THOUARS (ex-Rumanian)	Schneider, Chalon-sur-Saône	4.17	5 or 6.20	1921

NOTES

Requisitioned while building for the Rumanian Navy. DUPETIT-THOUARS was discarded in 1928, the other two in July 1935.

Below: **The submarine AMAZONE.**

Foot: **The submarine O'BYRNE.**

Captured Enemy Submarines
Roland Morillot – one ship

Displacement: 265 tons (surface), 291 (submerged).
Dimensions: 36·13m × 4·36m × 3·66m.
Machinery: 1 – 280 BHP 6-cylinder Daimler diesel, 1 – 280 SHP electric, 1 screw; speed 9 knots (surface), 5·7 knots (submerged).
Radius (nm): 45/4 knots (submerged).
Armament: 1 – 47mm gun, 2 – 500mm tubes (4 torpedoes).
Complement: 25.

NAME	BUILDER	LAID DOWN	LAUNCHED	COMPLETED
ROLAND MORILLOT (ex-UB.26)	A. G. Weser, Bremen	1915	14.12.15	1.16

NOTES
This enemy coastal submarine was caught in the net defence of Le Havre on April 5th, 1916 and depthcharged and shelled by the TB TROMBE and patrol boat NOELLA; she surfaced to save her crew then scuttled. Refloated she was incorporated in the French Navy on August 30th, 1917. Discarded in 1925.

Requisitioned Greek Submarines

After the events in Greece in 1916, the French Navy seized in December 1916 at Salamis the two submarines DELPHIN and XIPHIAS. Manned from 1916 to 1917 by French crews, they were returned in 1918. They had the following characteristics:

Laubeuf-Schneider type, built at Chalon-sur-Saône.
Displacement: 295 tons (surface), 350 (submerged).
Machinery: 2 sets Schneider-Carels engines, electric motors; 1850 BHP = 7·5 knots (surface), 8 knots (submerged).
Armament: 4 – 450mm tubes, 6 torpedoes.

Sloops

Amiens class – thirty ships

Displacement:	850 tons.
Dimensions:	72m × 8·71m × 3·20m.
Machinery:	2 Normand or du Temple boilers; 2 Parsons geared turbines, 2 screws; SHP 5000, speed 20 knots; fuel 200 tons oil.
Radius (nm):	3000/11 knots.
Armament:	2 – 138·6mm, 1 – 75mm, 4 – machine guns, D/C throwers, 20 depthcharges and other ASW gear.
Complement:	4 officers, 99 crew.

NAME	BUILDER	LAID DOWN	LAUNCHED	COMPLETED
AMIENS	Ch. de la Méditerranée, La Seyne	1918	1919	1920
ARRAS	Brest DY	1917	7.18	1918
BACCARAT	Ch. de Provence	1919	1921	1922
BAPAUME	Lorient DY	1917	1919	1920
BAR-LE-DUC	Lorient DY	1917	1918	1920
BELFORT	Lorient DY	1918	3.19	1920
BETHUNE	Ch. de Provence	1920	1921	
CALAIS	Ch. de la Méditerranée	1918	1919	1920
COUCY	Penhoët, St Nazaire	1918	1919	1920
CRAONNE	Ch. de la Méditerranée	1917	1920	1921
		1917	1920	1921
DUNKERQUE	Brest DY	1917	7.18	1918
EPERNAY	Ch. de la Méditerranée		1919	
EPINAL	Penhoët	1918	1919	1920
LASSIGNY	Ch. de Bretagne	1918	1919	1920
LES EPARGES	Ch. de Bretagne	1918	1919	1920
LIEVIN	Ch. de la Méditerranée	1917	1920	
LUNEVILLE	Ch. de la Méditerranée	1917	1920	
MONTDEMENT	Ch. de la Méditerranée		1920	
MONTMIRAIL	Ch. de la Méditerranée	1918	1920	
NANCY	Cherbourg DY	1917	1919	1920
PERONNE	Le Havre	1917	1920	
REIMS	Brest DY	1917	7.18	1918

The sloop BACCARAT.

REMIREMONT	F. et Ch. de la Gironde	1917	1920	
REVIGNY	F. et Ch. de la Gironde	1917	1920	
TAHURE	Ch. de la Loire	1918	1919	1920
TOUL	Ch. de la Loire	1917	1919	
VAUQUOIS	Ch. de la Loire	1918	1919	1920
VERDUN	Brest DY	1917	1918	1920
VIMY	Ch. de la Loire	1918	1919	1920
VITRY LE FRANCOIS	Ch. de la Loire	1918	1920	

NOTES

The following ships were ordered but never laid down: BETHENY CHALONS, CHATEAU-THIERRY, COMPIEGNE, DOUAUMONT FERE CHAMPENOISE, GERBEVILLER, NOYON, ROYE, SAINT DIÉ, SENLIS, SOISSONS and SOUCHEZ.

BAR-LE-DUC stranded on December 13th, 1920 near Lesbos while escorting General Wrangel's ships.

BAPAUME was after the war fitted with a flight deck for experimental purposes conducted by Lt. Teste (FN).

The sloop BAPAUME fitted with a forward flight deck.

The sloop DUNKERQUE.

The sloop VITRY LE FRANCOIS.

The sloop ALDEBARAN.

DUNKERQUE and VERDUN were respectively renamed YPRES and LAFFAUX in 1928.

All except the following were discarded before World War II:

LES EPARGES and YPRES (ex-DUNKERQUE) served as survey vessels; the former was captured by Germans and manned as M.6060 in 1943, her fate is unknown; the latter was scrapped April 30th, 1942.

BELFORT which served as a seaplane tender was used by the FNFL as an accommodation ship; she was scrapped November 26th, 1946.

AMIENS was also used by the FNFL as a depot ship. At Dunkirk in 1940 she was equipped with a new twin 37mm AA gun designed for the 35,000 ton battleships of the GASCOGNE class.

ARRAS was cannibalized for spares for AMIENS.

CALAIS was scrapped in 1946.

COUCY was seized by the British and used as a depot ship; scrapped 1946.

EPINAL also seized by the British was used as an accommodation ship; she was returned and scrapped in 1946.

LASSIGNY, condemned October 21st, 1941 was hulked at Bizerta, abandoned in December 1942, scuttled July 1943 by the Italians in Bizerta Lake.

TAHURE which was in Indochina was torpedoed and sunk by the US submarine FLASHER on September 24th, 1944.

VAUQUOIS was mined and sunk June 18th, 1940 off Brest.

British Flower class – eight ships

Displacement:	1470 tons (full load).
Dimensions:	81·5m × 10·5m × 4·2m.
Machinery:	1 set 4 – cylinder TE, 1 screw; SHP 2800, speed 17·5 knots. Coal 260 tons.
Radius (nm):	2400/12 knots.
Armament:	2 – 138·6mm, 4 – 47mm.
Complement:	6 officers, 97 crew.

NAME	BUILDER	LAID DOWN	LAUNCHED	COMPLETED
ALDEBARAN	Barclay Curle, Whiteinch, Glasgow	1916	19.5.16	3.7.16
ALGOL	Barclay Curle	1916	17.6.16	28.7.16
ALTAIR	Hamilton, Glasgow	28.2.16	6.7.16	14.9.16
ANTARES	Hamilton, Glasgow	8.3.16	4.9.16	30.10.16
BELLATRIX	Henderson, Glasgow	1916	29.5.16	17.7.16
CASSIOPEE	Barclay Curle	23.9.16	10.2.17	12.4.17
REGULUS	Barclay Curle	23.9.16	19.3.17	2.5.17
RIGEL	Henderson	1916	6.7.16	22.8.16

Above: The sloop ANTARES.

Below: The sloop BELLATRIX seen in dock.

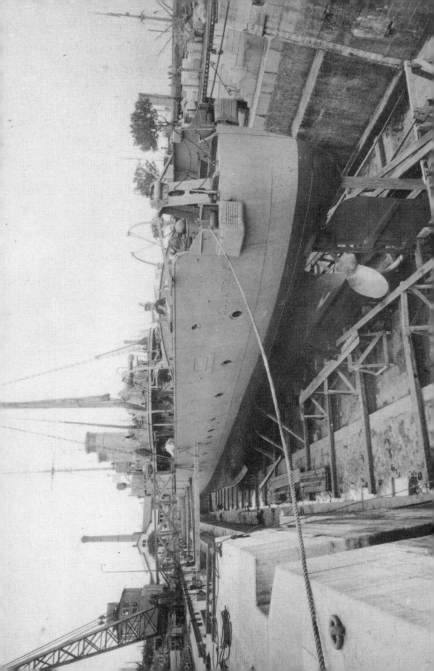

These excellent ships were practically the same as the famous British sloops of World War I. After the war the 4·47mm guns were replaced by 2·75mm guns. All were stricken between 1932 and 1936.

ALDEBARAN: 1916–18 Southern France patrol force; August 1st, 1916 with EPIEU and CATAPULTE attacked U.35 off Tunisia; August 23rd, 1916 chased U.34 with BELLATRIX; August 8th, 1917 depthcharged and damaged U.33.

ALGOL: 1916–18, Tunisia then Southern France patrol.

ALTAIR: same appointment.

ANTARES: commanding the division of ALDEBARAN, ALGOL, ALTAIR and BELLATRIX: August 5th, 1917 rammed U.39 on surface and damaged her, but she was able to reach her base.

BELLATRIX: same division; August 23rd, 1916 chased U.34; September 26th, 1916 attacked U.35; October 2nd, 1916 assisted the RIGEL.

CASSIOPEE: 1917–18 Atlantic patrol force.

REGULUS: 1917–18 Atlantic patrol force.

RIGEL: October 2nd, 1916 torpedoed by U.35 off Algiers.

Marne class – six ships

Displacement:	566 tons (MARNE 601).			
Dimensions:	78m × 8·90m × 3·40m.			
Machinery:	2 Normand or du Temple boilers; Parsons geared turbines, 2 screws; SHP 4000 (MARNE: 5000); speed 20 knots (MARNE 21). Fuel 143 tons oil.			
Radius (nm):	4000/11 knots, 1200/18 knots.			
Armament:	2 – 65mm.			
Complement:	4 officers, 109 crew.			

NAME	BUILDER	LAID DOWN	LAUNCHED	COMPLETED
AISNE	Lorient DY	1916	1917	1918
MARNE	Lorient DY	1916	25.11.16	1917
MEUSE	Rochefort DY	1916	1917	1918
OISE	Brest DY	1917	12.10.17	1917
SOMME	Brest DY	1916	3.17	1917
YSER	Rochefort DY	1916	1.17	1917

NOTES
1916 war programme. The engines were originally intended for the JOESSEL and LAGRANGE classes of submarines; MARNE and AISNE had two funnels, the others one only. Their armament was altered after the war to include 4 – 100mm and a 75mm army gun.

All six were serving in the Atlantic Patrol Force in 1918, and all except MARNE fitted with ultrasonic detecting devices.

A rare photo of the sloop AISNE seen in a dock.

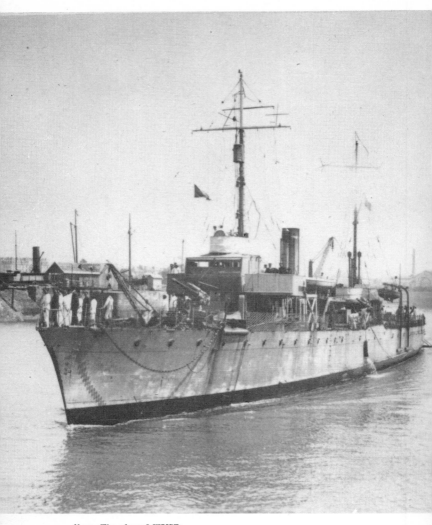

Above: **The sloop MEUSE.**

Above right: **The sloop OISE.**

Right: **The sloop YSER.**

MARNE was in the Baltic 1919–21; she was scuttled March 1945 at Can Tho, Indochina; raised and scrapped June 19th, 1957.

OISE on August 2nd, 1918 attacked UB.88; in 1919–21 she was in the Baltic.

SOMME was scrapped October 17th, 1941.

YSER was in the Black Sea 1919-20. She was scuttled November 27th 1942 at Toulon, raised 1943 and scrapped November 22nd, 1946.

Ailette class – two ships

Displacement:	492 tons.
Dimensions:	69·95m × 8·31m × 3·05m.
Machinery:	2 du Temple boilers; Parsons geared turbines, 2 screws; SHP 4000; speed 20 knots. Fuel oil 143 tons.
Radius (nm):	4000/11 knots, 1200/18 knots.
Armament:	4 – 100mm, 2 – 65mm.
Complement:	107.

NAME	BUILDER	LAID DOWN	LAUNCHED	COMPLETED
AILETTE	Brest DY	1917	3.18	1918
ESCAUT	Brest DY	1917	1918	1918

NOTES

1917 war programme. Externally camouflaged as mercantile vessels, gun being fitted behind movable panels on the four angles of the bridge.

Both served in the Atlantic Patrol Force 1918. AILETTE was scrapped during War War II and ESCAUT before the war.

Scarpe class – three ships

Displacement:	604 tons.
Dimensions:	76·20m × 8·68m × 3·27m.
Machinery:	2 du Temple boilers; Parsons geared turbines, 2 screws; SHP 5000; speed 20 knots. Fuel oil 143 tons.
Radius (nm):	4000/11 knots, 1200/18 knots.
Armament:	4 – 100mm, 1 – 65mm; depthcharges.
Complement:	107.

NAME	BUILDER	LAID DOWN	LAUNCHED	COMPLETED
ANCRE	Lorient DY	1917	1918	1918
SCARPE	Lorient DY	1917	31.10.17	1918
SUIPPE	Brest DY	1917	4.18	1918

NOTES

1917 war programme, these ships had a clipper bow.

ANCRE was in the Baltic 1919–21.

Below: **The sloop SCARPE.**

Foot: **The sloop SUIPPE.**

SUIPPE in 1918 in the Atlantic Patrol Force. In June 1940 she was seized by the Royal Navy and on April 14th, 1941 was bombed by German aircraft at Falmouth. Later salved, she was scrapped in June 1953.

SCARPE in 1918 was in the Atlantic Patrol Force and in the Black Sea 1919.

Ville d'Ys   – one ship

Displacement: 1121 tons.
Dimensions: 83·50m(oa), 75·40m(pp) × 12m × 5m.
Machinery: 2 cylindrical boilers; 1 set 4 cyl. TE, 1 screw; IHP 2675; speed 17 knots. Coal 270 tons.
Radius (nm):   2400/10 knots.
Armament: 3 – 100mm, 2 – 47mm AA; depthcharges.
Complement: 6 officers, 97 crew.

NAME	BUILDER	LAID DOWN	LAUNCHED	COMPLETED
VILLE D'YS	Swan Hunter & Wigham Richardson, Wallsend	26.12.16	6.17	15.8.17

NOTES
1916 war programme, ex-HMS ANDROMEDA and ordered to replace the lost RIGEL. Scrapped in June 1945.

Dubourdieu class – five ships

Displacement: 453 tons.
Dimensions: 64·92m(oa) × 8·20m × 3·10m.
Machinery: 2 du Temple boilers; Breguet geared turbines, 2 screws; SHP 2000; speed 16·5 knots. Fuel oil 140 tons.
Radius (nm):   2000/15 knots.
Armament: 1 – 138·6mm, 1 – 100mm; depthcharges.
Complement: 4 officers, 70 crew.

NAME	BUILDER	LAID DOWN	LAUNCHED	COMPLETED
DUBOURDIEU	Lorient DY	1917	4.18	1918
DU CHAFFAULT	Lorient DY	1917	9.18	1918
DUMONT D'URVILLE	Lorient DY	1917	6.11.18	1919
DU COUEDIC	Lorient DY	1918	7.19	1920
DUPERRE	Lorient DY	1918	12.18	1920

NOTES
1917 war programme.
    DUBOURDIEU was sunk by bombs and gunfire on November 8th, 1942 at Casablanca.

The sloop DUBOURDIEU.

DUMONT D'URVILLE was renamed ENSEIGNE HENRY on October 19th, 1929 when a colonial sloop of the same name was ordered in 1930. She was scuttled at Lorient on June 18th, 1940 but later salved and hulked as accommodation ship (she had been condemned since 1933).

DUPERRÉ was condemned in 1933, DU CHAFFAULT in 1938 and DU COUEDIC 1939.

Flamant – one ship

Displacement:	585 tons.
Dimensions:	50m(oa), 46·93m(pp) × 8·42m × 5·80m.
Machinery:	2 cylindrical boilers; reciprocating engine, 1 screw; IHP 1200; speed 14·5 knots. Coal 105 tons.
Radius (nm):	1200/10 knots.
Armament:	1 – 75mm, 1 – 47mm.
Complement:	53.

NAME	BUILDER	LAID DOWN	LAUNCHED	COMPLETED
FLAMANT	Rochefort DY	1913	12.16	1918

NOTES

Laid down in 1913, work was delayed between 1914 and 1917. She was renamed QUENTIN ROOSEVELT in 1918 in honour of one of the sons of President Theodore Roosevelt who had joined the French Air Force and and was killed on July 14th, 1918. Completed in April 1918 she was later assigned to fishery protection duties. She was seized by the British on July 3rd, 1940 and used for A/S training; returned 1945 she was scrapped in 1955.

ASW Gunboats

Ardent class – twenty-three ships

Displacement: 266 tons (except (a) 310).
Dimensions: 60·20m × 7·20m × 2·90m.
Machinery: Du Temple or Normand boilers; reciprocating engine, 1 screw (2 in (a)); SHP 1200 to 1500; speed 14 to 17 knots. Coal 85 tons.
Radius (nm): 2000/10 knots.
Armament: 2 – 100mm (except ARDENT, ETOURDI and SANS SOUCI: 2 – 145mm); depthcharges.
Complement: 55.

NAME	BUILDER	LAID DOWN	LAUNCHED	COMPLETED
AGILE (a)	Brest DY	1916	1916	1916
ALERTE	Rochefort DY	1916	1916	1916
ARDENT (a)	Brest DY	1916	5.3.16	1916
AUDACIEUSE	Ch. de Provence, Port de Bouc	1916	1917	1917
BATAILLEUSE	Ch. de Provence, Port de Bouc	1916	1917	1917
BELLIQUEUSE	Ch. de la Gironde, Bordeaux	1916	1916	1916
BOUDEUSE	Ch. de la Méditerranée, La Seyne	1916	1916	1916

The ASW gunboat AGILE.

The ASW gunboat ALERTE taken on August 8th, 1916.

The ASW gunboat BOUDEUSE.

The ASW gunboat COURAGEUSE moored in Cattaro harbour, 1919.

The ASW gunboat DEDAIGNEUSE.

CAPRICIEUSE	Ch. de la Loire, Nantes	1916	1916	1916
COURAGEUSE	Rochefort DY	1916	1916	1916
CURIEUSE	Lorient DY	1916	1916	1916
DEDAIGNEUSE	Ch. de la Gironde	1916	1916	1916
EMPORTE (a)	Ch. de la Loire	1916	1916	1916
ESPIEGLE (a)	Rochefort DY	1916	1916	1916
ETOURDI (a)	Lorient DY	1916	21.3.16	1916
EVEILLE (a)	Ch. de la Méditerranée	1917	1917	1917
GRACIEUSE	Lorient DY	1916	1916	1916
IMPETUEUSE	Ch. de la Gironde	1916	1917	1917
INCONSTANT (a)	Brest DY	1916	6.3.16	1916
MALICIEUSE	Ch. de Provence Port de Bouc	1916	1916	1916
MOQUEUSE	Lorient DY	1916	1916	1916
RAILLEUSE	Ch. de Provence Port de Bouc	1916	1916	1916
SANS SOUCI (a)	Lorient DY	1.12.15	1916	1916
TAPAGEUSE	Ch. de Provence Port de Bouc	1916	1916	1916

The ASW gunboat ETOURDI.

NOTES

1916 and 1917 war programmes. All had a clipper bow but varied a little in build; the illustrations given are believed to be typical of these ships. Some had been engined with machinery stripped from old coastal torpedo boats ('torpilleurs de défense mobile'). At the end of the war many of them were converted for minesweeping.

AGILE was condemned in 1933.

ALERTE: 1917–18 based on Rochefort, escort and patrol in the Bay of Biscay; February 10th, 1918 assisted the capsized patrol boat SARDINE in the Gironde estuary; condemned in 1936.

ARDENT: 1917–18 Channel Patrol Force; condemned 1936.

AUDACIEUSE: 1917–18 escort and patrol in the Bay of Biscay; scrapped January 1940.

BATAILLEUSE: 1917–18 Bay of Biscay; sunk as fleet target in 1938 off Quiberon.

BELLIQUEUSE: condemned in 1928.

BOUDEUSE: 1916 Otranto Straits patrol; October 7th, 1916 attacked the German U.35; 1917–18 9th Patrol Division, Aegean; 1920 unlisted and sold to Rumania to provide spares to the four FRIPONNE class (see page 186).

CAPRICIEUSE: 1917–18 9th Patrol Division, Aegean; April 16th, 1917 with MOQUEUSE attacked the German U.33 which had sunk the trooper SONTAY.

COURAGEUSE: fate unknown.

CURIEUSE: 1917–18 Algerian Patrol Force; condemned in 1926.

DEDAIGNEUSE: 1917–18 Algerian Patrol Force; May 29th, 1917 with ARBALETE and HM sloop LILY, attacked the German UC.74. On November 27th, 1942 she was scuttled at Toulon; later refloated and manned by the Italian Navy as FR.56 (1943). Captured by the Germans, she was armed as M.6920 (September 1943); fate unknown.

EMPORTE: 1917–18 escort duty in the Bay of Biscay.

ESPIEGLE: fate unknown.

ETOURDI: 1917–18 escort duty in the Bay of Biscay; scuttled June 19th, 1940 at Brest and scrapped in June 1941.

EVEILLE: 1917–18 escort and patrol, Bay of Biscay; December 13th, 1917 attacked U.103; condemned in 1928.

GRACIEUSE: 1917–18 Algerian Patrol Force; June 22nd, 1917 with IMPATIENTE, attacked the German U.63; condemned in 1938.

IMPETUEUSE: condemned in 1938.

INCONSTANT: 1917–18 Atlantic Patrol Force and Bay of Biscay; June 27th, 1917 assisted the sinking KLEBER; condemned in 1933.

MALICIEUSE: 1917–18 Tunisian Patrol Force.

MOQUEUSE: 1917–18 Tunisian Patrol Force; April 16, 1917 with CAPRICIEUSE attacked the German U.33; lost in 1923.

RAILLEUSE: 1917–18 Algerian Patrol Force; February 10th, 1917 attacked U.35; she was unlisted March 1st, 1920.

SANS SOUCI: condemned in 1936.

TAPAGEUSE: 1917–18 9th Patrol Division, Aegean; scrapped in 1944.

The ASW gunboat EVEILLE.

The ASW gunboat INCONSTANT.

Luronne – one ship

Displacement: 266 tons.
Dimensions: 60·20m(oa) × 7·16m × 2·90m.
Machinery: Fiat diesels, 2 screws; BHP 630; speed 13·7 knots.
Radius (nm): 3000/10 knots.
Armament: 2 – 100mm; depthcharges.
Complement: 54.

NAME	BUILDER	LAUNCHED	COMPLETED
LURONNE	Brest DY	1917	1917

NOTES
1916 war programme.
  1917–18 Atlantic Patrol Force; scrapped in 1941.

Friponne class – eight ships

Displacement: 315 tons.
Dimensions: 66·40m(oa) × 7·01m × 2·80m.
Machinery: 2 Sulzer diesels, 2 screws; BHP 900; speed 14·5 knots.
Oil 30 tons.
Radius (nm): 3000/10 knots, 1600/14 knots.
Armament: 2 – 100mm.
Complement: 54.

The ASW gunboat LURONNE.

The ASW gunboat DILIGENTE. Note her straight bow.

The ASW gunboat ENGAGEANTE.

Above: The ASW gunboat FRIPONNE.

The ASW gunboat SURVEILLANTE.

NAME	BUILDER	LAID DOWN	LAUNCHED	COMPLETED
BOUFFONNE	Lorient DY	1915	1916	1916
CHIFFONNE	Lorient DY	1916	1917	1917
DILIGENTE	Brest DY	1915	1916	1916
ENGAGEANTE	Brest DY	1916	17.12.16	1917
FRIPONNE	Lorient DY	1916	1916	1916
IMPATIENTE	Brest DY	1916	1916	1916
MIGNONNE	Brest DY	1916	1917	1917
SURVEILLANTE	Brest DY	1915	1917	1917

NOTES

1916 war programme; also included COQUETTE, HEROINE, JOYEUSE
and MUTINE ordered but cancelled. Generally of the same type as
ARDENT class but with diesel engines and no funnels except CHIF-
FONNE, ENGAGEANTE and MIGNONNE which had a dummy funnel.
DILIGENTE had a straight stem, others a clipper bow.

BOUFFONNE: 1916-18 Algerian Patrol Force; October 2nd, 1917
assisted the disabled RIGEL; unlisted in 1925.

CHIFFONNE: 1917–18 Atlantic Patrol Force; sold to Rumania in 1920
and renamed LOCOTENENT LEPRI REMUS.

DILIGENTE: 1916–18 Tunisian Patrol Force; assisted the disabled
RIGEL; scrapped in December 1946.

ENGAGEANTE: May 1918 with AMARANTE, made tests with Walser
hydrophonic device; unlisted 1944, sold for scrap in December 1946.

FRIPONNE: 1916–18 Tunisian Patrol Force; assisted the disabled
RIGEL; 1920 sold to Rumania, renamed LOCOTENENT-COMANDOR
STIHI EUGEN.

IMPATIENTE: 1916-18 Tunisian Patrol Force; 1920 sold to Rumania nd renamed CAPITAN DUMITRESCU C.

MIGNONNE: 1917-18 Atlantic Patrol Force; 1920 sold to Rumania and named SUBLOCOTENENT GHICULESCU.

SURVEILLANTE: 1916–18 Algerian Patrol Force; April 14th, 1917 ssisted the trooper GANGE, disabled by mine; May 15th, 1917 rammed d sank the Italian destroyer SCORPIONE; condemned in 1938.

aillante class – two ships

isplacement:	457 tons.
imensions:	66·40m × 7·90m × 2·80m.
achinery:	2 Sulzer diesels; 2 screws; BHP 1500; speed 17 knots.
	Oil 30 tons.
adius (nm):	3000/10 knots.
rmament:	2 – 100mm; depthcharges.
omplement:	54.

AME	BUILDER	LAID DOWN	LAUNCHED	COMPLETED
ONQUERANTE	Brest DY	1916	1917	1917
AILLANTE	Brest DY	1917	1917	1917

OTES

17 war programme; a modification of the FRIPONNE design with raighter bows.

CONQUERANTE was seized by the British in July 1940 and sunk by erman air attack at Falmouth on April 14th, 1941.

VAILLANTE was condemned in 1932.

e ASW gunboat CONQUERANTE.

Minelayers

Pluton class – two ships

Displacement:	660 tons (full load).
Dimensions:	59m × 8m × 3·15m.
Machinery:	Reciprocating, 1 screw; IHP 6000; speed 20 knots. Coal 150 tons.
Armament:	2 – 100mm, 1 – 75mm, 120 mines.

NAME	BUILDER	LAID DOWN	LAUNCHED	COMPLETED
PLUTON	A. Normand, Le Havre	1911	10.3.13	1913
CERBERE	Nantes	1911	13.7.12	1912

NOTES

PLUTON: 1914, 2nd Light Squadron, Channel; August 5th, 1914 captured the German cargo vessel PORTO in the Channel; October 17th, 1914 laid a minefield off Zeebrugge; October 22nd and November 2nd, 1914 with CERBERE laid minefields off Flemish ports and coast, refusing the proposed escort of British destroyers in order to be less obvious. Joined the Armée Navale 1915–18; December 1915 laid a field around Castellorizo Island; September 1915 to January 1916 Salamis and Athens operations; January 7th, 1916 laid 60 mines off Beirut, Syria; 1917 laid minefields off Salonika; August/October 1918 with HM minelayer BIARRITZ and others, laid 2500 mines off the Dardanelles entrance; 1921 unlisted and sold for scrap in 1923.

CERBERE: 1914 2nd Light Squadron, Channel; October 22nd and November 2nd, 1914 mining with PLUTON off the Flemish coast; 1916–18 continuous work on the Dover–Calais barrage; July 1917 laid 120 mines around the Vergoyer Bank in the Channel. Condemned in 1923.

Cassini class – two ships

Displacement:	925/960 tons.
Dimensions:	81·10m(wl) × 8·20/8·32m × 3·10m.
Machinery:	8 vertical small-tube Lagrafel d'Allest boilers; 2 sets quadruple expansion, 2 screws; IHP 5000; speed 21 knots. Coal 188 tons.
Protection:	Slight belt around machinery; protected deck 15mm.
Armament:	1 – 100mm, 3 – 65mm, 97 mines.

NAME	BUILDER	LAID DOWN	LAUNCHED	COMPLETED
CASSINI	F. et Ch. de la Méditerranée Graville, Le Havre	1.6.93	5.6.94	1895

Details of the minelayer CASSINI.

CASABIANCA	A. et Ch. de la Gironde, Bordeaux	11.92	1894	1896

NOTES

Designed by M. de Bussy and formerly 'avisos torpilleurs', they were converted into minelayers pre-war.

CASSINI: 1914 with the cruisers of the Armée Navale, patrols in the Otranto Straits; 1915 with LA HIRE, patrols near Crete and Rhodes; June 8th, 1916 shelled the German U.35 while she was sinking the British cargo boat BEACHY off Corsica; February 28th, 1917 sunk on a mine laid by UC.35 in the Bonifacio Straits.

CASABIANCA: 1914 with the cruisers of the Armée Navale, patrols in the Otranto Straits; 1915 patrols off Corfu; June 3rd, 1915 sunk on one of her own mines off Smyrna.

The minelayer CASABIANCA.

Minesweepers

Damier – one ship

Displacement: 155 tons.
Machinery: Reciprocating, 1 screw; IHP 340; speed 9 knots.
Armament: 1 – 47mm.
Complement: 15.

NOTES
A trawler purchased in 1910 and converted; unlisted in 1923.

Lorientais – one ship

Displacement: 433 tons.
Machinery: Reciprocating; IHP 370; speed 9·7 knots.
Armament: 1 – 47mm.
Complement: 15.

NOTES
A trawler purchased in 1910. 1918, 6th Patrol Division, Dunkirk; unlisted in 1919.

Alcyon I – one ship

Displacement: 300 tons.
Machinery: Reciprocating, 1 screw; IHP 320; speed 8·5 knots.
Armament: 1 – 47mm.
Complement: 15.

NOTES
Ex-trawler LIZZIE purchased in 1911. Served in the Calais Flotilla to 1918; unlisted 1919.

Iroise – one ship

Displacement: 240 tons.
Machinery: Reciprocating, 1 screw; IHP 430; speed 10 knots.
Armament: 1 – 47mm.
Complement: 15.

NOTES
Ex-trawler MARIE MARCELLE (1907) purchased in 1911. Unlisted 1919.

Orient – one ship

Displacement: 385 tons.
Machinery: Reciprocating, 1 screw; IHP 565; speed 10 knots.
Armament: 1 – 47mm.
Complement: 15.

NOTES
Ex-trawler built 1908 and purchased in 1910; unlisted 1919.

Herse class – four ships

Displacement: 255 tons.
Dimensions: 34m × 6·80m × 2·40m.
Machinery: Triple expansion, 1 screw; IHP 600; speed 12 knots.
Armament: 2 – 47mm QF.

HERSE, RATEAU, CHARRUE, PIOCHE:
All built by Forges et Ch. de la Méditerranée, La Seyne; laid down 1913
and completed 1914.

NOTES
All operated off the Dardanelles 1915. HERSE was unlisted in 1919 and the
others in 1923.

Granit class – five ships

Displacement: 360 tons.
Dimensions: 57·6om × 7·90m × 2·30m.
Machinery: 1 Belleville boiler from uncompleted FLANDRE
battleship; 1 Cochot reciprocating, 1 screw; IHP 600;
speed 12·5 knots.
Armament: 1 – 65mm.
Complement: 3 officers, 60 crew.

GRANIT, MARBRE, PORPHYRE, GRES, MICA:
First three built by Ch. de la Loire, Nantes; last two St Nazaire;
all launched and completed in 1918.

NOTES
GRANIT operated with a kite balloon in 1918 and was again in commission in 1939; she was scuttled November 20th, 1942 at Toulon. Refloated, she was used by the Germans as SG.26; her fate is unknown.
    MARBRE and GRES were condemned in 1920, PORPHYRE in 1932
and MICA 1938.

The minesweeper GRANIT.

Albâtre class – seven ships

Displacement: 380 tons.
Dimensions: 57·60m × 7·90m × 2·30m.
Machinery: 1 cylindrical boiler; 1 Cochot reciprocating, 1 screw; IHP 500; speed 10·5 knots.
Armament: 1 – 65mm.
Complement: 3 officers, 60 crew.

ALBATRE, GYPSE, PYRITE, QUARTZ, BASALTE, MEULIERE, SILEX: First four built by Ch. de la Loire, Nantes; last three by Ch. de la Loire, St Nazaire. All launched and completed in 1919. (1917 programme.)

NOTES
GYPSE and BASALTE unlisted 1919, probably not completed.
 ALBATRE sold 1920 as coaster of same name.
 PYRITE was lost in 1926 at Madagascar.
 SILEX sold 1920.
 QUARTZ unlisted in 1939..
 MEULIERE stranded May 24th, 1941 and lost in Corsica.

Auxiliary Minesweepers

The following five classes of auxiliary minesweepers were built under the 1917 programme; most were paid off after post-war mine clearance and sold to fishery owners:

Camelia class – ten ships

CAMELIA, DATURA, FRANCOA, FRESIA, GODETIA, IPECA, MAGNOLIA, PAULOWNIA, RESEDA, ZINNIA:

Builder: Ch. de Bretagne, Nantes.
Displacement: 124 tons.
Machinery: 1 cylindrical boiler; reciprocating engine; IHP 170; speed 8 knots.
Armament: 1 – 75mm.

NOTES
Of trawler type, all were completed early 1918. CAMELIA and DATURA were used as harbour tugs post-war and both scuttled at Toulon, the former on November 27th, 1942 by the French, the latter in August 1944 by the Germans.

Ajonc class – ten ships

AJONC, ASTER, CHARDON, GENET, JASMIN, LILAS, LUPIN,
MUGUET, MYOSOTIS, NENUPHAR:

Builder:　　　　Ch. Baudoin, Marseilles.
Displacement:　112 tons.
Machinery:　　 Oil engine; BHP 220; speed 9·5 knots.
Armament:　　 1 – 75mm.

NOTES
Four of these were completed before the armistice. They had been designed
with the view to transform them into 140-ton trawlers with a gas engine,
hulls being strengthened for this purpose.

Fanfaron class – ten ships

FANFARON, FANTASQUE, FAROUCHE, FAVORI, FLAMBANT,
FOUGUEUX, FOURRAGEUR, FRONDEUR, FULGURANT,
FURIEUX:

Builder:　　　　Ch. Niclausse, Paris.
Displacement:　154 tons.
Machinery:　　 1 Niclausse boiler; reciprocating engine, 1 screw; IHP 300;
　　　　　　　　speed 9 knots.
Armament:　　 1 – 90mm or 75mm.

NOTES
Of trawler type, all were completed in 1919 except FLAMBANT (1918);
this latter was later renamed MARECHAL FOCH and became a Rhone tug.

Amandier class – six ships

AMANDIER, BANANIER, COCOTIER, DATTIER, MURIER,
PALMIER:

Builder:　　　　Ch. Bocanini, Cannes.
Displacement:　78 tons.
Machinery:　　 Oil engine; BHP 160; speed 9 knots.
Armament:　　 1 light gun.

NOTES
Only AMANDIER and BANANIER were completed.

Campanule class – twelve ships

CAMPANULE, CLEMATITE, JACINTHE, JONQUILLE, LAVANDE, MARJOLAINE, PAQUERETTE, PERCE-NEIGE, RENONCULE, SAUGE, TULIPE, VIOLETTE:

Builders: Lorient DY (1st 6), Rochefort DY (2nd 6).
Displacement: 80 tons.
Machinery: Fiat oil engine, 1 screw; BHP 325; speed 13 knots.

NOTES
Ten completed before the armistice; CLEMATITE unlisted 1922, PERCE-NEIGE in 1934.

Briscard class – sixteen ships

BRISCARD, CHEVRONNE, GROGNARD, POILU, RENGAGE, VETERAN, MATHURIN, TROUPIER:
BOMBARDIER, CANONIER, MITRAILLEUR, PIONNIER:
FRANC-TIREUR, FUSILIER, SAPEUR, VOLONTAIRE:

Builders: Sud-Ouest, Bordeaux (1st 8);
             Baudouin, Marseilles (2nd 4);
             Sud-Ouest, Bordeaux (last 4).
Displacement: 370 tons.
Dimensions: 41m × 7·30m × 3·20m.
Machinery: Reciprocating; IHP 425; speed 11 knots (except MATHURIN and TROUPIER: petrol engine, BHP 420, 11 knots and the Marseilles vessels: Reciprocating; IHP 500, speed 11·5 knots).

NOTES
GROGNARD, POILU and RENGAGE were sold in 1922 to the Spanish Navy and renamed TETUAN, LARACHE and ALCAZAR respectively. BOMBARDIER was sold in 1922 and became a tug. VETERAN was sold in 1920 as a pilot boat (see same name on page 170 of 'French Warships of World War II').

Requisitioned Auxiliary Minesweepers

ALBATROS III, ALCYON, ATLANTIQUE, AUGUSTIN-NORMAND, BORDEAUX, CAMARGUE, CASTOR, CHEVRETTE, CORMORAN, COURLIS, DKD (M/S tug), DUCOUEDIC, FURET II, GOELAND II, GREBE I, GRILLON, HALICOR, HENRIETTE III, HERCULE (M/S tug), ISABELLE I, JEAN GUITTON, JERSEY, JULES COUETTE, KERNEVEN, LAVARDIN, LION I, MARIE ROSE IV, MARIUS

CHAMBON, MARSEILLAIS VIII (M/S tug), MARSEILLAIS XII
(M/S tug), MARSEILLAIS XIX (M/S tug), MARSEILLAIS XXVIII
(M/S tug), MOUETTE I, NORD, OUTARDE, PHOEBUS (mined
December 1st, 1917), PIERROT, POITOU (torpedoed December 8th,
1917), PROVENCE III, PROVENCE XV, PROVENCE XVII,
ROBUSTE (M/S tug), ROVE, SACHA, SAINT ANDRE I, SAINT
GUENAEL, SAINT PIERRE II, SOUFFLEUR, SUD, SUSSEX,
TROUVILLE, VENUS I, VILLE DE CANNES, VILLE DE GUJAN
MESTRAS, VILLE DE ROYAN.

Requisitioned Examination Vessels – fitted as Minesweepers

ACTIF, ALCYON III (lost June 27th, 1918), ANTOINETTE,
ARCHIMEDE II, ARLESIENNE, BALEINES, BERTHE VALÉRY,
CHACAL, COURRIER DU CAP, CYCLOPE, EIDER, FRANCE II,
FRANCOIS-NICOLAS, GARD II, GIRELLE, GOLIATH,
HIRONDELLE, HOLLAND, JACQUES CARTIER, JEAN BART III,
JEAN PIERRE, LA LYS, LAPRADE, LE CROZON, MADELEINE I,
MARSA, MENHIR, MESSIDOR II, MIREILLE, MYOTTE II,
NAUTILUS, NEPTUNE I, NOMADIC, ODET, RENEE-FERNANDE,
ROCHELAIS, ROLLAND, SAINT JOSEPH, SAINT LEON,
SAMSON, SEDJOUMI, SENEGALAIS, TARANAKI, TOUQUET,
TRAFFIC, VALENTINE-GERMAINE.

Gunboats

Surprise class – three ships

Displacement:	680 tons
Dimensions:	56m × 8m × 3·8m.
Machinery:	Reciprocating; IHP 900, 1 screw; speed 12·9 to 13·84 knots.
Armament:	2 – 100mm, 4 – 65mm, 6 – 37mm (except SURPRISE).
Complement:	7 officers, 96 crew.

NAME	BUILDER	LAID DOWN	LAUNCHED	COMPLETED
SURPRISE	A. Normand, Le Havre	1893	24.4.95	1896
DECIDEE	Lorient DY	1896	1989	1899
ZELEE	Rochefort DY	1898	18.10.99	1900

NOTES

SURPRISE: 1914 Cameroons; September 21st, 1914 sent a landing party to operate with infantry on Coco beach and also sank the German armed merchant ITOLO; September 22nd, 1914, bombardment of enemy positions; October 1914 with the BRUIX, capture of Victoria; 1915–16 Morocco Station; December 3rd, 1916 torpedoed by U.38 off Funchal.

ZELEE: 1914 Tahiti Station; August 12th, 1914, captured the German cargo ship WALKURE at Makatea Island; September 1914 disarmed at Papeete, her guns being landed for the defence of Tahiti; September 22nd, 1914 scuttled at Papeete entrance to prevent German cruisers from penetrating the harbour.

DECIDEE: 1914–17, Indochina Station; 1917–18, 7th Patrol Division in Syria; 1922 unlisted.

Requisitioned Greek gunboats – four ships

Displacement:	404 tons.
Dimensions:	44m × 8·30m × 3·40m.
Machinery:	Reciprocating; IHP 400; speed 11 knots.
Armament:	1 – old 152mm, 1 – 100mm (and 4 – MG in EUROTAS) (PENEIOS: 4 – MG only).

NAME	BUILDER	LAUNCHED	COMPLETED	MAJOR REFIT
ACHELOOS	Blackwall	1884	1885	1895
ALPHEOS	Blackwall	1884	1885	1895
EUROTAS	Dumbarton	1884	1885	1895
PENEIOS		1884	1885	1895

NOTES

Seized in December 1916 and armed under French flag; returned 1918 and unlisted 1928–30.

The gunboat ZELEE.

Dispatch Vessels

Chamois – one ship

Displacement:	431 tons.
Machinery:	Reciprocating, 1 screw; IHP 600; speed 12·6 knots.
Armament:	2 – 65mm.
Complement:	7 officers, 51 crew.

NAME	BUILDER	LAID DOWN	LAUNCHED	COMPLETED
CHAMOIS	Port-de-Bouc	1904	1906	1906

NOTES
Pilot School 1906–14; 1914–18, patrols in Mediterranean; pilot school again from 1919–23; unlisted 1925.

Ibis – one ship

Displacement:	254 tons (279 full load).
Machinery:	Reciprocating; IHP 340; speed 11·8 knots.
Armament:	2 – 65mm, 1 – 47mm.
Complement:	4 officers, 42 crew.

NAME	BUILDER	LAID DOWN	LAUNCHED	COMPLETED
IBIS	Rochefort DY	1882	1883	1884

NOTES
In 1899 with the storeship VIENNE, had made the first trials with wireless telegraphy in the French Navy. Unlisted 1920.

Jeanne Blanche – one ship

Displacement:	420 tons.
Machinery:	Reciprocating, 1 screw; IHP 820; speed 12 knots.
Armament:	4 – 37mm.
Complement:	4 officers, 39 crew.

NAME	BUILDER	LAID DOWN	LAUNCHED	COMPLETED
JEANNE BLANCHE	La Seyne	1893	1894	1895

NOTES
Originally a private yacht, given by her owner to the French Navy in 1908 to be used as the yacht of the French ambassador at Constantinople. She was rebuilt in 1913 and armed for patrol duties during World War I; unlisted 1920.

Kersaint – one ship

Displacement:	1243 tons.
Dimensions:	69m × 11m × 4·60m.
Machinery:	Reciprocating; IHP 1600; speed 15 knots. Coal 200 tons.
Radius (nm):	4000/10 knots.
Armament:	1 – 138·6mm, 5 – 100mm, 5 – 37mm.
Complement:	8 officers, 143 crew.

NAME	BUILDER	LAID DOWN	LAUNCHED	COMPLETED
KERSAINT	Rochefort DY	1895	28.8.97	3.11.98

NOTES

August 17th, 1914 disarmed at Noumea; December 19th, 1914 rearmed; 1915 patrols in South Pacific; 1916 refit at Saigon; 1917, S Pacific; 1918, China Sea; December 8th, 1918 at Vladivostock with the Allied Force; March 5th, 1919 fouled an uncharted coral reef at Moorea and classed as a constructive total loss July 18th, 1919.

Auxiliary Cruisers

Most of the French requisitioned passenger ships were alternatively used as auxiliary cruisers (generally in 1914), then as troopers (mostly for trooping to the Dardanelles and Macedonian fronts), and sometimes reverting to the cruising and patrolling role on theatres more or less remote, where true cruisers were scarce.

AMAZONE II (6007 GRT/built 1897, 19 knots); 1914–18 cruiser; 1919 unlisted.

BURDIGALA (12,000/97): 1914–16 cruiser, Mediterranean; November 14th, 1916 mined off Zea Island, Aegean.

CALEDONIEN (4130/82, 15 knots): 1914–17 cruiser, Mediterranean; June 30th, 1917 mined off Port Said.

CARTHAGE (5275/10, 19 knots): 1914 Mediterranean; 1915 Dardanelles; May 24th, 1915 landings at Seddul-Bahr and shore bombardment; July 4th, 1915 torpedoed by the German U.21 off Gallipoli.

DJEMNAH (3716/75, 13 knots): 1915–18 trooper; July 14th, 1918 torpedoed by the German UB.105 off Cyrenaica.

EUROPE (4838/06, 14 knots): 1914–15 cruiser; February 27th, 1915 captured the German cargo ship DACIA; 1915–18 trooper; 1919 unlisted.

FLANDRE (8450/14, 17 knots): 1914–17 cruiser and trooper; 1918–19 hospital ship; 1919 unlisted. 1939 requisitioned as trooper to June 1940;

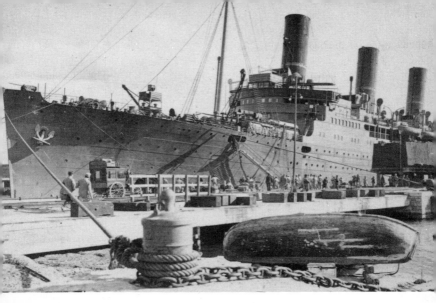

The auxiliary cruiser GALLIA.

The auxiliary cruiser PROVENCE II.

August 5th, 1940 taken by Germans at Bordeaux and mined September 13th, 1940 in the Gironde.

GALLIA (14,900/13, 21 knots): 1914–15 cruiser; 1916 trooper; October 4th, 1916 torpedoed by the German U.35 off Cape Matapan.

GANGE (6876/05, 13·5 knots): 1914–17 trooper; April 14th, 1917 mined off Bizerta.

GOLO II (1380/03, 18 knots, 2 – 65mm, 2 – 47mm guns): 1914 cruiser, patrols between Italy and Corsica; 1915–17 Western Mediterranean; August 22nd, 1917 torpedoed by the German UC.22 off Corfu.

HIMALAYA (5620/02, 14 knots): 1914–17 trooper; June 23rd, 1917 torpedoed by the German U.63 off Marrittimo, Sicily.

ITALIA (1305/04, 17 knots): 1914–17 trooper; May 30th, 1917 torpedoed by the Austrian U.4 south of Italy.

LORRAINE II (11,146/99, 21·5 knots): 1914 cruiser, patrols between Italy and Tunisia; 1915–18 Levant Squadron; 1919 unlisted.

LUTETIA (14,654/13, 20·5 knots): 1916–18 cruiser.

NEWHAVEN (1656/10, 24 knots): 1914 cruiser 2nd Light Squadron; 1915–18 patrols in the Channel. 1940 requisitioned for Flanders operations and Dunkirk withdrawal to June 1940; July 25th, 1940 seized by the Germans at Bayonne, renamed SKORPION then SKAGERRACK and became a depot ship; found at Kiel after the war; 1948 condemned.

NIAGARA (8590/90, 16 knots): 1914 cruiser, 2nd Light Squadron, Channel; 1915–18 patrol and trooping; 1919 unlisted.

POLYNESIEN (6363/90, 17 knots): 1914–18 trooper; August 10th, 1918 torpedoed by the German UC.22 in the Malta Channel.

PROVENCE II (13,753/06, 22·5 knots, 5 – 138·6mm, 4 – 47mm guns): 1914, cruiser, patrols off Sicily; 1915 Dardanelles; April 25th, 1915 landings at Seddul-Bahr and shore bombardment; October 1915 to February 1916 trooper between Levant and Greece; February 26th, 1916 torpedoed by the German U.35 off Cerigo Island.

SAVOIE (11,168/00, 21 knots): 1914 cruiser, 2nd Light Squadron, Channel; 1915–18 trooper; 1919 unlisted.

SANT-ANNA (9350/10, 16·5 knots): 1914–15 cruiser, Mediterranean; 1915–18 trooper; May 11th, 1918 torpedoed by the German UC.54 off Tunisia.

SONTAY (7236/07, 15 knots): 1914–17 trooper; April 16th, 1917 torpedoed by the German UC.54 off Tunisia.

TIMGAD: 1914 cruiser; 1915 hospital ship; 1916–18 trooper; January 11th/16th, 1917 Athens operations; 1919 unlisted.

TOURAINE (9429/91, 19 knots): 1914 cruiser, 2nd Light Squadron, Channel; 1915–18 trooper; 1919 unlisted.

Patrol Boats

Navarin class – twelve ships

Displacement:	640 tons.
Machinery:	Reciprocating; IHP 500; speed 11 knots.
Armament:	1 – 100mm.
Builder:	Canadian Car Co, Fort William.

NAME	LAID DOWN	LAUNCHED	COMPLETED
NAVARIN	From 25.5 to 3.6.18	29.7.18	20.9.18
MANTOUE	From 25.5 to 3.6.18	13.8.18	5.10.18
ST-GEORGES	From 25.5 to 3.6.18	21.8.18	26.10.18
LEOBEN	From 25.5 to 3.6.18	29.8.18	1.11.18
PALESTRO	From 25.5 to 3.6.18	19.8.18	16.10.18
LUTZEN	3.6.18	31.8.18	6.11.18
BAUTZEN	From 2.8 to 3.9.18	14.9.18	12.11.18
SENEF	From 2.8 to 3.9.18	20.9.18	15.11.18
CERISOLES	From 2.8 to 3.9.18	25.9.18	21.11.18
SEBASTOPOL	From 2.8 to 3.9.18	30.9.18	21.11.18
MALAKOFF	From 2.8 to 3.9.18	1.10.18	17.11.18
INKERMANN	From 2.8 to 3.9.18	3.10.18	21.11.18

NOTES
These trawlers suffered from very bad stability, as was shown when
CERISOLES and INKERMANN were lost with all hands on November
24th, 1918 on Lake Superior while on passage to Boston; hence it was
decided to disarm the ten survivors at Boston.

Bouvines class – thirty-eight ships

BOUVINES, AUSTERLITZ, FLEURUS, JEMMAPES, LODI,
MAGENTA, MARENGO, VALMY.
ALMA, ARCOLE, AUERSTAEDT, BASSANO, CASTIGLIONE,
DEGO, DENAIN, ECKMULH, ESSLING, HOHENLINDEN,
HONDSCHOOTE, ISLY, LENS, LES DUNES, LES PYRAMIDES,
LONATO, MARIGNAN, MINCIAO, MONDOVI, MONTEBELLO,
MONTENOTTE, POITIERS, ROCROI, SAMBRE-ET-MEUSE,
SOLFERINO, STEINKERQUE, TAGLIAMENTO, TILSITT,
WATTIGNIES, ZURICH.

Builders:	Foundation Co, Savannah, USA.
Displacement:	684 tons (full load).
Dimensions:	45m × 7·8m.
Machinery:	Reciprocating: IHP 500; speed 9·5 knots.
Armament:	2 – 100mm.

NOTES

These trawlers were ordered in 1918 and the Foundation Co of Savannah had decided to build a special shipyard for their construction. Because of the great delay in the building of this yard and from other reasons, no ship was complete by November 1918. Finally only the first eight were despatched to France where they were soon placed on the sale list; the others, completed in 1919, were sold in the USA.

At least nine of the class served in World War II:

AUSTERLITZ sold as LOON, became the French SABLAISE;

MARENGO sold as ULM then EMILIA PRIMEIRO, became the British SUNRISE;

VALMY sold as COOT, became the French ALGEROISE;

LONATO sold as PLOVER, became the French QUIMPEROISE;

MARIGNAN sold as MARIGNAM, became the British TEAL;

POITIERS sold as BRANDT, became the French ORANAISE;

ROCROI sold as CURLEW, became the British PANORAMA which was captured in November 1942 by a French aviso off West Africa and later returned;

SAMBRE-ET-MEUSE sold as KINGFISHER, became the British LUMINARY;

TILSITT sold as HERON, became the French CHERBOURGEOISE.
(See *French Warships of WW. II* and *British Warships of WW. II*.)

The patrol boat BOUVINES. Note the position of her gun.

209

Jacques Coeur class – fourteen ships

CHAMPLAIN, CHATEAURENAULT, D'ESTAING, JACQUES COEUR, LAPEROUSE, PRIMAUGUET, SEIGNELAY.
KERGUELEN, LA CLOCHETERIE.
COETLOGON, FORFAIT, HAMELIN, LAMOTTE-PICQUET.

Builders:	Brest DY (1st 7), Lorient DY (next 2), Ch. de la Loire, Nantes (last 4).
Displacement:	700 tons.
Dimensions:	51·25m × 7·9m × 4·25m.
Machinery:	2 cylindrical boilers; reciprocating, 1 screw; IHP 1100; speed 12 knots.
Armament:	2 – 100mm, 1 machine gun.

NOTES

D'ESTAING, renamed BEAUTEMPS-BEAUPRÉ in 1920, lengthened by 12m and tonnage increased to 781, became a survey ship; unlisted 1937.

LAPEROUSE, same conversion in 1920; scuttled March 13th, 1945 in Indochina.

PRIMAUGUET, renamed ALLIER in 1922 and unlisted 1938, and—
LAMOTTE-PICQUET, renamed ADOUR 1922, ALFRED DE COURCY 1924 and unlisted in 1937, were both used as naval transports.

CHAMPLAIN, COETLOGON, FORFAIT, HAMELIN and JACQUES COEUR were also fitted as transports circa 1922.

CHATEAURENAULT, KERGUELEN, LA CLOCHETERIE and SEIGNELAY were cancelled.

Gardon class – nine ships

EQUILLE, GARDON, GOUJON, LAMPROIE, MURENE;
CIGALE, COCCINELLE, LIBELLULE;
CRIQUET.

Builders:	Normand (1st 5), Port de Bouc (next 3), Le Trait (last 1)
Displacement:	665 tons.
Machinery:	EQUILLE, LAMPROIE, MURENE fitted with Belleville boiler from uncompleted FLANDRE; others had a diesel engine; speed 10 knots.
Armament:	1 – 100mm, 1 – 47mm, ASW equipment.

NOTES

Of trawler type and all built between 1917 and 1918 and all unlisted in 1919 except CRIQUET which was used as a transport in 1920 and unlisted in 1921.

Barbeau, and similar, type – eight ships

ABLETTE, ANGUILLE II, BARBEAU, BREME, BROCHET, PERCHE, TANCHE, TRUITE.

Builders: Various.
Displacement: 315 tons.
Machinery: Reciprocating; IHP 365; speed 9 knots.
Armament: 1 – 90mm army gun, 1 – 47mm.

NOTES
Of trawler type and all unlisted in 1919.

Mauviette, and similar, type – thirty ships

ALOUETTE II, BECFIGUE, BERGERONETTE, CAILLE II, CANARD, CHARDONNERET II, COLIBRI II, CORNEILLE II, ENGOULEVENT, ETOURNEAU II, FAUVETTE II, GRIVE II, LINOTTE III, LORIOT, MARTINET, MARTIN-PECHEUR, MAUVIETTE, MERLE II, MOINEAU II, ORTOLAN, PASSEREAU II, PERRUCHE II, PIE II, PIERROT II, PINSON II, PIVERT, ROITELET II, ROSSIGNOL II, ROUGE-GORGE II, SANSONNET.

Builders: Ch. de la Méditerranée, La Seyne *or* Le Trait, Normand.
Displacement: 420/460 tons.
Dimensions: 43·50 × 7·30m × 3·40 to 4·20m.
Machinery: 1 cylindrical boiler; reciprocating, 1 screw; speed 10 knots. Coal 120 tons.
Armament: 1 – 90mm army gun, 1 – 47mm.

NOTES
Trawler type. PASSEREAU II fitted as minesweeper.

The following trawlers of this class were converted after the war into survey ships:

MARTIN-PECHEUR renamed ALIDADE;
MAUVIETTE renamed ASTROLABE;
ORTOLAN renamed GASTON RIVIER;
PERRUCHE renamed SENTINELLE;
PIE II renamed ESTAFETTE;
PINSON II renamed BOUSSOLE;
PIVERT renamed OCTANT.

All of these were in commission at the start of World War II.

ASTROLABE was bombed and sunk by US naval aircraft off Tourane, Indochina on February 26th, 1944.

ESTAFETTE was forced to beach off Casablanca on November 8th, 1942 after being bombed by USN aircraft and shelled by the destroyer TILMAN.

GASTON RIVIER was seized by the Royal Navy in July 1940 and returned in 1945; she was scrapped in 1946.

OCTANT was bombed and sunk by USN aircraft at Saigon, Indochina January 12th 1945.

SENTINELLE was scrapped November 14th, 1947.

The unconverted trawlers were unlisted in 1919 except ROITELET II and ROSSIGNOL II which were stricken in 1920 and PASSEREAU II which was unlisted in 1946.

Canna class – six ships

CANNA, LANTANIA, LOBELIA, NEMESIA, THUYA, YUCCA.

Builder:　　　　Ch. de Saint-Quentin, Nantes.
Displacement:　129 tons.

NOTES
Trawler type and laid down in 1917; none were completed until after the armistice.

Abricotier class – ten ships

ABRICOTIER, CERISIER, CITRONNIER, FIGUIER, MARRONIER, MERISIER, NEFLIER, PECHER, POMMIER, PRUNIER.

Builder:　　　　Ch. de Saint-Quentin, Nantes.
Displacement:　130 tons.
Machinery:　　1 boiler; reciprocating engine, 1 screw; IHP 200.

NOTES
Only the first four named were completed.

Aussiere class – fourteen ships

CAPELAGE, COSSE, DROSSE (all launched 1917), AUSSIERE, BATAYOLLE (both 1918), RIDOIR (1919), BOSSE, BOUT-DEHORS, CABILLOT, CALEBAS, CALIORNE, FAUX-BRAS, GRELIN, TOULINE.

Builder:　　　　Barreras—Vigo, Spain.
Displacement:　43 to 66 tons.
Length:　　　　From 20 to 29m.
Machinery:　　Reciprocating, 1 screw; IHP 120 to 150; speed 10 knots.
Armament:　　1 light gun.

NOTES
These small trawlers were ordered in 1917 and unlisted in 1919; CAPELAGE was renamed ELLE in 1923.

Loup class – four ships

LOUP, MARCASSIN, RENARD I, SANGLIER.

Builder:	Ch. de la Méditerranée, La Seyne.
Displacement:	285 tons.
Machinery:	1 Belleville boiler from uncompleted battleship FLANDRE; reciprocating engine, 1 screw; IHP 600; speed 10 knots.
Armament:	1 – 75mm.

NOTES

These were patrol tugs and commissioned in 1917.

RENARD was mined October 19th, 1917 in the Iroise.

SANGLIER was unlisted in 1940; LOUP and MARCASSIN were scuttled at Toulon on November 27th, 1942, the latter being refloated October 6th, 1943 and on July 5th, 1944 bombed and sunk by Allied aircraft at Toulon.

Hippopotame class – four ships

HIPPOPOTAME, RHINOCEROS, MASTODONTE, MAMMOUTH.

Builders:	Penhoët (1st two), Ch. de Normandie (2nd two).
Displacement:	970 tons.
Machinery:	2 d'Allest boilers; reciprocating, 1 screw; IHP 1800; speed 12 knots.
Armament:	2 – 75mm.

NOTES

Patrol tugs completed 1917–19. All served in World War II; MAMMOUTH and MASTODONTE were seized by the British and returned in 1945; RHINOCEROS was captured by the Germans at Bizerta on December 8th, 1942 and bombed and sunk March 25th, 1943 by Allied aircraft at Sousse. HIPPOPOTAME was unlisted 1952.

Pluvier class – fifteen ships

HERON, PIGEON, PINGOUIN II, PINTADE, PLUVIER,
PERDREAU II, TOURTERELLE, VANNEAU II;
CANARI, COLOMBE, COQ, FAISAN, GELINOTTE, PAON,
RAMIER.

Builders:	Ch. de la Loire, Nantes (1st 8).
	Ch. de la Loire, St Nazaire (last 7).
Displacement:	680 to 780 tons.
Machinery:	Reciprocating, 1 screw; IHP 750.

A trawler type patrol boat flown over by an airship.

A patrol boat fitted with a 90mm gun.

Tugs used as patrol boats; all were completed early in 1918.

CANARI unlisted 1919, PLUVIER and VANNEAU II 1920, COLOMBE 1922; COQ unlisted 1919, sold 1920 as SAINT-CHARLES civilian tug and requisitioned 1939–45. She then had 2 – 20mm Oerlikons.

PERDREAU was rammed and sunk August 14th, 1918 by the Italian steamer SALVATORE off Dakar.

PINGOUIN II, PINTADE, FAISAN and RAMIER all seized in July 1940 by the British and returned 1945/46; they were respectively unlisted in 1949, 1945, 1945 and 1949.

TOURTERELLE scuttled November 9th, 1942 at Oran, was raised in 1943 and recommissioned; condemned in 1956.

HERON was scuttled November 27th, 1942 at Oran, raised in 1946, unlisted in 1949.

PAON was taken by the Germans in November 1942 at Toulon and renamed M.7601; she was sunk October 2nd, 1944 at La Spezia by internal explosion.

GELINOTEE was unlisted in 1951.

Aurochs class – four ships

AUROCHS, ELAN, RENNE, ZEBU.

Builder:	Ch. de Bretagne.
Displacement:	290 tons.
Machinery:	1 d'Allest boiler from old battleships CARNOT and CHARLES MARTEL; reciprocating engine, 1 screw; IHP 650; speed 10 knots.
Armament:	1 – 90mm, 1 – 47mm.

NOTES

Tugs used as patrol vessels. All were completed before 1918 and were in commission at the outbreak of World War II.

ELAN, renamed ELAN II, was seized by the British in July 1940, and used as a barrage balloon vessel then as a target tug; she was returned 1945.

RENNE was sunk February 7th, 1943 by Allied air attack at Lorient.

ZEBU foundered June 12th, 1940 off Le Havre.

AUROCHS was captured in June 1940 by the Germans; recovered 1945 and unlisted 1949.

Clameur class – six ships

CLAMEUR, FRACAS, VACARME, TAPAGE, TINTAMARRE, TUMULTE.

Builders:	Ch. de la Ciotat (1st 3), Ch. de la Gironde (2nd 3).
Displacement:	370 tons.

Machinery:	2 cylindrical boilers; 2 sets reciprocating, 1 screw; IHP 720; speed 12 knots.
Armament:	1 – 90mm army gun.

NOTES

Tugs used as patrol boats, completed after the armistice.

CLAMEUR was unlisted in 1940, TAPAGE in 1925, TINTAMARRE in 1931.

FRACAS disarmed at Bizerta was taken by the Germans and possibly scuttled in the same area in May 1943.

TUMULTE was bombed by German aircraft at Dunkirk May 21st, 1940.

VACARME foundered August 6th, 1942 off the Zafarrina Islands

Athlete class – three ships

ATHLETE, GLADIATEUR V, LUTTEUR.

Builder:	Brest DY.
Displacement:	585 tons.
Machinery:	1 Belleville boiler from uncompleted FLANDRE; 2 Sisson steam engines; IHP 500; speed 12 knots.
Armament:	2 – 120mm.

NOTES

These tugs were completed 1918–19.

GLADIATEUR V was unlisted in 1920.

LUTTEUR was scuttled June 18th, 1940 at Brest; refloated by the Germans and renamed URSUS (V.1801), she was later lost in circumstances and place unknown.

ATHLETE was also scuttled at Brest on June 18th, 1940.

Crabe class – twelve ships

CRABE, HOMARD, CALMAR, TOURTEAU;
CHENE, HETRE, ORME, PEUPLIER, CEDRE, ERABLE, FRENE, PLATANE.

Builders:	Brest DY (1st 4), Lorient DY (others).
Displacement:	360 to 370 tons.
Machinery:	1 Belleville boiler from DESCARTES; 1 Fraser and Chulmar steam engine, 1 screw; IHP 400; speed 9 to 10 knots.
Armament:	1 – 90mm.

NOTES

All these tugs were completed between 1918 and 1920 and served in World War II.

CRABE, FRENE, PEUPLIER and TOURTEAU were all seized by the

British and used as gate vessels; returned in 1945 except PEUPLIER, sunk April 30th, 1941 at Plymouth, probably bombed.

HOMARD, captured by Germans 1942, was sunk October 2nd, 1944 by Allied A/C at La Spezia.

CALMAR, also captured by the Germans, was bombed July 5th, 1944 and sunk at Toulon.

ERABLE, captured in November 1942 by Germans at Toulon and renamed M.6024, was sunk March 11th, 1944 at the same place by Allied A/C; raised and unlisted in 1963.

ORME was scuttled May 21st, 1940 at Boulogne; raised by Germans, renamed FH.02, she was sunk August 2nd, 1944 by Allied A/C at Le Havre.

CEDRE became a kite-balloon ship.

CHENE was scuttled at Oran November 8th, 1942.

HETRE scrapped in 1946.

Trawlers requisitioned during the war

The armament of these varied according to their size; the smallest generally had one 47mm, the largest one or more 75mm, 90mm or sometimes 100mm guns. Most of them also had A/S equipment.

ADRIEN, ADRIENNE, AFRIQUE II, AGATHE, AIGLON, AILLY, AIGRETTE II, ALBATROS II*, ALCYON II, ALEXANDRA (torpedoed March 8th, 1918), ALEXANDRINE, ALGERIE I, ALICE, ALPRECHT, ALSACE I, AMBROISE-PARE, AMERIQUE (mined March 25th, 1917), ANDRE, ANDRE LOUIS, ANGELE, ACHAQUE, ANGUILLE, ANJOU (mined June 17th, 1917), ARMEN, ASCENSION, ASIE, AUBEPINE, AUNIS, AU REVOIR (torpedoed February 27th, 1916), AUTOMNE, AUTRUCHE; BAMALOU (lost October 4th, 1917), BAR I, BAR II, BERCEUSE, BERNADETTE, BISSON II, BLANC-NEZ (mined October 28th, 1916), BONITE I, BONITE II, BON PASTEUR, BRISE (stranded March 24th, 1917, salved post-war); CACHALOT, CANADA II (lost September 12th, 1915), CANCHE, CARIBOU, CARPE (stranded August 6th, 1918), CECILLE, CHAMPAGNE II, CHARISSON, CHARITE, CHARLES, CHARLOTTE, CHAUVEAU, CONFIANCE, CORDOUAN, CORNE (wrecked October 23rd, 1917), COTENTIN, CRABE IV; DAMIER II, DAUPHIN III, DIEU ET PATRIE, DENISE, DORADE (storeship, lost 1917 and later raised); EDERRA, EDOUARD CORBIERE (torpedoed June 1917), EL HADJ, ELISABETH (mined March 12th, 1917), ELISABETH II, EMBRUN, EMERALD, EMMA I, EMMANUELLA, EMILE ET MARIE, EOLE, EOLE II, ESPERANCE (mined August 17th, 1917), ESTAFETTE (mined April 21st, 1916), ESTEREL, ETOILE DE L'EST, EUGENIE, EUROPE II, EYLAU; FASI, FELIX FAURE, FLAMENT, FLAMME, FLORE AUGUSTINE, FOI, FOURMI, FRANCETTE, FRIEDLAND,

* Awarded the 'Croix de Guerre'.

The patrol boat ALBATROS in 1917.

The 535 tons patrol boat LEGER. Note her two 75mm army guns.

A patrol boat fitted with a 37mm gun.

GABRIELA, GAULOIS II, GINETTE (mined March 20th, 1916),
GLOIRE DE MARIE (lost in collision August 16th, 1918), GOELAND I
(lost January 4th, 1918), GOELAND III, GRAZIELLA, GRIS-NEZ
(lost March 9th, 1915); HARDI, HARLE, HENA, HENRIETTE II,
HENRIETTE V; IENA, INES, ILES CHAUSEY (lost in collision
May 22nd, 1916), ISOLE; JEAN, JEAN II, JEAN DORE, JEAN
EDMEE, JEANNE I (lost in collision September 7th, 1917), JEANNE II,
JEANNE ANTOINETTE, JEANETTE, JEANNE D'ARC II,
JEANNE D'ARC III, JEANNOT, JESUS-MARIA (torpedoed
November 1915), JUBARTE, JULES (mined June 23rd, 1917),
JUPITER I (mined July 10th, 1917), JUPITER II; KERBIHAN
(mined January 23rd, 1918), KERYADO (torpedoed May 2nd, 1917);
LA BEAUDROIE, LABRADOR, LA COUBRE, LAITA,
LA MANCHE II, LA SLACQ, LEGER, LIANE, LIBERTE,
LICORNE II, LILLOIS, LOUISE-MARGUERITE,
LOUISE-MARIE; MADELEINE, MARGOT, MARGUERITE II,
MARGUERITE IV, MARGUERITE V, MARGUERITE-MARIE,
MARGUERITE-MARIE II, MARIE (mined February 24th, 1915),
MARIE I, MARIE-FREDERIQUE (mined May 16th, 1918*),
MARIE-LOUISE I, MARIE-ROSE I, MARIE-ROSE II, MARIS-
STELLA, MARIE-THERESE (lost April 17th, 1917, mined?), MAROC,

* Posthumously awarded the 'Croix de Guerre'.

MARRAKCHI, MARS, MARSOUIN, MARTE ET SOLANGE, MAUMUSSON (to Italian Navy May 25th, 1915 – MONSONE; mined February 25th, 1916), MAURITANIE, MEKNASSI, MIRA, MORSE, MONREVEL, MONTAIGNE (sunk October 27th, 1916 by 5 German destroyers), MONTESQUIEU, MOUETTE II, MOUETTE III; NELLY, NEPTUNE II, NOELLA (mined February 7th, 1917), NORD CAPER (boarded and captured Turkish schooner 1916; awarded Croix de Guerre), NORMANDIE, NOTRE-DAME DES DUNES, NOTRE-DAME DE LOURDES I, NOTRE-DAME DE LOURDES II, NOTRE-DAME DE LA MER, NOTRE-DAME DE LA SALETTE; OCEAN, ONAGRE, PARIS II (sunk October 13th, 1917 by Turkish shore batteries*); PETREL, PETREL II, PICARDIE, PRECURSEUR, PRINTEMPS (wrecked May 1st, 1917), PROVIDENCE (lost in collision September 2nd, 1916), PROVENCE IV, RAILEUR, RASCASSE, RELIANCE, REQUIN II, RESURRECTION, RICHELIEU, ROCHEBONNE, ROLLON, ROMA, RORQUAL, ROSEMONDE, ROSITA, SAINT ANDRE II, SAINT HERVE, SAINT HUBERT (mined October 30th, 1916), SAINT JACQUES (mined June 19th, 1916), SAINT JEAN, SAINT JEAN II (lost March 22nd, 1918), SAINT JEAN BAPTISTE DE LA SALLE, SAINT JOACHIM, SAINTE CECILLE, SAINTE JEHANNE, SAINT LOUIS II, SAINT LOUIS III (mined March 31st, 1917), SAINT LOUIS IV (lost in collision August 28th, 1916), SAINT MATHIEU (lost January 1st, 1918), SAINT PIERRE I (torpedoed on September 25th, 1915), SAINT PIERRE II, SAINT PIERRE III (lost in collision January 14th, 1917), SAINT WANDRILLE, SAINTONGE, SALAMBO (torpedoed April 19th, 1918), SATURNE, SAVOIE II, SEMPER, SENTINELLE, SHAMROCK II, SIRIUS, SOLE, SOMME II, STELLA (mined October 4th, 1917)*, STELLAMARIS, SURMULET (see *French Warships of World War II*, p. 121), SUZANNE CELINE, SUZANNE MARIE, SUZE, SUZE MARIE, TAROUDANT, TARTARIN, TURBOT, VAUBAN, VEGA, VENSUS, VENUS III, VERDON, VICTOR ET MARIE, VILLE DE WAGRAM, WALKYRIE, WIMEREUX, YVONNE.

* Posthumously awarded the 'Croix de Guerre'.

Trawlers etc purchased abroad during the war (in parentheses: former names and tonnage)

The armament varied between one or two 75mm, 90mm or 100mm guns in larger vessels and one 47mm in smaller craft. Most of them also had A/S equipment.

Eight purchased in Belgium 1916-17

BECASSE, BÉCASSINE, CAILLE, CIGOGNE, COUCOU, ROUGE GORGE (ex-*B.9*, *B.15*, *B.8*, *B.16*, *B.62*, *B.61* respectively; all 40 tons) GRILLON (ex-*Walcheren*, 180), GUEPE (ex-*Lloyd*, 637).

Four purchased in Brazil 1916-17

GIRAFE (ex-*Palomita*, 150), KANGOUROO (ex-*Almerante*, 160), LION (ex-*Ernestina*, 270), PANTHÈRE (ex-*Ruth*, 115).

Twenty-three purchased in Great Britain

BERNICLE (ex-*Norseman*, 422), BOA (ex-*Titania*, 108), BUSE (ex-*Stirling Hill*, 50) (stranded March 24th, 1917), COCCINELLE (ex-*Yostel*, 227), CORNEILLE (ex-*Medea*, 112), CHARDONNERET (ex-*Kerpion*, 152), COURAGEUX (ex-*Bramley More*), CROTALE (ex-*Ulna*, 156), CYPRIEN (ex-*Winifred*, 135), ELIANE (ex-*Norian*, 62), GOBIE (ex-*Nita*, 73), GRIVE (ex-*Skeandlan*, 110), HIBOU (ex-*Cherfol*), JOYEUSE (ex-*Joyeuse*, 267), LEVRIER (ex-*Chrysalis*, 165), LUCIOLE (ex-*Lady Sophia*, 300), MERLE (ex-*Vola*, 172) (lost after collision February 1st, 1918), MILAN (ex-*Sirocco*, 121), PALOURDE II (ex-*Belindra*, 225), PHALENE (ex-*Stratherrick*, 186), PHOENIX (ex-*Garland*, 234), VIGOUREUX (ex-*Gladston*), (ex-*Cestria*).

Eight purchased in Greece 1917

ALOUETTE (ex-*Ithaca*, 220), AMIRAL DE RIGNY (ex-*Amphitritis*), BENGALI (ex-*Evan Gelistria*, 200), COLIBRI (ex-*Volga*), ELEPHANT (ex-*Maria Grech*, 286) (torpedoed January 31st, 1918), FAUVETTE (ex-*Chrysalis*), LINOTTE (ex-*Alkyon*), MESANGE (ex-*Praxi*, 150).

Ten purchased in Iceland 1917

CHIMPANZÉ (ex-*Thorsf Ingolf*), GIBBON (ex-*Baldur*), GORILLE (ex-*Egert Olafson*), GUENON (ex-*Earl Mereford*), MAKI (ex-*Jarlinn*), ORANG-OUTANG (ex-*Thor*), OUISTITI (ex-*Bragi*), SAJOU (ex-*Mai*), SAPAJOU (ex-*Avril*), SINGE (ex-*Ing-Anarson*). All these were of 600 tons and fitted as minesweepers.

One purchased in Italy 1915

GASPARE (ex-*Tirreno*, 358) (wrecked March 19th, 1915, probably with civilian crew)

Thirty-four purchased in Japan 1916

ANEMONE (ex-*Giusiu Maru*, 200), AZALEE (ex-*Tenyo Maru*, 200), BALSAMINE (ex-*Swai Maru*, 196), BEGONIA (ex-*Ottawa Maru*, 200), BLEUET (ex-*Shinkoku Maru*, 200), CAPUCINE (ex-*Yebisu Maru*, 209), CHRYSANTHEME (ex-*Jakai Maru*, 220), COQUELICOT (ex-*Hakuta Maru*, 215), CYCLAMEN (ex-*Sambo Maru*, 215), DAHLIA (ex-*Yayoi Maru*, 157), FOUGERE (ex-*Korijo Maru*), FUCHSIA (ex-*Yeiryo Maru*, 215), GERANIUM (ex-*Daichi Maru*, 185), GIROFLEE (ex-*Nagato Maru*, 140), GLAIEUL (ex-*Sachi Maru*, 199), GLYCINE (ex-*Yebisu Maru*, 140), HELIOTROPE (ex-*Serwo Maru*, 215), HORTENSIA (ex-*Hatsuhara Maru*, 200), IRIS (ex-*Chidore Maru*, 200), LISERON (ex-*Yebisu Maru*, 195), LOTUS (ex-*Simoneski Maru*, 200), MIMOSA (ex-*Mandai Maru*, 180), NARCISSE (ex-*Khaumion II Maru*, 200), ORCHIDEE (ex-*Khaumion I Maru*, 185), PAVOT (ex-*Kychyo Maru*, 220) (mined November 6th, 1918), PENSEE (ex-*Hinode Maru*, 380), PERVENCHE (ex-*Fukukaku Maru*, 200) (lost February 13th, 1919), PETUNIA (ex-*Iokiwa Maru*, 183), PIVOINE (ex-*Harada Maru*, 233), PRIMEVERE (ex-*Tamahime Maru*, 200), SERPOLLET (ex-*Yeki Maru*, 250), TUBEREUSE (ex-*Shinko Maru*, 212) (mined December 6th, 1917), VERVEINE (ex-*Yebisu Maru*, 195), VOLUBILIS (ex-*Rikoku Maru*, 240).

Eleven purchased in the Netherlands 1916

BELETTE (ex-*Holland*, 180), CHACAL (ex-*Admiral van Batz*, 350), DANAE (ex-*Jeannic*), FOUINE (ex-*Groningen*, 180), HANNETON (ex-*Greta*), HYENE (ex-*Val Duchene*, 115), JASON (ex-*Frederika*), MEDEE (ex-*Delfzyl*), NIOBE (ex-*Concordia*), PAPILLON II (ex-*Vesta*), PHEBUS (ex-*Edison*).

Forty-three purchased in Norway

ALOSE (ex-*Goukana*, 138) (mined October 6th, 1915), AMBITIEUX (ex-*Whangaroo*, 117), ANTILOPE (ex-*Egeland*, 250), BICHE (ex-*Fell*, 146), BOUVREUIL (ex-*Funding*, 100), BOULEDOGUE (ex-*Klem*, 150),

The patrol boats COQUELICOT and DATURA. The COQUELICOT is armed with a 75mm army gun.

CAMELEON (ex-*Eagle*) (mined May 4th, 1917), CAPRICORNE
(ex-*Busta*, 115), CHIMERE (ex-*Larsen*, 150), CIGALE (ex-*Horta*, 110),
CONDOR (ex-*Rusheen*, 117), CONGRE (ex-*Formosa*, 137),
COULEUVRE (ex-*Dean Peregrine*, 180), CRIQUET (ex-*Svend*, 107),
CYGNE (ex-*Lingao*, 116), DAUPHIN (ex-*Kuysna*, 138), DRAGON
(ex-*Sir Liege*, 181), ENGAGEANTE (ex-*Vilna*, 117) (lost in collision
February 5th, 1918), FANTASQUE (ex-*Diaz*, 106) (lost August 22nd,
1916), GAZELLE (ex-*Apsmith*) (lost March 8th, 1918), INDISCRET
(ex-*Frithjof*, 125), JAGUAR (ex-*Norrana*, 116), LEOPARD (ex-*Niall*,
150), LEZARD (ex-*Hawk*), PAPILLON (ex-*Powell*, 171), PELICAN
(ex-*Dore*, 138), PERDREAU (ex-*Peregrine*, 180), PERRUCHE (ex-
Palmer, 111), RAIE (ex-*Zitzckama*, 137), ROITELET (ex-*Hawken*, 112),
ROUGET (ex-*Plettemberg*, 115), SAGITTAIRE (ex-*Crozet*, 150),
SALAMANDRE (ex-*Heard*, 162), SARDINE (ex-*Briton*, 116)
(capsized May 27th, 1915), SAUTERELLE (ex-*Durbane*, 131),
SCARABEE (ex-*Carmen*, 106), SCORPION (ex-*Saldana*, 130),
SERPENT (ex-*K.D.J.*, 98), TAUREAU (ex-*Fynd*, 150), TIGRE
(ex-*Nordebale*, 105); also ex-*Kolter* (lost), ex-*Hwalen* and ex-*Thekla*, both
transferred to the Russians.

Three purchased in Sweden 1916-17

LYNX (ex-*Swona*, 226), PERDRIX (ex-*Sole*, 326), ROSSIGNOL
(ex-*Odin*, 351).

Ninety-eight purchased in Spain

BRAVE (ex-*Maria del Carmen*, 250), FIER (ex-*San Rafael*, 237), HARDI
(ex-*San Jose*, 250), RUSE (ex-*Dragon*, 174), SEDUISANT (ex-*Finisterre*,
265), VALEUREUX (ex-*San Miguel*, 212) (all purchased in 1915).
AIGLE (ex-*Bash*, 156), ALOSE (ex-*Rodeiro*, 40), ASPIC (ex-*Lucas*, 234)
burnt December 18th, 1918), BLAIREAU (ex-*Uruguay*, 49), BONITE
(ex-*Foruna*, 50), CARTHAGINOIS (ex-*Manuel Maria*), CERF (ex-
Carmen), COBRA (ex-*Grancanaria*, 150), CREVETTE (ex-*Mugardos*, 40),
DAIM (ex-*Jubia*), ECUREIL (ex-*Beloval*, 180), EPERLAN (ex-*Olga*),
EPERVIER (ex-*Franconia*, 154), ESTURGEON (ex-*Balea*, 40),
FAUCON (ex-*Dalmacia*, 155), FOURMI (ex-*Arcadia*, 155), FRELON
(ex-*Bohemia*, 155), FURET (ex-*Robin*, 134), GRONDIN (ex-*Joachim
Costa*, 52), HARENG (ex-*Cajal*, 52), HERMINE (ex-*Aragons*, 40),
HERON (ex-*Anita*, 187), LOUTRE (ex-*Lerroux*, 40), MARTRE (ex-
Soriano, 40), MEDUSE (ex-*Torremolinos*, 49), MERLAN (ex-*Doncella*,
30), OEILLET (ex-*Carmen*, 158), OTARIE (ex-*K. Lele*, 80), OURSIN
(ex-*Torrox*, 47), PIERROT (ex-*Union IV*, 69), PIEUVRE (ex-*Sagosta*,
70), PINSON (ex-*Union III*, 60), PLIE (ex-*Helios*, 37), PLONGEON
(ex-*Jose Castro*, 40), PUTOIS (ex-*Iberia*, 42), SAUMON (ex-*Delen*, 40),
THON (ex-*Marconi*, 60), TRUITE (ex-*Saltillo*, 40), VAUTOUR
(ex-*Onuba*, 152), VIEILLE (ex-*Javier*, 37), VIPERE (ex-*Gijon Musel*, 55),

The patrol boat PINSON (to right) and OTARIE.

ZIBELINE (ex-*Maria Christina*, 40) (all purchased in 1916).
AMURE (ex-*Carmen*, 22), ARTIMON (ex-*Asturias*, 50), BARRA-QUETTE (ex-*Conchita*, 30), BEAUPRE (ex-*Cinco Hermanos*, 38),
BONETTE (ex-*Ramona*, 49), BOSSOIR (ex-*Maria Rosa*), BOULINE
(ex-*Dolores*, 22), BRAS (ex-*Rogelia*, 50), BRIGANTINE (ex-*Nieva
Marcella*, 46), CABESTAN (ex-*V. Moleton*, 45), CACATOIS (ex-*Luis*,
50), CAPELAN (ex-*Espartero*), CHAUMARD (ex-*Sophia*) (lost in
collision May 15th, 1918), CHOUQUE (ex-*Relanpago* (lost February 6th,
1918), CLIN-FOC (ex-*Jemeny*, 43), CORNE (ex-*Dos Hermanos*) (wrecked
October 23rd, 1917), DRAILLE (ex-*J. Manuel I*, 63), DRISSE (ex-*Rio
Santiago*, 79), ECOUTE (ex-*Emilia*, 22), ECUBIER (ex-*Diamant*),
ELINGUE (ex-*A. Hondo*, 45), ENFLECHURE (ex-*Rodriguez*, 53),
ESTROPE (ex-*Thano*, 53), ETAI (ex-*Alberto III*, 35), ETALINGURE
(ex-*G. Romon*), FLECHE (ex-*Emilia*, 40), FOC (ex-*Angel*, 40),
GALHAUBAN (ex-*Extramadura*, 34), GRENOPE (ex-*Sirius*, 40),
HAUBAN (ex-*Leonor*, 39), HAUMIERE (ex-*Santa Librada*, 48),
HUNIER (ex-*Nieva Providencia*, 43), MISAINE (ex-*Venus*, 41),
MARTINGALE (ex-*Santa Christina*, 30), PERROQUET (ex-*San
Fernando*, 36), SOUS BARBE (ex-*Adolfo*), TAPECUL (ex-*Asuncion*, 40),
TOURNEVIRE (ex-*Clementina*, 43), TRAVERSIERE (ex-*Tres Hermanos*
60), TRINQUETTE (ex-*Napoleon*, 43), VERGUE (ex-*Juan Manuel II*,
31) (all purchased in 1917).
ANNIBAL (ex-*Arana*, 270), BARBUE (ex-*Zenobia*, 145), ETOURNEAU
(ex-*Mamelena VIII*, 155), HEROS (ex-*Seoneber*, 270), LIEVRE (ex-*Maria Gregorio*, 150), PASSEREAU (ex-*Mamelena X*), SARRIGUE
(ex-*H. Capa Paez*, 282), SERIEUX (ex-*Monserrat II*, 190), SEVERE (ex-*Mesirecordia*, 270) (all purchased later).

Thirteen purchased in the USA

APACHE (ex-*Easton*), ATALA (ex-*Susquehanna*), BUFFALO (ex-*Doric*), HURON (ex-*Obcott*), INCA (ex-*Maywood*), IROQUOIS (ex-*Colorado*), LOUP-CERVIER (ex-*Villot*), MOHICAN (ex-*Elm City*),
PEAU-ROUGE (ex-*Emerson*), RENARD BLEU (ex-*Henlopen*), RENE
(ex-*Racine*), SIOUX (ex-*United Shores*), SEMINOLE (ex-*Cape Ann*).

Eight purchased elsewhere

ALSACE II, CAROLINE V, CROCODILE (ex-*Whale*, 300 GRT),
EURVIN, MONTE DE ORO, PIE (ex-*Rodriguez*, 32 GRT), SARCELLE
(ex-*Guillerme*, 120 GRT), TABARKA (ex-*Sea Queen*).

Armed Yachts

In parenthesis – gross tonnage and year built.

ALMEE (80/87), AMPHITRITE II, ANDRE II, ANNETTA (seized in Greece), ARA (870/15) (Captain, Brittany Patrol Division), ARIANE II (630/98) (Flagship of R. Admiral Commanding Syria Division 1917–18), ATMAH (1746/98) (Flagship of R. Admiral Commanding Aegean Patrol Force), BACCHANTE (973/91) (Flagship of R. Admiral Commanding S France Patrol), BEG-HIR (121/92), BERTHIC (34/02), BUTTERFLY (20/12), CAROLINE V (311/10), CECILE, CHIMERE II (37/90), DALGUA, DIANA (815/96) (1400 tons, 10 knots, 2 – 75mm army guns; acquired 1918, Levant Station 1919–33, unlisted 1935), EROS (1020/05) (Senior Officer Tunisian Patrol Force 1917–18; in service in World War II, renamed INCOMPRISE II on November 27th, 1942; scuttled at Toulon, raised by Germans, renamed UJ.2216; torpedoed September 14th, 1944), FILLE SAUVAGE, FORT DE FRANCE, GREBE III, HELENE (538/01) (Senior Officer Aegean Patrol Force 1917–18), HENRIETTE I (89/10), ISIS, JEANNE BLANCHE (see Dispatch Vessels), KENER, LINOTTE II (90/88), MAGDA (58/96), MARGARET ELISABETH, MONIQUE, MYOTTE II, NELLY II (40/13), NOCHETTE (20/04), ONDINE II, ORB (147/78), ORPHEE (181/87), ORVET, POUPEE (326/86) (Senior Officer Dardanelles Sweeping Force 1915), PRINCESS HELENE (Greek), RENARD (ex-*New Crown*, 285 GRT), RESOLUE (840 GRT/10), RIVOLI, ROLAND, SAMARA (108/93), SAMVA (222/99), SIMONE, VONNA (144/14), WILDWAVE (128/89).

The armed yacht DIANA.

Submarine Chasers (Chasseurs)

C.1 to C.100 – 100 boats

In 1917 the French Navy purchased 50 subchasers from the US Navy and in 1918 a further 50. The first boat was delivered in July 1917 and the last in October 1918. They crossed the Atlantic under their own power, under escort of patrol boats, via Bermuda and the Azores, a notable achievement because of their small size and poor sea-keeping capabilities.

Being hurriedly constructed, most of them lasted for only a short time in service; at the outbreak of World War II only eight were in commission—C.25, 51, 56, 58, 74, 81, 95 and 98. (See *French Warships of World War II* p. 110.)

Displacement:	60 tons (75 full load) (wooden hull).
Dimensions:	35·55m(oa), 32m(pp) × 4·70m × 2·30m.
Machinery:	Petrol motors, 3 screws; BHP 660; speed 15·5 knots.
Armament:	1 – 75mm army gun, 1 – 'Y' depthcharge thrower.
Complement:	19.

NOTES

C.2 was bombed in September 1914 by German A/C in Dunkirk harbour; probably the first French warship to be so sunk.

C.43 was lost by fire on June 2nd, 1918 at Dunkirk.

A third of this type (ex-American SC.141) was lost with all hands in the Atlantic on passage to France; her French number is not known.

The subchaser C.67.

The subchaser 72. Note her forward 75mm army gun.

C.101 to C.117 – seventeen boats (37 ordered)

Builders:	Normand, Le Havre (8 boats); La Loire, Nantes (10 boats); Dubigeon, Nantes (7 boats); Lorient DY (8 boats); Dyle et Bacaclan, Bordeaux (4 boats).
Displacement:	128 tons (150 full load).
Dimensions:	43·40m(oa), 41·40(pp) × 5·24m × 2·40m.
Machinery:	2 small-tube Normand or du Temple boilers; reciprocating engine, 2 screws; IHP 1300; speed 16·5 knots.
Armament:	1 – 75mm army gun, 1 – MG, 8 depthcharges (75 kilos), 1 Pinocchio apparatus.
Complement:	31.

NOTES

Ordered in March and April 1918, By September 1918 their construction had hardly started and by the end of the year twenty had been cancelled; the others (Le Havre and Nantes boats) were completed in 1919–20.

They were of steel construction and steam driven with the funnels set to port and starboard of the centre line. All had the 'C' prefix altered to 'Ch' after the war.

Only four of this class (C.106, 107) and CDT BOURDAIS (ex-C.111) and AVALANCHE (ex-C.112) and fitted for service in the Far East, were in commission in 1939.

Motor Boats

Rated as Vedettes a Moteur

After having made a study of several ASW-boat designs, the French Navy finally purchased the following 73 boats. By 1925 only two were still in commission.

V.1 to V.40 – forty boats

These had been ordered originally by the Royal Navy from Elco of Bayonne, USA through Vickers of Montreal and were part of the British ML.114-548 series.

Displacement: 40 tons.
Dimensions: 24m × 3·80m × 1·05m.
Machinery: 2 standard petrol motors; BHP 440; speed 20 knots (max).
Armament: 1 – 75mm army gun, 1 or 2 – MG, 1 'Y' thrower, 1 – 'C' tube ASW system.

NOTES
The first four (V.1–4) arrived at Cherbourg in May 1916 and joined the Dunkirk Torpedo Flotilla. The fate of V.4 is not known, but the other three took part in Channel patrols until the end of the war; later, via Paris and Strasbourg they joined the Rhine Flotilla.

V.5–12 were based at Corfu for the Otranto Patrol.

V.13–28 were assigned to patrol divisions in Algeria and Tunisia; V.2 grounded on August 23rd, 1917 near Cape Bougaroni.

V.32–5 joined the Dunkirk Flotilla and later went to the Rhine.

V.36–40 operated off the coast between Le Verdon and La Rochelle; V.3 was lost November 24th, 1917 by explosion at Les Sables D'Olonne. V.3 and V.39 also joined the Rhine Flotilla in 1919–20.

V.41 to V.53 – thirteen boats

Displacement: 40 tons (wooden hull).
Dimensions: 25m × 3·70m × 1·05m.
Machinery: 2 Panhard petrol motors; speed 20 knots (max).
Armament: 1 – 75mm army gun, 1 or 2 – MG, 1 'Y' thrower, 1 – 'C' tube ASW system.

NOTES
Designed by M. Despujols and ordered from his yard at Neuilly near Paris to be delivered between November 1916 and March 1917.

Due to engine difficulties, the first four boats of this type were not ready

The motor boat V.29 and two floatplanes.

The subchaser C.11 and the motor boats V.32, V.39, and V.64 moored in the Rhine River in a German city after the war.

until September 1917 when they joined the Biscay Patrol Division. They were based at Bayonne in May 1918 while the following six were assigned to the 2nd Patrol Squadron at Dunkirk. The three remaining boats were cancelled. All were paid off in November 1919.

V.54 to V.61 – eight boats

Displacement: 40 tons.
Dimensions: 26·50m × 4m × 1·30m.
Machinery: 2 American Wolverine petrol motors; BHP 360; designed
                   speed 16·5 knots (14·5 only in service).

NOTES
Ordered in August 1916 from the Gustave Cornilleau yard near Marseilles. The first boat was delivered in January and the last in June 1917; they were assigned to the patrol divisions of Provence, except two (V.54 and V.55) which joined the naval air stations of Saint-Raphael and Port-Vendres respectively.

V.62 to V.73 – twelve boats

Displacement: 41 tons.
Dimensions: 23·40m × 3·77m.
Speed: 19 knots.

NOTES
Built by Vickers, Montreal to be delivered in May 1918, but because of delayed trials the first four were not in service until two days after the armistice when they arrived at Le Havre. They were on the Channel patrol and later, V.69 and V.71 went to the Rhine.

Q Ships

The following were fitted out as submarine decoy vessels:

FRANCIS MARIE (fishing ketch), HIRONDELLE IV (motor schooner), JEANNE D'ARC VII (see Armed Ketches), JEANNE ET GENEVIEVE (see Storeships), JEAN D'UST (3-masted schooner, 210 GRT; stranded November 16th, 1917 on the beach at Philippeville, Algeria; raised February 22nd, 1918 and repaired), KLEBER (schooner), MADELEINE III (motor schooner, 145 GRT; torpedoed and sunk April 7th, 1918 by UB.50 north of Bizerta), MARGUERITE VI (see Storeships), MEG 1 (Armed whaler on loan from the Royal Navy 1916), MEG, MICHEL ET RENEE, NORMANDY (3-masted schooner, 700 GRT purchased in the USA; 4 – 75mm army guns, 2 machine guns; June 26th, 1917 in action with the German UC.71 in the Channel; renamed JEAN then paid off), TROPIQUE (see Armed Ketches), VENUS II (235 GRT, built 1908; mined and sunk January 1st, 1917).

The Q ship KLEBER. She was awarded the 'Croix de Guerre' pennant.

Below: **The Q ship MARGUERITTE VI.**

Foot: **The Q ship MEG.**

Armed Fishing Ketches

In parentheses – gross tonnage/year built and armament.

AMI DE DIEU (45/06, 1 – 65mm, 1 tube) (lost September 2nd, 1918),
ANDRE III (38/06, 1 – 47mm), ARMIDE II (40/12, 1 – 47mm),
AVENIR (59/06, 1 – 75mm), BARON DAVILLIERS (1 – 47mm),
BERCEAU DE L'OCEAN (56/14, 1 – 47mm), BIENHEUREUX
MICHEL NOBLETZ (106/13, 1 – 65mm), CALYPSO (59/14, 1 – 47mm),
CLEMENTINE (34/06, 1 – 47mm), COMMANDANT DANYCAN
(60/14, 1 – 47mm), DIAMANT (37/08, 1 – 47mm), GENERAL
LYAUTEY (102/13, 1 – 65mm, 1 – tube), HYACINTHE-YVONNE
(43/07, 1 – 47mm) (lost March 18th, 1917), KENAVO (22/07, 1 – 47mm),
JEANNE D'ARC VII, JEANNE-EUGENIE (57/14, 1 – 47mm),
JEANNE-MARIE (1 – 47mm), PALOURDE (1 – 47mm), LION II
(38/08, 1 – 47mm), RÉDEMPTEUR (63/13, 1 – 47mm), ROSSIGNOL
(1 – 47mm), SAINT-BARTHELEMY (33/97, 1 – 47mm), TROPIQUE
(102/13, 1 – 47mm), VILLARET DE JOYEUSE (30/98, 1 – 47mm).

River Gunboats

Doudart de Lagrée – one ship

Displacement:	183 tons.
Dimensions:	54·40m(oa), 52·30m(pp) × 6·70m × 1m.
Machinery:	2 boilers; reciprocating, 2 screws; IHP 900; speed 14 knots.
Armament:	1 – 75mm army, 2 – 37mm, 4 – MG (from 1917), 6 – 37mm (originally).
Complement:	4 officers, 55 crew (+7 Chinese).

NAME	BUILDER	LAUNCHED	COMPLETED
DOUDART DE LAGREE	A. et Ch. de Bretagne, Nantes	5.1.09	4.2.09

NOTES
Ordered March 11th, 1908 for China service and similar to BALNY but
with one funnel in place of two. 1917–18 in the Far East; laid up at Shanghai
in 1939 and scrapped in 1941.

The river gunboat LA BRUTALE of the first type.

Two river gunboats moored in a canal near the front.

Balny – one ship

Displacement: 201 tons (226 full load).
Machinery: 2 Fouché water-tube boilers; reciprocating, 2 screws;
IHP 900; speed 14 knots. Coal 27 tons.
Armament: 1 – 75mm, 2 – 37mm, 4 – 8mm MG.
Complement: 4 officers, 55 crew.

NAME	BUILDER	LAUNCHED	COMPLETED
BALNY	Ch. de Bretagne, Nantes	6.14	1920

NOTES
Work was delayed between 1914 and 1918, one of her engines being trans-
ferred to the Q-ship MEG. She was again in service at the outbreak of
World War II but was laid up at Chungking 1940 and scrapped in 1944.

Vigilante class – two ships

Displacement: 130 tons.
Machinery: Reciprocating, 1 screw; IHP 1150; speed 13 knots.
Armament: 2 – 90mm, 4 – 37mm.
Complement: 2 officers, 51 crew.

NAME	BUILDER	LAID DOWN	LAUNCHED	COMPLETED
ARGUS	Thornycroft	1899	1900	1900
VIGILANTE	Thornycroft	1899	1900	1900

NOTES
Built for use in Indochina and both in the Far East 1914–18.

Pei-Ho – one ship

Displacement: 123 tons.
Machinery: Reciprocating, 1 screw; IHP 1150; speed 13 knots.
Armament: 2 – 90mm, 4 – 37mm.
Complement: 2 officers, 51 crew.

NAME	LAUNCHED	COMPLETED
PEI-HO	1901	1901

NOTES
Ex-LIEUTENANT CONTAL renamed in 1905 for use in Indochina.
She was in the Far East 1914–18 and unlisted 1922.

Gunboats for French rivers

These were built during the war for service with the army in France. Their construction was decided upon in 1915 and three types were designed by naval constructors of which two were retained; one fitted with a 138·6mm and the other with two 100mm guns. Officially designated by letters (A, B, C etc) but given names by their ships' companies (ARDENTE, BRUTALE, CRUELLE, DECIDEE, etc).

Eight of the first type were ordered in May 1915 from the naval dockyards of Brest and Lorient and delivered in July. Four of the second type were built by the same yards between July 1915 and September 1915. Gunboat 'C' was sunk on July 16th, 1916 by a 150mm shell on the Somme but soon raised and repaired. Two others were lost on October 4th, 1918 in bad weather while on tow to Cherbourg.

First type:

Displacement:	110 tons.
Dimensions:	28·50m × 5m × 1·20m.
Machinery:	Reciprocating; speed 9 knots.
Protection:	Guns, magazine and machinery protected by 20mm plating.
Armament:	1 – 138·6mm 1893 model, 2 – 47mm AA guns.

Second type:

Displacement:	180 tons.
Machinery:	1 boiler; reciprocating; speed 10 knots.
Armament:	2 – 100mm, 2 – 47mm AA guns.

NOTES

The first 'battery' of gunboats fired the following shots:

In Belgium (June 1915 to March 1916) 1450 rounds of 138·6mm, 3000 of 47mm;

In the Somme (March 1916 to January 1917) 11,300 rounds of 138.6mm;

In the Oise (January 1917 to March 1917) 300 rounds;

In Champagne (April 1917 to July 1917) 3855 rounds;

In Belgium (July 1917 to December 1917) 3855 rounds.

The second 'battery' fired the following:

In Champagne (July 1915 to March 1916) 5680 rounds of 138·6mm;

On the Oise and Aisne rivers (March 1916 to July 1917) 2730 rounds of 138·6mm and 1961 rounds of 47mm.

In Belgium (July 1917 to November 1917) 2740 rounds of 138·6mm and 2785 of 100mm.

The third 'battery' remained in Champagne from September 1915 to September 1917 then operated on the River Aisne region of Vailly from October 1917 to November 1917. It fired:

3272 rounds of 138·6mm and 8076 of 100mm in Champagne;

2563 rounds of 138·6mm and 3806 of 100mm on the Aisne.

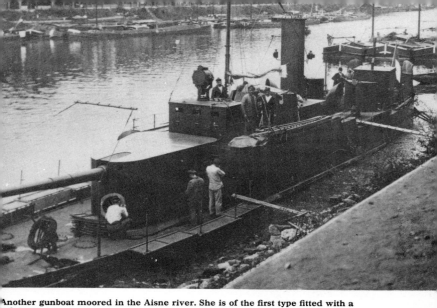

Another gunboat moored in the Aisne river. She is of the first type fitted with a c38·6mm gun.

Details of a river gunboat of the second type showing her forward 100mm gun.

The canal boat SAVERNE fitted with a 240mm gun.

A total of 40,524 rounds of 138·6mm and 16,628 of 100mm were from July 1915 to the end of November 1917, fired at the enemy by these gunboats.

They were put out of commission at the end of 1917; however, four gunboats of the first type ('C', 'G', 'H' and 'I') were recommissioned in November 1918 and December 1918 for the Rhine Flotilla and renamed AISNE, MARNE, OISE and SOMME with modified armament to include 75mm army guns only.

Armed Canal Boats

These were used by the French army though manned by the navy and operated on canals around Verdun, in Champagne and in Flanders.

The first two boats were requisitioned in 1914 for use along canals and the River Meuse near Verdun, between the locks of Croix-sur-Meuse and Samogneux; these two each had a 138·6mm gun, removed in January 1916. Two others were requisitioned in 1915 but not armed.

Two boats (ALSACE-LORRAINE and JEAN GOUIN) were scuttled in February 1916 during the German offensive on Verdun. One 138·6mm gun was in July 1916 remounted on a barge which however was not used.

Two barges were requisitioned at the end of 1914, each with a 164·7mm gun; one operated on the canal between the Marne and the Rhine and later between the Aisne and Marne, taking part in the 1915 Champagne offensive; she was disarmed in October 1915. A second boat worked in May and June 1915 around Loe on the Belgian canal, firing at the 380mm long-range enemy gun of Clerken which was shelling Dunkirk; she also was put out of commission in 1915.

In 1916, the use of canal boats fitted with 1870–93 models of 194 and 240mm was proposed to the Army High Command; consequently the barge MARCELLE was given a 194mm gun and operated in Champagne along the Marne/Aisne canal. A second boat, named JEANNE D'ARC took part in these operations. In June 1917 a third barge (SAVERNE) was requisitioned and armed with a 240mm gun; she fired her first shot on September 8th. These three boats formed in January 1918, the 5th Group of *canonniers marins* which took part in operations until the end of the war, mainly in the Aisne and Oise rivers. On June 12th, 1918 the MARCELLE was hit by a heavy shell and put out of action. A new barge named MARCELLE II soon replaced her and with her sisters, took part in the brilliant offensive of the 4th Army (General Gouraud).

On October 8th, 1918 the 5th Group left the Champagne for the Rhine canal and arrived at Lanauville-sur-Nancy on the day after the armistice; later it joined the Rhine Flotilla.

Submarine Depot Ships

Tourville – one ship

Displacement: 5445 tons.
Dimensions: 105m × 15m × 6·70m.
Machinery: Reciprocating; IHP 2700; speed 14 knots. Coal 806 tons.

NAME	BUILDER	LAID DOWN	LAUNCHED	COMPLETED
TOURVILLE (ex-Gironde)	Bordeaux	1880	1884	1885

NOTES
Ex-GIRONDE renamed 1909; gunnery school 1909–14; depot ship for submarines based on Malta 1915–16; depot ship at Corfu 1917–18; renamed RHIN 1924; gunnery school 1924–29; reserve officers school 1929–33; signal school 1933–39; disarmed 1939 and abandoned 1942 at Toulon; condemned 1944.

The obsolete battleship MARCEAU was also used as a depot ship for submarines of the Adriatic Division.

The very old battleship MARCEAU fitted as a submarine depot ship.

Oilers, Colliers and Storeships

Rhône – one ship

Displacement: 2781 GRT, 4000 tons dw.
Dimensions: 112·47m(oa) × 13·70m × 7·60m.
Machinery: 2 cylindrical boilers; reciprocating, 1 screw; IHP 2100; speed 11 knots.
Armament: 1 – 100mm.
Complement: 57.

NAME	LAUNCHED	COMPLETED
RHONE (ex-Radioleine)	1910	1911

NOTES
Supply ship for the 'Armée Navale' 1914–18. She was sunk December 19th, 1940 by the German U.37 off Cape Juby.

Garonne – one ship

Displacement: 3533 GRT, 5800 dw.
Dimensions: 120m × 15·40m × 8·30m.
Machinery: 2 cylindrical boilers; reciprocating, 1 screw; IHP 2600; speed 11 knots.
Armament: 2 – 100mm.
Complement: 65

NAME	BUILDER	LAID DOWN	LAUNCHED	COMPLETED
GARONNE (ex-Lucellum)	Sunderland	1912	1913	1913

NOTES
Ex-British LUCELLUM purchased on July 21st, 1913; on loan to the British February 1916 to 1918. She was scuttled at Toulon November 27th, 1942, salved April 21st, 1944 and expended as blockship there on June 20th, 1944.

Dordogne – one ship

Displacement: 7333 tons, 12,500 dw.
Dimensions: 161·50m × 20·27m × 8·84m.
Machinery: 2 cylindrical boilers; reciprocating, 1 screw; IHP 4100; speed 11 knots.

NAME	BUILDER	LAUNCHED
DORDOGNE	Armstrong,	1914
(ex-San Isidro)	Newcastle	

NOTES
Ex-mercantile, purchased. Was on loan to the British 1917–19, under the name of SILVERSLIP. She was on the disposal list when she was scuttled June 18th, 1940 at Brest.

Var – one ship

Displacement:	5500 tons.
Dimensions:	82m × 11·50m × 6·60m.
Machinery:	4-cylinder reciprocating, 2 screws; IHP 1000; speed 13·5 knots.
Armament:	1 – 76mm, 1 – 47mm.

NAME	BUILDER	LAID DOWN	LAUNCHED	COMPLETED
VAR	Schichau,	1895	1895	1896
(ex-Tsar Nicolas II)	Danzig			

NOTES
Ex-German tanker seized in August 1914 at Bizerta and used until 1929 when she was scrapped.

The ex-German tanker TSAR NICOLAS II.

Aube class – three ships

Displacement: 1055 GRT, 1500 dw.
Dimensions: 74m × 11·58m × 4·80m.
Machinery: 2 boilers; Breguet turbine, 1 screw; SHP 1100; speed
10·5 knots.

NAME	BUILDER	LAUNCHED	COMPLETED
AUBE	Lorient DY	7.1920	1920
DURANCE	Lorient DY	1920	1920
RANCE	Lorient DY	7.1921	1921

NOTES
These three were ordered during the war but not completed until 1920–21.
AUBE, renamed DROME in 1940, was scrapped on January 6th, 1956.
DURANCE was scuttled November 27th, 1942 at Toulon, refloated May
7th, 1943 and scrapped January 6th, 1956. RANCE was scuttled at Toulon
November 27th, 1942, refloated May 30th, 1943 and rescuttled at Marseilles
in August 1944.

Requisitioned oilers – three ships

PROMETHEUS (3000 tons) seized in Greece in December 1916 and
returned in 1918.

KANGUROO (2493 GRT/12): torpedoed and sunk December 3rd, 1916 by
the German U.38 off Funchal.

MOTRICINE (4047 GRT) sunk May 17th, 1918 in a gunfire action with the
German U.55 off Ushant.

Colliers

At the beginning of the war the French Navy requisitioned a great number
of mercantile colliers which it is not possible to list here. Of these, the
following were war losses:

ARTHUR CAPEL (822/10): torpedoed on January 14th, 1918 by the
German UB.80 off Barfleur.

BALAGUIER (2274 GRT): torpedoed March 15th, 1917 by the German
U.70 off Bishops Rock.

BAYONNAISE (2425/11): torpedoed June 7th, 1918 by the German
UC.53 south of Italy.

BRETON (3739/86): torpedoed August 8th, 1917 by the German UC.37
off Tunisia.

BUFFALO (2359 GRT): torpedoed September 18th, 1918 by the German
UB.117 off Trevose Head.

CAP BRETON (1464/12): torpedoed July 14th, 1918 by the German
UB.103 off the Gironde estuary.

CHARLES LE COUR (2352/03): torpedoed March 11th, 1917 by the
German UC.47 off the Cornish coast.

CONSTANCE (2468/13): torpedoed August 23rd, 1917 by the Austrian U.14 off Malta.

MEUSE (4075/14): torpedoed May 15th, 1917 by the German U.48 off the Fastnet.

OLGA (2884/10): torpedoed June 18th, 1916 by the German U.35 off Minorca.

P.L.M.4 (2550 GRT): torpedoed December 27th, 1917 by the German UC.71 off Barfleur.

SOCOA (2772/12): torpedoed August 25th, 1916 by the German U.63 off Pantellaria.

SUZETTE FRAISSINET (2288/92): torpedoed May 11th, 1918 by the German UB.52 south of Sardinia.

SYDNEY (2695/03): sunk by gunfire January 14th, 1917 in action with the German U.48 off the NW coast of Spain.

THERESE ET MARIE (1615/93): sunk August 19th, 1917 by the German UC.21 off Le Croisic, Brittany.

THISBE (1091/10): torpedoed September 6th, 1917 by the German UB.35 off the Lizard.

TUNISIE (3246/07): torpedoed June 19th, 1917 by the German U.43 off the Fastnet; no survivors.

Storeships

The following are a few of the many storeships used during the war:

Drome – one ship

Tonnage: 3236 GRT.
Machinery: Reciprocating, 1 screw; speed 11 knots.

NAME	BUILDER	LAID DOWN	LAUNCHED
DROME	Saint Nazire	1885	1887

NOTES
1915: supply ship for the Dardanelles fleet; mined January 1st, 1918 off Marseilles.

Loiret – one ship

Displacement: 2200 tons.
Dimensions: 73m × 9·98m × 5·40m.
Machinery: Reciprocating; IHP 1060; speed 11 knots. Coal 193 tons.
Armament: 1 – 65mm.

LOIRET (ex-Paris): mercantile, purchased in 1900; unlisted 1937.

The LOIRET.

Seine – one ship

Displacement: 3160 tons (5770 full load).
Dimensions: 81·40m × 11·05m × 5·40m.
Machinery: Reciprocating, 1 screw; IHP 1950; speed 12·6 knots.
Coal 285 tons.
Armament: 2 – 100mm, 1 – 47mm.

NAME	LAID DOWN	LAUNCHED	COMPLETED
SEINE	1912	1913	1913

NOTES

1915–16 supply ship, Aegean Flotillas; December 20th, 1932 sprang a leak in heavy seas and foundered in tow December 21st, 1932 off Oleron Island.

Jeanne et Genevieve – one ship

Displacement: 620 tons.
Dimensions: 44·80m × 7·31m × 3·80m.
Machinery: 1 cylindrical boiler; reciprocating, 1 screw; IHP 600;
speed 11 knots.
Armament: 1 – 75mm.

NAME	BUILDER	LAID DOWN	LAUNCHED	COMPLETED
JEANNE ET GENEVIEVE	Nantes	1916	1917	1917

The storeship SEINE.

While in use as a Q-ship, was seriously damaged on August 6th, 1917 in action with the German U.61 off the Gironde; awarded the 'Croix de Guerre'. While at Plymouth in July 1940 she was seized by the British and used as a kite-balloon depot ship. Returned in 1945 and scrapped in May 1948.

Captured or requisitioned vessels

ALESIA (6030/02): ex-German cargo boat PRINZ ADALBERT; torpedoed by the German UC.69 and finished by UC.50 on September 6th, 1917 off Ushant.

BOUVET (936/04): ex-Austrian SALONA seized 1914; sunk September 12th, 1917 in collision with trawler ORQUE in the Mediterranean.

DINORAH (4208/12): ex-Austrian cargo boat captured 1914; torpedoed September 25th, 1917 by the German UC.63 off Penmarks.

JEAN BART II (475/08): torpedoed February 2nd, 1916 by the Austrian U.4 off Durazzo.

LA CHAUSSADE (4494 GRT): ex-Japanese ASAMA MARU purchased in 1917; torpedoed by the German UC.27 north of Tunisia August 13th, 1918.

MEMPHIS (2382/91): ex-mercantile BYZANTION; disabled by mine February 16th, 1916, beached near Durazzo but lost.

MIRA (3050/95): ex-mercantile CAYO BLANCO; sunk May 15th, 1916 by gunfire in action with the German U.34 off Sicily.

RAVITAILLEUR (2813/01): ex-Austrian cargo boat GRADAC captured 1914; sunk September 17th, 1915 by gunfire from the German U.35 off Cape Matapan.

YSER (3545/99): ex-German cargo boat DACIA captured February 27th, 1915 by the auxiliary cruiser EUROPE; used as cable-ship and sunk November 6th, 1915 by gunfire from the German U.38 off Philippeville, Algeria.

MOGHRAB (1087/83): ex-Austrian FLORA seized in 1914; lost August 18th, 1918 by unknown cause in the Aegean.

BERTHILDE (672/87): ex-German coaster seized in Greece in November 1916; torpedoed July 12th, 1917 by the Austrian U.4 south of Italy.

MARGUERITE VI (1440 tons, 9 knots, built 1907): This Danish cargo boat was on charter to a German company and was seized at Rouen in 1914. In 1915 converted to Q-ship (4 – 75mm, 4 – MG) and sailed in February 1915. In May 1916 her two forward 75mm guns were replaced by two Japanese 47mm. She was damaged March 15th, 1917 in action with a U-boat; repaired at Rochefort and guns replaced by four 75mm, 1916 model; again damaged after actions with two further U-boats in 1917 and guns again changed (to 2 – 100mm, 3 – 75mm and 2 – 57mm). She was used as a transport from March 1918, paid off in November 1919 and awarded the 'Croix de Guerre' pennant.

Hospital Ships

Bien-Hoa class – two ships

Displacement: 5500 tons.
Dimensions: 105m × 15m × 6·70m.
Machinery: Reciprocating; IHP 2700; speed 13 knots.

NAME	BUILDER	LAID DOWN	LAUNCHED	COMPLETED
BIEN-HOA	Le Havre	1878	1880	1882
VINH-LONG	Bordeaux	1878	1881	1883

NOTES
Ex-navy transports; 1914: storeships with the 'Armée Navale'; 1915–19
hospital ships; BIEN-HOA condemned 1923; VINH-LONG burnt by
accident and lost December 16th, 1922 off Constantinople.

Duguay-Trouin – one ship

Displacement: 5445 tons.
Dimensions: 105m × 15m × 6·70m.
Machinery: Reciprocating; IHP 2700; speed 13 knots.

NAME	BUILDER	LAID DOWN	LAUNCHED	COMPLETED
DUGUAY-TROUIN (ex-Tonkin)	La Seyne	1876	1878	6.79

The hospital ship BIEN-HOA.

The hospital ship ANDRE LEBON.

NOTES

Ex-trooper; 1900–12 Cadets' training ship; 1912–14 disarmed; August 1914 converted to hospital ship; 1915 Dardanelles; 1916–18 Aegean; 1919 Black Sea; 1922 renamed MOSELLE; 1927 hulked for Engineer and Stoker school; 1936 condemned and sold for scrap in 1937.

A number of requisitioned passenger ships were alternately used during the war as troopers or hospital ships:

AMIRAL DUPERRE (5037/01, 12 knots): 1914 hospital ship; 1915–18 trooper.

ANDRE LEBON (13,681/15, 15 knots): 1915–18 trooper; 1919 hospital ship.

ASIE (9058/14, 16 knots): 1914 hospital ship; 1915–18 trooper; 1942 taken by Italians and renamed ROSSANO; May 10th, 1944 sunk by Allied aircraft at Genoa.

BRETAGNE (6756 GRT, purchased 1912, 17 knots): 1914–15 hospital ship; 1916–18 trooper; 1919 unlisted; 1921 renamed ALESIA; 1923 condemned.

CEYLAN (8223/07): 1914–16 hospital ship; 1916–18 trooper and store carrier; 1919 returned to owners.

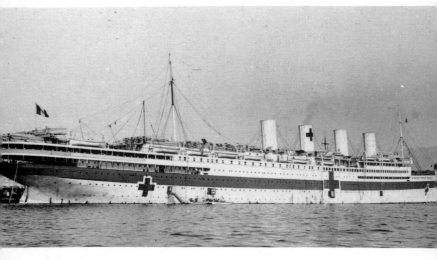

The hospital ship FRANCE IV.

CHARLES ROUX (4104/08, 20 knots): 1914–16 trooper; 1916–17 hospital ship; 1917–18 storeship; 1919 unlisted; scrapped 1936.

CANADA (9684/12, 14 knots): 1914 hospital ship Mediterranean; 1916 auxiliary cruiser; 1917–18 patrol duty and trooping. 1939 again requisitioned as hospital ship until 1943 then trooper; returned 1946.

DIVONA (ex-British ORMUZ 6484/86): 1914 hospital ship; 1915–18 trooper; 1919 returned.

FRANCE IV (23,666/12, 24·5 knots): 1915–16 trooper; 1917–18 hospital ship; 1919 unlisted.

LAFAYETTE (12,220/15, 18·5 knots): 1916–17 trooper; 1918–19 hospital ship; 1920 returned and renamed MEXIQUE. In 1939 requisitioned as auxiliary cruiser and mined June 19th, 1940 in the Gironde estuary.

LOUQSOR (6889/04, 13 knots): 1914–16 hospital ship; 1917–19 trooper.

NAVARRE (6373/92, 17 knots): 1914–16 trooper; 1916–18 hospital ship; 1919 returned.

PORTUGAL (5358/87, 16·8 knots): In the Black Sea at start of the war and requisitioned 1915 as hospital ship in Russian service with French crew; torpedoed and sunk at anchor on March 30th, 1916 by the German U.33 in the Black Sea.

SPHINX (11,374/15, 17 knots): 1915 hospital ship, Mediterranean to 1918; 1919 returned. 1939 requisitioned as auxiliary cruiser; 1941 disarmed; May 25th, 1943 seized by Italians and renamed SUBIACO; January 5th, 1944 sunk by Allied aircraft in Genoa harbour.

TCHAD: 1914–16 trooper; 1916–19 hospital ship; 1920 unlisted.

Tugs

Navy tugs

BOEUF, BUFFLE, CEPET, LAMALGUE, MEHARI, MILON (ex-Abeille III purchased 1912), TONKINOIS.

Requisitioned tugs

ALGERIENNE (51/08), ATLAS (rammed and cut in two by the British freighter MERREDIO off Brest January 22nd, 1917),

AUDACIEUX II, BOIS ROSE (wood, 65/81),

CAUDAN (340 tons; mined December 19th, 1918 off Smyrna),

CYDNUS (small ex-Turkish tug taken June 4th, 1915 by the JEANNE D'ARC at Mersina; sunk November 4th, 1917 by Turkish batteries at Ruad Island; raised and repaired), EUROPE I (116/09),

LAURENT SCHIAFFINO (small wood tug), GLADIATEUR II (54/74),

GLADIATEUR III (38/07, fitted as M/S), GLADIATEUR IV,

PHOCEEN I (257/88), PHOCEEN II (29/02),

TENEDOS (400/06, ex-Greek tug and minelayer),

TRAVAILLEUR II (81/77), ZAGHOUAN (ex-Portuguese SAO JOAO),

ZAZITA (214/64, Marseilles harbour tug and probably the oldest of all requisitioned vessels).

(See also Tugs listed under 'Patrol Vessels')

Colouring of Ships

In 1914 all large warships were painted a bluish shade of battleship grey, with white bands around the funnels and black tops to distinguish them and their divisions. It is probable that from 1916 the paintwork on the main turrets was polished by defaulters with fatty cotton waste which, combined with the corroding effects of the salt atmosphere, gave them an attractive shade of brown.

Destroyers were also painted a bluish shade of battleship grey. In order to identify them and the different flotillas belonging to the 'Armée Navale', they bore pendant letters on the bows and bands around the funnels, indicated as follows:

Leader: BOUCLIER—no pendant letters or bands. (Tricoloured ensign of the Captain D)

First Flotilla—Organized on November 20th, 1916
(Blue pendant letters and bands)

FUNCTIONS	NAME	PENDANT LETTERS
Leader (1)	CASQUE	CQ
Other ships	DAGUE	DG
	FOURCHE	F
	FAULX	FX
	CIMETERRE (2)	CM
	BOUTEFEU (Since 1913)	BF
	MANGINI (Since 1914)	MG
	PROTET (Since 1914)	OT

Second Flotilla—Organized in 1912
(White pendant letters and bands)

FUNCTIONS	NAME	PENDANT LETTERS
Leader (1)	CARABINIER	E
Other ships	SPAHI	SI
	LANSQUENET	L
	MAMELUK	MK
	ENSEIGNE HENRY	EH
	ASPIRANTE HERBER	AH

Third Flotilla—Date of constitution uncertain
(Red pendant letters and bands)

FUNCTIONS	NAME	PENDANT LETTERS
Leader (1)	FANTASSIN	FN
Other ships	CHASSEUR	CH
	CAVALIER	CV
	JANISSAIRE	J
	TIRAILLEUR	T
	VOLTIGEUR	V

Fourth Flotilla—Organized in August 1912
(Green pendant letters and bands)

FUNCTIONS	NAME	PENDANT LETTERS
Leader (1)	HUSSARD	MD
Other ships	SAPE	SP
	PIERRIER	PR
	MASSUE	MS
	MORTIER	MT
	HACHE	H

Fifth Flotilla—Organized in October 1912
(Black pendant letters but grey funnel tops)

FUNCTIONS	NAME	PENDANT LETTERS
Leader (1)	POIGNARD	PG
Other ships	TRIDENT	TR
	FANFARE	FF
	SABRETACHE	SM
	COGNEE	CG
	COUTELAS	CT

Sixth Flotilla—Organized in early 1914
(Buff pendant letter and bands)

FUNCTIONS	NAME	PENDANT LETTERS
Leader (1)	COMMANDANT RIVIERE	RV
Other ships	DEHORTER (3)	DM
	BISSON	BS
	RENAUDIN	RD
	CIMETERRE (2)	CM
	COMMANDANT BORY	BR
	MAGON (4) (Since 1914)	MN
	COMMANDANT LUCAS (Since 1914)	LA

OBSERVATIONS

(1) Bears a blue triangle.
(2) In early 1914, CIMETERRE was transferred from the First to the Sixth Flotilla.
(3) She remained in the Sixth Flotilla until she became the submarine leader ship.
(4) In 1916, MAGON was transferred to the North Squadron.
During the war, some small ships, like the destroyers or escort vessels, were also camouflaged.

Naval Ordnance

French naval artillery, from lessons learned from the Russo-Japanese war, had made great progress before World War I and gunnery had been much improved, due to the work of Admiral Germinet when he commanded the Mediterranean fleet 1906–7.

A sea fire-practice school had been created in 1906 and shortly afterwards a special naval artillery corps of engineers was founded to replace the old 'Colonial Artillerists' so long in charge of naval ordnance. A special powder-control service was then established to remedy deficiencies of organization and manufacture that had been disclosed after the accidents in IENA and LIBERTE.

These reforms gave good results; French guns gained a reputation for accuracy and for the training of their crews. However, there were some deficiencies: the maximum range was generally shorter than that of recent foreign battleships. It seems that French gunnery experts had not considered the possibility of firing beyond 15,000 yards, a range thought to be quite adequate considering the usual sea visibility and consequently the siting of the guns was too low.

Range-finders were mediocre as regards their accuracy and it was only between the wars that French warships were given good rangefinders and fire-control systems.

From intelligence reports on Austrian gun-range, it was decided circa 1916 to increase the range of French guns; this was fairly easy in the case of deck-mounted weapons, the cradle trunnion height had merely to be raised, though for some ships this modification was discarded because of the amount of work involved, the naval yards' activities being reserved for urgent ASW work.

The navy also used a great number of 75, 90 and 120mm army guns for requisitioned ships.

The 'Canonniers Marins' used some ninety old 120 and 155mm army guns, besides naval 138·6 and 164·7mm modified for increased range, etc, but long delays were necessary to transport these heavy weapons from place to place. So, the Navy studied the possibility of giving them relative mobility; as an example, the moving of several heavy guns as a single load with the aid of two or three motor tractors. It is interesting to note that before the arrival of the famous G.P.F. 155mm gun, the naval weapons were the only ones with range sufficient to reach special targets behind the enemy lines.

The Navy also used some ALVF batteries (heavy railway artillery) while numerous navy or coastal guns were converted for army use, such as the 340mm which had been ordered for the NORMANDIE class battleships. The ALVF weapons used by the sailors were the 194mm Schneider railway truck gun (1870–93 model) and the 305mm Batignolles cradle support gun (1893–6 model).

Forward main turrets, blockhouse, charthouse and searchlights of the dreadnought BRETAGNE.

Astern 340mm main turrets of the dreadnought BRETAGNE.

Heavy and Medium Guns

CALIBRE IN MM	MODEL	SHIP CLASSES	LENGTH OF BORE CALIBRE	MUZZLE VELOCITY M/SEC	WEIGHT OF PROJECTILE IN KILOS / EXPLOSIVE CHARGE	RATE OF FIRE PER MINUTE	MAXIMUM RANGE IN METRES
340	1912 M	NORMANDIE, LYON	45	800	540/22	1	16,500
340	1912	BRETAGNE	45	790	540/22	1	14,500, 18,000 (LORRAINE only)
305	1910	COURBET	45	783	432	1	14,500
305	1906	DANTON	45	826	440/13	1	13,000 to open the fire
305	1902	VERITE; REPUBLIQUE	45	815	340/10·5	1	12,500 12,500, 10,000 to open the fire
305	1893–6	SUFFREN	40	780	340	1	12,000
305	1893	CHARLEMAGNE, BOUVET	40	780	340	1	12,000
305	1887	JAUREGUIBERRY	45	780	340	1	10,000
274	1893–6	HENRI IV, REQUIN	40	815	255	1	12,000
274	1891–3	BOUVET	45	780	255	1	12,000
274	1887	JAUREGUIBERRY	45	780	255	1	10,000
240	1902	DANTON	45	800?	220/6·5	2	13,000, 18,000 in 1918
240	1893	D'ENTRECASTEAUX	40	800	170	1	12,000
194	1902	VERITE, W. ROUSSEAU	50	875	115	2	14,000 18,000 in 1918

CALIBRE IN MM	MODEL	SHIP CLASSES	LENGTH OF BORE CALIBRE	MUZZLE VELOCITY M/SEC	WEIGHT OF PROJECTILE IN KILOS/EXPLOSIVE CHARGE	RATE OF FIRE PER MINUTE	MAXIMUM RANGE IN METRES
194	1893–6	AL. AUBE and LEON GAMBETTA; J. MICHELET, E. RENAN	45	840	86	2	12,000 to 12,500
194	1893	POTHUAU; J. D'ARC and GUEYDON	45	770	86	2	9500
194	1887	AL. CHARNER	40	750	86	2	12,500
164·7	1893–6 and 1893–6 M	REPUBLIQUE; SUFFREN; GUEYDON; KLEBER, AL. AUBE and LEON GAMBETTA; JULES MICHELET, E. RENAN	45	865	52	2/3	9000 / 10,800 except the guns in casemates 9000
164·7	1887–93	GUICHEN; JURIEN DE LA GRAVIERE; CHATEAURENAULT	45	765	52	2/3	10,000
164·7	1887	FRIANT, DESCARTES	40	?	52	2	8000
138·6	1910	LYON, NORMANDIE, BRETAGNE and COURBET	45			8/10	
138·6	1891–3	HENRI IV, BOUVET, CHARLEMAGNE, J. D'ARC; GUICHEN D'ENTRECASTEAUX; CHATEAURENAULT; D'ESTREES; LAVOISIER	45		6·5	4/5	
138·6	1887	AL. CHARNER; SURCOUF	45		6·5	4/5	

Top: The astern main turret of the battleship PATRIE.

Above: A single 194mm turret of a battleship of the VERITE class.

Top: **Astern 194mm twin turret of the armoured cruiser JULES MICHELET.**

Above: **A 164·7mm gun of the protected cruiser CHATEAURENAULT.**

Light Guns

CALIBRE IN MM	MODEL	SHIP CLASSES	LENGTH OF BORE CALIBRE	MUZZLE VELOCITY M/SEC	WEIGHT OF PROJECTILE IN KILOS/ EXPLOSIVE CHARGE	RATE OF FIRE PER MINUTE	MAXIMUM RANGE IN METRES
100	1893	CHARLEMAGNE; SUFFREN; REQUIN; KLEBER; GUEYDON; AL. AUBE; D'ESTREES; 800-ton destroyers	45	710	1·7	8/10 5/7	9000 to 9500 11,500 max 6000 normal
100	1891	BOUVET; FRIANT; DESCARTES; LAVOISIER	45	710		6/8	9000 max 5000 to 6000 normal
75 SCHNEIDER model	1906	DANTON	65			14	6000 normal
65	1902	REPUBLIQUE and VERITE, E. RENAN; W. ROUSSEAU; 300-, 450- and 800-ton destroyers	45			10/12	9000 to 10,500 max 5000 to 6000 normal
65	1891	AL. CHARNER; 300-ton destroyers	50			10/12	9000 max
47	1902	REPUBLIQUE and VERITE; SUFFREN; HENRI IV; J. D'ARC; AL. AUBE and LEON GAMBETTA; J. MICHELET; GUICHEN; 300-ton destroyers	50				4000 max

CALIBRE IN MM	MODEL	SHIP CLASSES	LENGTH OF BORE CALIBRE	MUZZLE VELOCITY M/SEC	WEIGHT OF PROJECTILE IN KILOS/ EXPLOSIVE CHARGE	RATE OF FIRE PER MINUTE	MAXIMUM RANGE IN METRES
47	1885	JAUREGUIBERRY, BOUVET; CHARLE-MAGNE; REQUIN; POTHUAU; AL CHARNER; KLEBER; and GUEYDON; D'ENTRE-CASTEAUX, CHATEAU-RENAULT, JURIEN DE LA GRAVIÈRE, FRIANT, DESCARTES; 300-ton destroyers	50				4000 max

An old 100mm gun aboard a patrol boat.

A 90mm gun aboard a patrol boat.

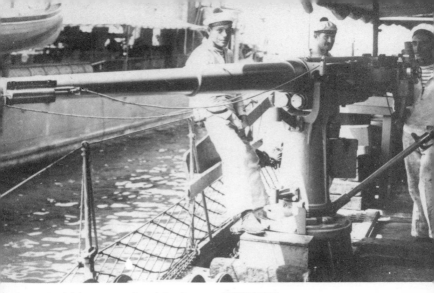

A 1902 model 65mm gun aboard the destroyer FANTASSIN.

A 65mm gun aboard a patrol boat.

A 37mm gun aboard a patrol boat.

An unknown type of light gun fitted aboard a trawler.

ASW Weapons

1. *Bomb throwers:* (a) De Maubeuge type, designed 1915 from the 58 mm army mortar; it was fitted on to a 47mm gun mounting – 23 kilo bomb, 750m range – 200 of these and 4000 bombs were fitted in destroyers and patrol boats. They proved inadequate and were replaced by – (b) the V.D. type, designed by the Belgian Major Van Deuren and also derived from the trench mortar – calibre 58mm, weight 21·5 or 37 kilos, rate four shots per minute.

2. *Depthcharges* – 'Grenades anti-sous-marines': (a) 500 emergency charges were first made, using an explosive charge of 30 kilos of gun-cotton. These were suitable only when a submarine had been located at short depth or when caught in defence nets.

(b) Guiraud type, invented 1915 by Lt Guiraud (FN) and 4000 units delivered initially. Weight was 45 kilos, perchlorate charges replacing gun-cotton in 1916. Firing was hydrostatic.

(c) Naval artillery type: 203 'grenades' (86 of 75 kilo and 117 of 45 kilo) were ordered in 1916. Designed to explode with simple percussion or at definite depth. Forty-five of 40 kilo charge were also ordered in 1917. Each large destroyer and sloop received one charge of this type.

(d) CM type: A 35 kilo depthcharge with melinite explosive. This weapon included a float connected to the charge by a 35m long steel cable; this cable was attached to the fuse and actuated it by traction. When the weapon was dropped overboard, the charge sank with the float remaining on the surface; the cable suddenly parted and caused the explosion. About 4000 of this type were supplied in late 1917 and 100 of heavier type (100 to 500 kilo) were made in March 1918.

(e) Duchene type: This had the advantage of sinking obliquely in order to reduce the danger of a premature explosion in the vicinity of the launching ship. It was cancelled after inconclusive trials.

(f) British and American depthcharges: By 1918, British ships were using three types: the 'D' of 190 kilos (containing 136 kilos of amatol); the 'DI', 131 kilos with 54–68 kilos of amatol; the 'G' of 36 kilos, 18 kilos of amatol. The fuses were of two types, both hydrostatic; one permitted to adjust immersion at 12 and 25m, the other at various depths from 15 to 60m. The USN used a depthcharge containing 23 kilos of TNT; the firing system was similar to the French CM grenade.

3. *Depthcharge throwers:* (a) The Thornycroft type: At the end of the war the French Navy purchased 134 throwers of this type from Britain; it was one of the best of its time. The full installation allowed for the firing of two 'D' type charges on each side of the ship while two others were dropped at close intervals astern on the centre line. One thousand depthcharges were ordered in Great Britain but none had been delivered before the armistice. The same type was also ordered from French manufacturers, but none delivered by November 1918.

(b) The 'Y' thrower: At the beginning of 1918, the US Navy had a thrower named the 'Y' because of its shape. The subchasers were fitted with two of this type. Its tactical use was as follows: one charge was dropped astern, 50m ahead one fired on each beam, and another 50m further on a fourth was dropped astern, thus forming a square pattern of explosions.

4. *Towed torpedoes:* (*a*) the Exelmans system, designed 1915 by Captain Exelmans, CO of the cruiser MARSEILLAISE. Briefly, the towed torpedo, containing 22 kilcs of perchlorate, was exploded by the tension in a lanyard connecting it to the towing vessel, the tension being activated if one of four mobile hooks on the end of a steel wire should encounter an obstacle. About 280 of these devices were made but their use was difficult and needed considerable maintenance.

(*b*) The Pinocchio system was more effective than (*a*). It was lighter despite its 30 kilo explosive charge and could be launched at 15 knots and towed at 25. Two models were manufactured: the 1916 model with between 15 and 25m submersion and the 1917 type for use against submarines at depths between 25 and 50m. This system was also adopted in the Italian navy.

ASW Equipment – Listening Devices

After testing several types, the French navy chiefly used the following:

(*a*) The Perrin microphone: a microphone in a swivelling casing handled from the deck of the ship. The ship had to stop to listen for the noise of the enemy's propeller, turning the casing until the noise was at its maximum; in

A 450mm single torpedo tube of a 450 tons destroyer.

fine weather its range was about 2000m. Some 250 sets were ordered in 1917 and a training school was set up at Bandol for training operators.

(*b*) The Walser microphone: this was also a microphonic device based on the concentration of sound waves with an acoustic diopter.

(*c*) The 'C' tube: an American device which gave good results and used mainly in small craft. In September 1918, all motor boats, subchasers, nine destroyers and a number of submarines had this apparatus.

(*d*) The Langevin-Colin system: this later gave birth to the famous 'asdic' of the Royal Navy and was to become the prototype of the modern sonars. Based on echo detection, a beam of acoustic waves emitted from the hunting ship, echoed back, this echo occurring only when the transmitter was pointing in the direction of the target, thus giving its direction. The time taken for the return of the echo indicated the distance from the target. Trials made in June and July 1918 indicated its great effectiveness and its use was strongly recommended, but lapsed at the end of the war in the French Navy, though perfected in the Royal Navy.

Torpedoes

The following torpedoes were in service during World War I:

Model	Calibre in mm	Length	Weight in kilos	Explosive charge in kilos	Speed in knots	Max range/ max speed
1887	356	4·99m	318	42	27	400m/27
1887	381	5·68m	423	42	28	400m/28
						600m/27
1892	450	5·05m	530	75	31	400m/31
						600m/29
						800m/27
1904	450	5·07m	627	72	36·5	1000m/32·5
						1500m/27
						2000m/24·5
1906	450	5·07m	648	86·8	36·5	d°
1906 mod.	450	5·07m	650	d°	d°	d°
1909 R	450	5·25m	683	d°	38	1000m/38
						2000m/34
						3000m/29

Mines

The French Navy had never displayed any great interest in mining and on the outbreak of the war it possessed only small stocks of mines, of the following types:

Breguet: In this contact mine a pin was sheared and a cocked spring released by the movement of an external firing bridle.

The Admiral Ronarch's minesweeping device.

Sauter-Harle: An excellent pattern which made use of hydrostatic pressure to activate the firing mechanism. The fracture of any one of the horns admitted water to a switch, the pressure releasing a cocked spring which forced a striker into a percussion detonator. Another type of Sauter-Harle mine was fired by means of an inertia switch.

Schneider: This mine was under development for laying from submarines but was never used. Two AMPHITRITE class submarines were converted into minelayers and two new ships were laid down in 1917 but not completed until after the war.

Minesweeping

In order to counter the numerous mines laid by the enemy, the French Navy used a system devised by Admiral Ronarch and which was developed by the British into the well known Oropesa sweep.

From the stern of the minesweeper, a steel wire was trailed which, at about 50 metres from the ship, divided into two diverging wires, 200m in length, fitted with cutters. In order to keep these cutters at the required depth of immersion a sheet-metal 'diver' was fitted at the fork of the 'Y'. When the mine cable was caught by a wire it slid along until it met the jaws of the cutter which severed it and freed the mine which was then destroyed on the surface.

Naval Aviation

On August 1st, 1914 the French Navy had only eight aircraft in service. On January 1st, 1918 it had 690 of them and on November 11th, 1918 the naval aviation amounted to the considerable total of 1264 floatplanes, seaplanes and aircraft and also 37 airships and 200 kiteballoons.

At the beginning of the war, the naval aviation was mostly used for reconnaissance and patrol duties. The aircraft were armed with light bombs which prevented them from undertaking open assaults. They merely reported the enemy submarines to patrol boats which would attack them or to merchant ships which would avoid them.

But from mid-1917, planes were equipped with more powerful bombs which considerably increased their offensive capability. Attack processes, sighting devices and bomb racks were improved.

Finally, French Navy used during the following aircraft:

FBA	
Donnet-Denhaut	} Floatplanes for observation and ASW duties.
Tellier	
Sopwith	} Seaplanes for fighting duties.
Hanriot-Dupont	
Spad 200	

The floatplanes were fitted with 130, 150, 160 or 200 HP Clerget, Lorraine or Hispano engines giving them a maximum speed of 140 to 160 km per hour. They had a crew of three or four men (one or two pilots, two observers). Their armament included two bombs containing eleven to fifty kilos of explosive charge, machine-guns and sometimes a 47mm gun. New bombs containing 120 kilos of explosive were being manufactured at the end of the

A floatplane of the FBA type moored in the port of Dunkirk.

war but were not used because of the armistice. Special float-bombs were also manufactured; they permitted the bombing of the subs at very low height without causing damage to the aircraft.

The fighters were land aircraft which had been fitted with floats. Their armament included one or two machine-guns and a 37mm gun on the Spad 200. Their speed varied from 160 to 180 km per hour.

The naval aerostation was created in 1916–17 with the transfer to the Navy of six Army airships (LORRAINE, TUNISIE, CHAUSSIN, CHAMPAGNE, D'ARCANDES and MONTGOLFIER) of which it had not the use because of their extreme vulnerability to air attacks and AA guns. It included non-rigid airships and also kiteballoons which were chiefly used for convoying merchant boats and screening combat ships for ASW, while the airships were almost exclusively used to convoy merchant ships and to search mine fields.

The Naval aviation was operating in co-operation with surface patrols. The airbases were under the same naval authority as the patrol boats. When flying, the intercommunication was insured by visual signals (signal flags, flares, etc) or by radio. Each division of floatplanes or each airship had a sending set to which the bases were permanently listening while in reconnaissance flight. Carrier pigeons were also used as a sort of emergency communication means.

Finally 155 submarines were attacked by the French Naval aviation (124 by the floatplanes or aircraft and 31 by the airships). By mid-1918, with special bases created for antisubmarine warfare the Naval aviation was able to protect all coasts of France and of its colonies. Thus by compelling the enemy U-boats to stand offshore, the Naval aviation was able to insure an efficient protection for merchant coastal shipping.

A floatplane of the Tellier type.

Motor and twin machineguns of Donnet Denhaut type floatplane.

A Sopwith seaplane.

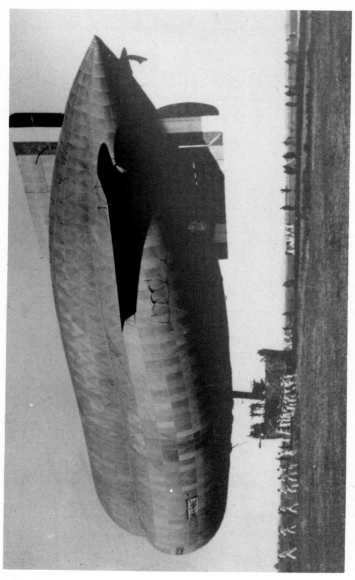

An airship of the AT type.

French Naval Airships Characteristics

Type	Volume cubic metres	Engines	Speed	Autonomy	Armament
LORRAINE, TUNISIE	10,500		35kts		Bombs and a 47mm gun
CAUSSIN	9100		35kts		
CHAMPAGNE, D'ARCANDES, MONTGOLFIER	14,000		35kts		
CHALAIS-MEUDON (CM 1, 2, 3, 4)	6500	2 × HP 150 Renault	40kts	10h/40kts	120 kilos of bombs
ASTRA-TORRES (AT 1, 2, 3, 4)				20h/25kts	
AT 5, 6, 7, 8, 9	7600	2 × HP 260	40kts		250 kilos of bombs
ZODIAC (Z 1, 2, 3, 4, 5)					one 48mm gun on ATR and ZD5
CM 5, 6, 7, 8	10,000		40kts	14h/40kts	One 75mm aircraft type gun (muzzle velocity: 400m/sec)
AT 10, 11, 12, 13, 14, 15					
ZD 6, 7, 8				30h/30kts	400 kilos of bombs
CM (T. type)	5600	2 × HP 230 Salmson	50kts		

NOTES: The 10,000 cu.m. airships were not completed at the end of the war. French Navy also purchased two SSZ British type airships (1960 cu.m., one HP 75 Hawk engine).

Order of Battle of the 'Armee Navale' (August 1st, 1914)

Battleships
COURBET   Flag ship of Vice-Admiral Boué de Lapeyrere, C in C the 'Armée Navale'
JEAN BART

Cruiser
JURIEN DE LA GRAVIERE   Repeating ship

First line squadron
Battleships
DIDEROT (F)*   (First division VA Chocheprat)
DANTON
CONDORCET
VOLTAIRE (F)   (Second division RA Lacaze)
MIRABEAU
VERGNIAUD

Second line squadron
Battleships
VERITE (F)   (First division VA le Bris)
DEMOCRATIE
JUSTICE
PATRIE (F)   (Second division RA Tracou)
REPUBLIQUE
PARIS
FRANCE

Complement division
Battleships
SUFFREN (F)   (RA Guepratte)
SAINT LOUIS
BOUVET
GAULOIS

First light division
Cruisers
JULES MICHELET (F)   (RA de Ramry de Jugny)
ERNEST RENAN
EDGAR QUINET
WALDECK ROUSSEAU

* (F) Flagship.

Second light division
Cruisers
LEON GAMBETTA (F)   (RA Senes)
JULES FERRY
VICTOR HUGO

Special division
Battleships
JAUREGUIBERRY (F)   (RA Darrieus)
CHARLEMAGNE

Cruisers
D'ENTRECASTEAUX
POTHUAU
CASSARD
COSMAO
BRUIX
AMIRAL CHARNER
LATOUCHE-TREVILLE

Minelayers
CASABIANCA
CASSINI
LA HIRE

Aircraft carrier
FOUDRE

Transports
VINH-LONG
BIEN-HOA
RHONE

Destroyer flotilla
BOUCLIER

1st squadron	2nd squadron
CASQUE	LANSQUENET
DAGUE	ASPIRANT HERBER
BOUTEFEU	ENSEIGNE HENRY
FOURCHE	MAMELUK
FAULX	SPAHI
MANGINI	

3rd squadron	4th squadron
FANTASSIN	HUSSARD
JANISSAIRE	SAPE
CAVALIER	PIERRIER
TIRAILLEUR	MORTIER
VOLTIGEUR	HACHE
CHASSEUR	MASSUE

5th squadron	6th squadron
POIGNARD	CDT RIVIERE
FANFARE	CIMETERRE
SABRETACHE	MAGON
COUTELAS	BISSON
TRIDENT	RENAUDIN
COGNEE	CDT BORY
	PROTET

Submarine flotilla

Destroyer
DEHORTER (F)

1st squadron	2nd squadron
Destroyers	*Destroyers*
ARBALETE	MOUSQUETON
HALLEBARDE	SARBACANE
	ARC

Submarines	*Submarines*
MONGE	JOULE
GAY-LUSSAC	FARADAY
AMPERE	COULOMB
PAPIN	BERNOUILLI
MESSIDOR	ARAGO
CUGNOT	LE VERRIER
FRESNEL	CURIE
	CIRCE

ORDER OF BATTLE OF THE ADRIATIC FRENCH DIVISION (JUNE 1st, 1915)

1st destroyer squadron
BOUCLIER. CDT RIVIERE. MAGON. BISSON, PROTET. CDT BORY.
2nd destroyer division
CARABINIER. SPAHI. MAMELUK. ENSEIGNE HENRY. ASPIRANT HERBER. LANSQUENET.
Submarines
Old battleship MARCEAU fitted as submarine depot-ship.
   CUGNOT. MESSIDOR, PAPIN. MONGE. AMPERE. FRESNEL.
Torpedo-boats and submarines of Toulon
Torpedo-boats: BOREE. ARVERNE. Nos 281, 288, 349, 360, 368, 369.
Submarines: CIGOGNE. ARGONAUTE.

ORDER OF BATTLE OF THE 'ARMEE NAVALE'
(April 15th, 1916)

Battleship
PROVENCE   Flagship of Vice-Admiral Dartige du Fournet C in C the
'Armée Navale'

Cruiser
CHATEAURENAULT

First line squadron
Battleships
BRETAGNE (F)   (VA Gauchet)
LORRAINE
FRANCE
PARIS
COURBET
JEAN BART

Second line squadron
Battleships
DIDEROT (F)   (VA Favereau)
DANTON
VERGNIAUD
VOLTAIRE (F)   (RA Daveluy)
MIRABEAU
CONCORCET

Third line squadron
Battleships
VERITE (F)   (VA Moreau)
DEMOCRATIE
JUSTICE
PATRIE (F)   (RA Habert)
REPUBLIQUE
SUFFREN

First light division
Cruisers
WALDECK-ROUSSEAU (F)   (RA de Gueydon)
EDGAR QUINET
ERNEST RENAN

Second light division
Cruisers
JULES MICHELET (F)   (RA Charlier)
VICTOR HUGO
JULES FERRY

Third light division
Cruisers
BRUIX
LATOUCHE-TREVILLE

Division of Syria
Cruiser
POTHUAU (F)   (RA de Spitz)

Battleships
JAUREGUIBERRY
REQUIN

First flotilla (Based on BRINDISI)
BOUCLIER (F)

1st squadron	6th squadron	Submarines
CASQUE	CDT RIVIERE	CUGNOT
FOURCHE	MAGON	MESSIDOR
MANGINI	BISSON	PAPIN
BOUTEFEU	CDT BORY	AMPERE
FAULX	PROTET	ARCHIMEDE
	CDT LUCAS	BERNOUILLI

Second flotilla
DEHORTER (F)

2nd squadron	3rd squadron	4th squadron
CARABINIER	FANTASSIN	HUSSARD
ASPIRANT HERBER	JANISSAIRE	MORTIER
SPAHI	OPINIATRE	COUTELAS
ENSEIGNE HENRY	TEMERAIRE	SARBACANE
LANSQUENET	CIMETERRE	VOLTIGEUR
MAMELUK		TIRAILLEUR

5th squadron	7th squadron	Reserve
POIGNARD	ARBALETE	MOUSQUETON
FANFARE	PIQUE	ARC
TRIDENT	HACHE	HALLEBARDE
SABRETACHE	CHASSEUR	
COGNEE	MASSUE	
SAPE	PIERRIER	

Submarines

COULOMB	LE VERRIER	FARADAY
GUSTAVE ZEDE	ARAGO	FOUCAULT
GAY LUSSAC	ARGONAUTE	FRANKLIN
ATALANTE	CIGOGNE	GORGONE
ARTEMIS	CIRCE	VOLTA

ORDER OF BATTLE OF THE 'ARMEE NAVALE' (July 1st, 1918)

First squadron
1st Division
Battleships
PROVENCE   Flagship of the VA Gauchet C in C the 'Armée Navale'
BRETAGNE

2nd Division
LORRAINE (F)   (RA Sagot-Duvauroux)
FRANCE

Second squadron
1st Division
Battleships
DIDEROT (F)   (VA Darrieux)
MIRABEAU
VERGNIAUD

2nd Division
JUSTICE (F)   (RA Amet)
VERITE
DEMOCRATIE

Reserve battleships: VOLTAIRE
Light Division
EDGAR QUINET (F)   (RA Allemand)
WALDECK-ROUSSEAU
ERNEST RENAN
JULES MICHELET

Repeating ship: JURIEN DE LA GRAVIERE

Aircraft carrier: PLUTON

1st destroyer squadron (Mudros)
CASQUE (F)
COMMANDANT LUCAS
BISSON
MANGINI

3rd destroyer squadron (Corfu)
ALGERIEN (F)
ARABE
HOVA
MAROCAIN
TONKINOIS
CAVALIER
JANISSAIRE

6th destroyer squadron (Mudros)
COMMANDANT RIVIERE (F)
COMMANDANT BORY
CIMETERRE
DEHORTER
PROTET
11th destroyers squadron (assigned to escort between Taranto and Itea)
TOUAREG (F)
BAMBARA
KABYLE
SAKALAVE
SENEGALAIS
SOMALI
ANNAMITE
3rd submarine squadron
FRIANT (cruiser fitted as submarine depot-ship)
ANTIGONE
AMAZONE
ARMIDE
RUBIS
EMERAUDE
and detached from the 2nd submarine squadron
TOPAZE
OPALE
GAY-LUSSAC
WATT
BERTHELOT
GIFFARD
VENTOSE
CUGNOT
Division of Salonica
Battleships
PATRIE (F)   (RA du Varney)
REPUBLIQUE (in reserve)
Cruiser:
BRUIX (in reserve)
10th destroyer squadron
SABRE
FAUCONNEAU
BOMBARDE
BALISTE
CARABINE
FLAMBERGE
Trawler squadron of Salonica
Torpedo-boats nos 309, 311, 353
9 trawlers
Division of Syria
Yacht
ARIANE II (F)

Battleships
REQUIN
JAUREGUIBERRY (in reserve)
7th destroyer squadron
ARBALETE
COUTELAS
PIERRIER
HACHE
VOLTIGEUR
DARD
7th patrol squadron
MAROC (F)
CANADA II
NORD-CAPER
CORDOUAN
PENSEE
DECIDEE
Aegean Sea Division
Yacht
HELENE (F)
2nd destroyer squadron
MAMELUK
LANSQUENET
SPAHI
ENSEIGNE HENRY
ASPIRANT HERBER
CARABINIER
6th patrol squadron
13 trawlers
9th patrol squadron
10 trawlers
ASW gunboats
CAPRIEUSE
BOUDEUSE
COURAGEUSE
TAPAGEUSE
AGILE
Patrol Division of Provence
Yacht
BACCHANTE (F)
4th destroyer squadron
HUSSARD (F)
TIRAILLEUR
MORTIER
PIQUE
MASSUE
SARBACANE
8th destroyer squadron
MOUSQUETON

HALLEBARDE
PISTOLET
FRONDE
ARC
EPEE
Sloops
ANTARES (F)
ALTAIR
ALDEBARAN
BELLATRIX
CASSIOPEE
4th patrol squadron
8 trawlers
5th patrol squadron
11 trawlers
Listening offensive groups
2 trawlers
6 chasers
Minesweeper squadron of Provence: 6 minesweepers
Patrol Division of Algeria
Trawler
TOURTERELLE (F)
5th destroyer squadron
TRIDENT
SABRETACHE
FANFARE
COGNEE
COUTELAS
POIGNARD
ASW gunboats
RAILLEUSE
CURIEUSE
GRACIEUSE
DEDAIGNEUSE
BOUFFONNE
SURVEILLANTE
8th patrol squadron: 13 trawlers
10th patrol squadron: 13 trawlers
Listening offensive groups: 3
Minesweeping squadron of Algeria: 5 minesweepers
Patrol Division of Tunisia
Yacht
EROS (F)
9th destroyer squadron
CATAPULTE
ARQUEBUSE
RAPIERE
EPIEU
SAGAIE

BELIER
ASW gunboats
FRIPONNE
DILIGENTE
IMPATIENTE
MOQUEUSE
MALICIEUSE
Dispatch vessels
LA HIRE
D'IBERVILLE
ALGOL (sloop)
2nd patrol squadron: 13 trawlers
3rd patrol squadron: 13 trawlers
3 listening offensive groups
Minesweeping squadron of Tunisia: 5 minesweepers

ORDER OF BATTLE OF THE SECOND LIGHT SQUADRON AT THE OUTBREAK OF THE WAR

1st Armoured Cruiser Division
MARSEILLAISE   Flagship of the RA Rouyer Commanding the Second
Light Squadron
AMIRAL AUBE
JEANNE D'ARC
2nd Armoured Cruiser Division
GLOIRE
GUEYDON
DUPETIT-THOUARS
Protected cruiser
LAVOISIER
Destroyers
DUNOIS, FRANCIS GARNIER, CAPITAINE MEHL
1st destroyer squadron
OBUSIER, BRANLEBAS, ORIFLAMME, TROMBLON, ETENDARD,
CARQUOIS
2nd destroyer squadron
GLAIVE, GABION, FANION, STYLET, FLEURET, CLAYMORE
3rd destroyer squadron
CATAPULTE, BOMBARDE, RAPIERE, EPIEU, BELIER,
ARQUEBUSE
Destroyers in reserve
BALISTE, FLAMBERGE, SAGAIE, HARPON
Minelayers
PLUTON, CERBERE
1st submarine squadron (Cherbourg)
Destroyers
FRANCISQUE (F)
FAUCONNEAU

287

SABRE
Submarines
PRAIRIAL, FLOREAL, GERMINAL, PLUVIOSE, VENTOSE, WATT,
BERTHELOT, GIFFARD, FRUCTIDOR
2nd submarine squadron (Calais)
Destroyers
ESCOPETTE (F)
DURANDAL
Submarines
MARIOTTE, BRUMAIRE, NEWTON, FRIMAIRE, VOLTA,
NIVOSE, EULER
3rd submarine squadron (Cherbourg)
Destroyers
JAVELINE (F)
EPEE
Submarines
AMIRAL BOURGEOIS, ARCHIMEDE, MONTGOLFIER,
FOUCAULT, THERMIDOR
Minesweepers (Boulogne)
Trawlers
MARIS STELLA, BLANC NEZ, TURBOT, EUROPE II
MOBILE DEFENCE OF DUNKIRK
First-class torpedo-boats
SIMOUN (F)
RAFALE
Torpedo-boats (torpilleurs numérotés)
224, 251, 258, 259, 279, 280, 317, 318, 319, 320, 321, 322, 323, 341, 342, 343,
344, 345, 350, 351

The following ships joined the Second Light Squadron in 1914
    2 armoured cruisers: DESAIX, KLEBER.
    5 cruisers: GUICHEN, CHATEAURENAULT, SURCOUF,
FRIANT, D'ESTREES.
    2 destroyers: INTREPIDE, AVENTURIER.
    8 auxiliary cruisers: FLANDRE, TOURAINE, NIAGARA, SAVOIE,
ROUEN, NEWHAVEN, NORD, PAS DE CALAIS.

ORDER OF BATTLE OF FRENCH NAVAL FORCES IN THE NORTH ARMIES AREA (October 1918)

1. *DIVISION DES FLOTTILLES DE LA MER DU NORD*
    Destroyer squadron
    MAGON, CAPITAINE MEHL, FRANCIS GARNIER, ENSEIGNE
    ROUX, BOUCLIER, MECANICIEN PRINCIPAL LESTIN
    Torpedo-boat flotilla of Dunkirk
    at Dunkirk OBUSIER, ORIFLAMME
    nos 305, 318, 320, 321, 322, 323, 345, 351
    At Calais nos 314, 341, 342, 343, 344, 346, 350, 365

motor boats nos 1, 2, 3, 33, 34, 35
2nd patrol squadron
SIRIUS, BAR II, AGATE, INDISCRET, EMILE ET MARIE,
CYGNE, TIGRE, CAPRICORNE
ALBATROS, BON PASTEUR, YVONNE, COTENTIN,
REDEMPTEUR
motor boats nos 45, 46, 47, 48
6th patrol squadron (minesweepers)
SAINT JOACHIM, JEANNOT, SUZANNE ET MARIE,
LORIENTAIS, LAITA, JUBARTE, GOELAND II, SEMPER,
TROUVILLE, GUEPE, JERSEY, AUGUSTIN NORMAND,
GRILLON, SEINE, NORD, PAS-DE-CALAIS
Interrogation ships
at Dunkirk: FRANCE II, HIRONDELLE, EUROPE II,
PROVIDENCE II.
at Calais: ALCYON I, EMMA II, PROVDENCE III, MADELEINE I

2. *DIVISION DES FLOTTILLES DE LA MANCHE ORIENTALE*
Torpedo boats of Boulogne
SIMOUN, RAFALE, nos 224, 231, 258, 259, 279, 280
3rd patrol squadron (trawlers)
EURVIN, CRIQUET, JEANNE D'ARC, CHAMPAGNE,
AUBEPINE, LIMANDE, PERRUCHE, LOUISE-MARIE, DENIS
PAPIN, JOYEUSE, RELIANCE, AMBITIEUX, MAKI, VILLE DE
BOULOGNE, ORANG-OUTANG, MARIE III
Chasers: 4, 5, 6, 7, 8
4th patrol squadron (auxiliary minesweepers)
FELIX FAURE, EUROPE II, MARIE-STELLA, ANDRE-LOUIS,
PICARDIE, GAULOIS II, SAINT LOUIS I, SAINTONGE,
LILLOIS, ALEXANDRINE, MADELEINE II, AMBROISE PARE,
BAR I, MARIE THERESE
ONDINE, EMILLA, N.D. DU PERPETUEL SECOURS, JEANNE
D'ARC?, ALBATROS
5th patrol squadron (trawlers)
ROITELET, HENRIETTE V, RESURRECTION, SAINT
WANDRILLE, ADRIENNE, BECASSINE, ANNONCIATION,
DIEU-PATRIE, ND DE LA SALETTE, NEPTUNE II, PELICAN,
MIRA, MOUETTE, NELLY, CAILLE, BECASSE,
MARGUERITE MARIE II, CIGOGNE, COUCOU, NANCY II,
EUTERPE, ZANETTE, SADO
1st patrol squadron
CHARLES, MARIE LOUISE I, JEAN EDMEE, JEAN BAPTISTE
DE LA SALLE, ASCENSION, NOTRE DAME DE LOURDES,
ALSACE, AIGRETTE, FLAMAND, STELLA MARIS, MANCHE
II, MARIE ROSE II, BONITE, SUZETTE, CAIMAN
Interrogation ships
at Boulogne: HOLLAND, VICTOR ET MARIE, MEDEE, JEANNE,
MARGUERITE II, REIBELL

War Losses

Battleships: four
BOUVET   Mined, Dardanelles   18.3.1915
DANTON   Sunk by submarine U.64 south-west of San Pietro   19.3.1917
GAULOIS   Sunk by submarine UB.47, Aegean   27.10.1916
SUFFREN   Sunk by submarine U.52 off Lisbon   26.11.1916

Cruisers: five
AMIRAL CHARNER   Sunk by submarine U.21 off Beirut   8.2.1916
CHATEAURENAULT   Sunk by submarine UC.38 off Cephalonia   14.12.1917
DUPETIT-THOUARS   Sunk by submarine U.62 off Brest   7.8.1918
KLEBER   Mined (from UC.61) off Brest   27.6.1917
LEON GAMBETTA   Sunk by Austrian submarine U.5 in the Straits of Otranto   27.4.1915

The old battleship BOUVET sinking.

Destroyers: fifteen

BRANLEBAS   Mined off Nieuport   29.9.1915
BOUTEFEU   Mined (from UC.25) off Brindisi   15.5.1917
CARABINIER   Stranded and scuttled off Latakieh, Syria   13/15.11.1918
CASABIANCA (M/L)   Lost on one of her own mines off Smyrna 3.6.1915
CASSINI (M/L)   Mined (from UC.35) in the Bouches de Bonifacio 28.2.1917
CATAPULTE   Lost in collision with British ss WARRIMOO off Bizerta 18.5.1918
DAGUE   Mined off Antivara   24.10.1915
DOXA (ex-Greek)
ETENDARD   Sunk by German destroyers off Dunkirk   25.4.1917
FANTASSIN   Collision with MAMELUCK off Fano, Ionian Sea 5.6.1916
FAULX   Collision with MANGINI, Straits of Otranto   18.4.1918
FOURCHE   Sunk by Austrian submarine U.15 in the Straits of Otranto 23.6.1916
MOUSQUET   Sunk by German cruiser EMDEN at Poulo-Penang 28.10.1914
RENAUDIN   Sunk by Austrian submarine U.6 off Durazzo   17.3.1916
YATAGAN   Collision with British ss TEVIOT   4.11.1916

Torpedo boats: ten

251   Collision with destroyer ORIFLAMME in the Channel   26.10.1914
289   Stranded near Nabeul, Tunisia   1918
300   Mined (from UC.26) off Le Havre   1.11.1916
317   Mined (from UC.1) off Calais   27.12.1916
319   Mined off Nieuport   19.1.1915
325   Mined (from UC.27) off Kerkenah Island   22.1.1919
331   Collision with British ss ARLEIA off Harfleur   13.4.1915
333   Collision with British ss HOSANGER off Kelibia   12.3.1918
347   Collision with TB.348   9.10.1915
348   Collision with TB.347   9.10.1915

Submarines: fourteen

ARIANE   Torpedoed by submarine UC.22 off Bizerta   19.6.1917
BERNOULLI   Mined off Durazzo   15.2.1918
CIRCE   Torpedoed by submarine U.47 off Cattaro   20.9.1918
CURIE   Captured at Pola; refloated, became Austrian U.14; returned 1918   20.12.1914
DIANE   Lost in the Atlantic   11.2.1918
FLOREAL   Collision with HMS HAZEL off Mudros   2.8.1918
FOUCAULT   Bombed by Austrian A/C L.132 and L.135   15.9.1916
FRESNEL   Sunk by Austrian destroyer VARASDINIER   5.12.1915
JOULE   Mined, Dardanelles   1.5.1915
MARIOTTE   Turkish gunfire, Dardanelles   27.7.1915
MONGE   Sunk by gunfire, Adriatic   29.12.1915
PRAIRIAL   Collision with British ss TROPIC   25.4.1918

SAPHIR   Mined, Dardanelles   15.1.1915
TURQUOISE   Turkish gunfire and beached, Sea of Marmara; became
    Turkish MUSTADIER OSMAHI   30.10.1915 but never commissioned

Gunboats and sloops: three
RIGEL (sloop)   Sunk by submarine U.35 off Algiers   2.10.1916
SURPRISE   Sunk by submarine U.38 off Funchal   3.12.1916
ZELEE   Scuttled and finished by gunfire from German SCHARNHORST
    and GNEISENAU, Tahiti   22.9.1914

Auxiliary cruisers: eight
BURDIGALA   Mined (from U.73), Canal of Zea   14.11.1916
CALEDONIEN   Mined (from UC.34) off Port Said   30.6.1917
CARTHAGE   Sunk by submarine U.21 off Galipolli   4.7.1915
GALLIA   Sunk by submarine U.35 35 nautical miles off San Pietro Island
    4.10.1916
GOLO II   Sunk by submarine UC.22   22.8.1917
ITALIA   Sunk by submarine U.4, 30 nautical miles off Taranto   30.5.1917
PROVENCE II   Sunk by submarine U.35 west of Cerigotto   26.2.1916
SANT'ANNA   Sunk by submarine UC.54 between Bizerta and Malta
    11.5.1918

Patrol boats (trawlers, tugs, minesweepers etc): eighty-two
ALCYON III   Collision in the Channel   27.6.1918
ALEXANDRA   Sunk by a bomb in a drifting Turkish boat, Gulf of
    Adalia   8.3.1918
ALOSE   Mined (from UC.6), North Sea   6.10.1915
AMERIQUE   Mined off Penmarch   25.3.1917
ANJOU   Mined (from UC.48) off Bayonne   17.6.1917
ASPIC   Lost by fire off Constantinople   18.12.1918
AU REVOIR   Sunk by submarine UB.18 off Le Havre   27.2.1916
BAMBALOU   Lost by fire   4.10.1917
BLANC NEZ   Mined (from UC.26) off Boulogne   27.10.1916
BUSE   Stranded and lost at Lezardieux   24.3.1917
CAMELEON   Mined off Argostoli   4.5.1917
CANADA II   Stranded and lost at Agadir   12.9.1918
CARPE   Stranded at Raz de Sein   6.8.1918
CAUDAN   Mined, Gulf of Smyrna   19.12.1918
CERISOLES   Lost in a storm on Lake Superior, USA   24.11.1918
CHAUMARD   Collision with French FRANCETTE, Gironde entrance
    13.5.1918
CHOUQUE   Stranded off Audierne   7.2.1918
CORNE   Foundered from a leak, Bay of Biscay   24.10.1917
CORSE   Sunk by submarine UC.67 off La Ciotat   24.1.1918
EDOUARD CORBIERE   1917
ELEPHANT   Sunk by submarine UC.79 off Lezardieux   31.1.1918
ELISABETH   Mined (from UB.12) off Dunkirk   12.3.1917
ENGAGEANT   Collision with tug MENHIR off the river Charente
    5.2.1918

ESPERANCE   Mined (from UC.64) off Le Treport   17.8.1917
ESTAFETTE   Mined near Dyck   24.4.1916
ETIENNE   German batteries, Ostend   3.3.1915
FANTASQUE   Stranded and capsized, Oleron Island   22.8.1916
FUSCHIA   Stranded off Leixoes   2.11.1918
GAZELLE   Stranded at Cap de la Hague   8.3.1918
GINETTE   Mined (from VC 14) off Corfu   20.3.1916
GLOIRE DE MARIE   Collision with British ss WAR MATRON
   19.8.1918
GOELAND II   Sunk by submarine U.93 off Penmarch   4.1.1918
GRIS-NEZ   1915
HIRONDELLE IV   Stranded off Bizerta   16.10.1917
HYACINTHE YVONNE   Sunk by submarine UC.70, Atlantic   18.3.1917
ILES CHAUSEY   Collision with British ss AL'T off Le Havre   22.5.1916
INDIEN   Sunk by submarine U.34 off Rhodes   8.9.1915
INKERMANN   Lost in a storm on Lake Superior, USA   24.11.1918
JEAN BART II   Sunk by Austrian submarine U.4 off Durazzc   2.2.1916
JEANNE I   Collision with British ss KINTUCK off Port Vendres
   7.9.1917
JEANNE D'ARC VII   Stranded and lost, coast of Brittany   17.12.1917
JESUS-MARIA   Mined (from UB.17) off Dunkirk   9.11.1915
JULES   Mined (from UC.27) off Sfax   23.6.1917
JUPITER I   Mined (from UB.12) off Dunkirk   10.7.1917
KERYADO   Sunk by submarine UC.72 off Yeu Island   2.5.1917
KERBIHAN   Mined (from UC.67) off Marseilles   23.1.1918
LORRAINE III   Collision with British ss TYNEFORD off Boulogne
   18.3.1917
MADELEINE III   Sunk by submarine UB.50 off Bone   7.4.1918
MARIE   Mined off Nieuport   24.2.1915
MARIE FREDERIQUE   Mined (from UC.54) off Bone   16.5.1918
MARIE THERESE   Probably by drifting mine, Channel   17.4.1917
MAUMUSSON   Mined (from UC.14) in the Adriatic   25.2.1916
MERLET   Collision with TB.252 off Cherbourg   1.2.1918
MONTAIGNE   Gunfire from five German destroyers off Cape Gris Nez
   27.10.1916
NOELLA   Mined (from UC.20) near Le Havre   7.2.1917
PARIS II   Gunfire, Avova Bay   13.10.1917
PAVOT   Mined off Alexandretta   6.11.1918
PERVENCHE   Stranded off Sevastopol   13.2.1919
PERDREAU II   Collision with Italian SALVATORE, Mauritanian coast
   14.8.1918
PHOEBUS   Mined (from UC.67) off Toulon   1.12.1917
POITOU   Stranded off les Sables d'Olonnes   8.12.1917
PRINTEMPS   Stranded at Quenocs   1.5.1917
PROVIDENCE I   Collision with auxiliary cruiser GALLIA west of
   Sardinia   2.9.1916
RENARD   Mined in the Iroise   19.10.1917
SAINT ANDRE II   Stranded, north coast of Stampalie   27.9.1915
SAINT CORENTIN   Mined (from UC.6) off Gravelines   24.4.1916

SAINT HUBERT   Mined (from UC.26) off Cherbourg   30.10.1916
SAINT JACQUES   Mined (from UC.6) off Le Havre   19.6.1916
SAINT JEAN II   22.3.1918
SAINT LOUIS III   Mined (from UC.71) off St Valery en Caux   31.3.1917
SAINT LOUIS IV   Rammed by British ss HUANCHACO off Milo
22.8.1916
SAINT MATHIEU   6.1.1918
SAINT PIERRE I   Sunk by submarine UB.17 near the Dyck   25.9.1915
SAINT PIERRE III   Rammed by HMS GREYHOUND off Gravelines
14.1.1917
SALAMBO   Sunk by submarine U.38 off Crete   19.4.1918
SARDINE   Capsized in the Gironde estuary   10.2.1918
SOUS-BARBE   Stranded near Les Sables d'Olonnes   7.1.1918
STELLA II   Mined (from UC.67) near Bougaroni   4.10.1917
TAPIR   Mined off Beg Melen   24.3.1917
TUBEREUSE   Mined (from UC.38) off Corfu   6.12.1917
UTRECHT   Shelled by submarine UB.49, Tyrrenian Sea   18.3.1918
VENUS II   Mined (from UC.23) off Milo   1.1.1917

French-river gunboats: two
'B'   Sunk in a gale while in tow   4.10.1918
'F'   Sunk in a gale while in tow   4.10.1918

Chasers: four
No. 2   Bombed by German A/C at Dunkirk   9.1917
No. 3   Lost by fire at Dunkirk   2.6.1918
No. 43   Collision with destroyer FRONDE   3.7.1918
No. 141   Foundered in the Atlantic on passage from builders to France
15.12.1917

Motor boats: three
No. 21   Lost by fire at Algiers   4.5.1917
No. 23   Stranded near Delhys   23.8.1917
No. 37   Internal explosion, Les Sables d'Olonnes   24.11.1917

Storeships: five
BERTHILDE   Sunk by Austrian submarine U.4 south of Italy   12.7.1917
BOUVET   Collision with trawler ORQUE, Mediterranean   12.9.1917
DROME   Mined (from UC.67), Gulf of Lyon   22.1.1918
LA CHAUSSADE   Sunk by submarine UC.27 north of Tunisia   13.8.1918
MOGHRAB   Lost by accident, Aegean   18.8.1918

Bibliography

ANTIN DE VAILLAC (Arnaud d'): *Les canonnières du Yang Tse* (France Empire, Paris).

BALINCOURT (Cdt de): *Les Flottes de Combat 1904. Les Flottes de Combat 1910. Les Flottes de Combat 1917.*

BELOT (Rear Admiral de) and A. REUSSNER: *La puissance navale dans l'histoire* (Editions maritimes et d'Outre-Mer, Paris).

BREYER (Siegfried): *Schlachschiffe und Schlachtkreuzer 1905.* 1970 (Lehmanns, Munich).

CHACK (Paul). Several books.

FRACCAROLI (Aldo): *Italian Warships of WW I* (Ian Allan).

GAMBIEZ (Général) and SUIRE (Colonel): *Histoire de la Première Guerre Mondiale* (Fayard, Paris).

GAUDET (MM): *Historique des batteries de canonniers marins et des canonières fluviales* (Imprimerie Nationale, Paris).

Jane's Fighting Ships 1014 and *1918.*

LABAYLE-COUHAT (Jean): *French warships of WW I* (Ian Allan).

LAURENS (Commander): *La guerre sous-marine. L'organisation des forces de patrouille* (Naval Historic Service, Paris).

LE MASSON (Henri): *Propos Maritimes* (Editions Maritimes et d'Outre-Mer, Paris). *Du Nautilus au Redoubtable* (Presses de la Cité, Paris). Very interesting French submarine technical story. *Histoire du torpilleur en France* (edited by Académie de Marine). This very important work is a true summary of the French destroyer and torpedo-boat technical history.

LA RONCIERE and CLERC RAMPAL: *Histoire de la Marine française* (Larousse).

MEIRAT (Jean): *Chronique du 'Ship lover'*, revue maritime.

SOKOL (H.): *La Marine austro-hongroise dans la guerre mondiale* (Payot, Paris).

THOMAZI (Captain A.): *La guerre navale en Méditerranée* (Payot, Paris). *La guerre navale dans la zone des armées du Nord* (Payot, Paris). *La guerre navale en Adriatique* (Payot, Paris).

TRAMOND (Joannes) and REUSSNER (André): *Eléments d'histoire maritime et coloniale contemporaine* (1815–1914) (Editions Maritimes et d'Outre-Mer, Paris).

WILSON (H. W.): *Les flottes de guerre au combat* (Payot, Paris), translated from 'Fighting Fleets' by Captain Thomazi).

WEYERS: *Taschenbuch der Kriegsflotten 1914* (Lehmann's, Munich).

Photo Credits

Marius Bar: 13 (foot), 21, 22, 24, 30, 32, 35 (foot), 36, 52, 59, 60, 61, 62, 63, 65 (foot), 79 (foot), 95, 96, 97 (top), 98, 99, 100, 102, 103, 105 (foot), 107, 109 (foot), 110, 112 (top), 113 (foot), 119 (top), 123 (top), 129 (foot), 133, 135 (foot), 136 (top), 137, 139 (foot), 142 (top), 149, 150, 153 (foot), 154, 155, 156, 158, 161, 167 (foot), 168 (foot), 177 (top), 180, 181, 252, 253, 254, 259 (top), 262 (top)

Etablissement Cinématographique des Armées: 106, 129 (top), 142 (foot), 175 (foot), 177 (foot)

Froger Collection: Title page (top), 8, 16 (top), 39, 44, 48, 54 (foot), 56, 57 (foot), 66 (foot), 68, 69, 74 (top), 76, 88 (foot), 91 (top), 93 (foot), 97 (foot), 105 (top), 109 (top), 114, 119 (foot), 120, 123 (foot), 125, 130, 138, 139 (top), 141, 143, 146, 147, 157, 163 (top), 166, 167 (top), 168 (top), 171, 173, 174, 175 (top), 179, 182, 183, 185 (top), 190, 197, 203, 206 (top), 214 (foot), 223, 225, 230, 231, 233, 235, 236, 238, 241, 242, 244, 262 (foot), 263 (top), 267 (top), 270

Colonel Guiglini: 40, 41

HLM Collection: 170, 185 (foot), 186, 187, 188, 189, 193, 194, 214 (top), 219, 227, 228, 229, 263 (foot), 266, 267 (foot), 268, 272, 276

Imperial War Museum: 11, 15 (foot), 27 (top), 47, 51 (top), 57 (top), 65 (top), 70 (foot), 84 (foot), 112 (foot), 206 (foot), 290

JLC Collection: Title page (centre and foot), 13 (top), 15 (top), 16 (foot), 19 (top), 26, 27 (foot), 31, 34, 35 (top), 49, 51 (foot), 54 (top), 66 (top), 70 (top), 72, 74 (foot), 75, 79 (top), 82, 84 (top), 85, 87, 88 (top), 91 (foot), 93 (top), 113 (top), 116, 118, 135 (top), 136 (foot), 144, 151, 153 (top), 163 (foot), 209, 219, 259 (foot)

Musée de l'air: 273, 274, 275

Admiral Rouyer: 19 (foot)

Index